UNQUIET EAGLE

Memory and Desire in the Idea

of American Freedom, 1815–1860

ASCENSION AÉROSTATIQUE,

EXÉCUTÉE PAR

E. ROBERTSON,

EN PRÉSENCE DU

Général Lafayette,

NEW-YORK, 9 JUILLET, 1825.

O Peuples, levez-vous ! L'Aigle républicaine ,
A la voix d'un Héros , s'élance vers les cieux.
C'est l'Aigle des Brutus , c'est l'Aigle américaine ;
Elle oppose aux tyrans son vol audacieux.

Ils dorment les tyrans sur la pourpre royale ;
Aux éclats de la foudre ils seront réveillés !
La mort plane sur eux. Leur pompe triomphale
Insulta trop long-temps aux Peuples dépouillés...

De l'immense Univers, image trop fidèle !
La moitié de ce globe est dans l'obscurité ,
L'autre repand l'éclat d'une gloire immortelle :
L'Imposture partage avec la Vérité !

Mais , sur le globe entier l'Aigle étend son empire
Et la Liberté sainte enchaîne les mortels :
Les trônes sont brisés ; le Peuple enfin respire.
WASHINGTON , LAFAYETTE ont partout des autels.

E. L.:

*L'un des hémisphères de l'aérostat représente l'Aigle et les Etoiles
de la République des Etats-Unis , l'autre n'offre aucun emblème.*

UNQUIET EAGLE

Memory and Desire in the Idea

of American Freedom, 1815–1860

BY FRED SOMKIN

Cornell University Press

ITHACA, NEW YORK

First published 1967

Library of Congress Catalog Card Number: 67-23763

PRINTED IN THE UNITED STATES OF AMERICA
BY VAIL-BALLOU PRESS, INC.

To Bodil

Acknowledgments

During the years that I have been writing this book I have held a John L. Senior Graduate Fellowship in American Civilization at Cornell University and have received several Summer Faculty Grants from Queen's University at Kingston, Ontario. The frontispiece, from the *Archives La Fayette* in the Arthur H. and Mary Marden Dean Collection of Cornell's Olin Library, is reproduced with the permission of Cornell University. For courtesy and helpfulness I wish to thank the staffs of the following libraries: the Olin Library; the Library of Congress, especially in the Newspaper and Rare Book divisions; the New York Public Library; the Lafayette College Library, Easton, Pennsylvania; the University of Toronto Library; and Queen's University Library.

A book like this necessarily rests upon the labors of many scholars, and I am aware that my intellectual indebtedness to those who have enriched the field of American cultural history by formulating new categories and approaches is but inadequately indicated by specific citations. My deepest obligation in this respect, and for criticism, counsel, and encouragement, is to David Brion Davis, Ernest I. White Professor of History at Cornell University. It was at his suggestion that the study was begun, and through the long course of its gestation he helped me avoid many errors of fact and interpretation. Those that remain are my own responsibility.

F. S.

Kingston, Ontario
May 1967

A Note on the Frontispiece

The frontispiece reproduces the French version of a handbill that was printed in two languages and scattered over New York City by a French balloonist in honor of Lafayette's visit, July 9, 1825. Four to five thousand people, including Lafayette himself, witnessed the ascent from Castle Garden. The following English translation was printed in the *New-York American* for July 11, 1825:

AEROSTATIC ASCENSION

BY

E. ROBERTSON,

IN THE PRESENCE OF

General Lafayette,

NEW-YORK, 9TH JULY, 1825

Rise, Nations arise!—The Eagle's free breast
  At the voice of a Hero shall glance to the sky;
'Tis the Eagle of Brutus—America's crest,
  At the rush of whose wings Tyrants turn them and fly.

Sleep, Tyrants! sleep on in your purple and gold,
  'Til roused by the burst of the thunder's coil;
Death poises his wing—their triumphs are told
  That insulted the world by their pomp and their spoil . . .

Of the Universe wide, a type, ah! too true,
  One half of this globe is bereft of all light,
The other is beaming with glory's own hue,
  Like the pure rays of Truth, and Imposture's dark night.

But the Eagle is shading the world with his wing,
  And millions are gaining, have gained Liberty;
Thrones crumble—and Nations enfranchised now sing,
  WASHINGTON, LAFAYETTE, 'twas YOU made us free.

One of the hemispheres of the balloon represents the Eagle and Stars of the United States, the other is without any device.

Contents

xi

UNQUIET EAGLE

*Memory and Desire in the Idea
of American Freedom, 1815–1860*

The actual focus of any history is a problem that has been generated by a tension developed between newer and older human ways of acting and believing.

—JOHN HERMAN RANDALL, JR.

Introduction

"A man who gives a good account of himself," wrote George Orwell, "is probably lying, since any life when viewed from the inside is simply a series of defeats." [1] Orwell's remark, extended to the writing of American history, raises a disquieting question. Our historians have traditionally given a good account of the national biography. High expectation and overfulfillment have in general been their theme. In the history books America has been the story of those who succeeded, making those who did not, by implication, non-American, or in the modern phrase, un-American. The Godly Commonwealth, the agrarian republic, the small, decentralized federal government, vanished one by one from the American scene. But an idea of America remained, and the continuing process of American self-definition carried the obligation of doing justice to the past.

Since Americans have always been more or less satisfied with themselves, their official story has been one that

[1] *Dickens, Dali and Others* (New York, 1946), p. 170.

would suit a satisfied people. Yet from the beginning there were those whose idea of America refused to compromise with time. John Taylor of Caroline, Henry Adams, and Albert Jay Nock were, like Ernest Hemingway, unwilling "to pretend that a country which is finished is still good." [2] Almost alone among American historians, Vernon Louis Parrington saw American history in Orwellian terms, as "a series of defeats." [3] *Main Currents in American Thought* portrayed the downfall of Parrington's Jeffersonian America in terms of classic tragedy. The protagonist appears in many ages and plays many roles: he is Roger Williams, Sam Adams, Jefferson, Emerson, Whitman, and Wendell Phillips. Always he is humanitarian, individualistic, freedom-loving, devoted to agrarianism, decentralized government, and idealism, for "the idealist has always seen deeper into the spirit of America than the realist." [4] Time after time he goes down to defeat not under the onslaught of alien forces but because of his own inner flaws. At a time when they were in a position to resist, the farmers let the Constitution be foisted upon them, passively allowing their necks to be put in the yoke of property rule. With Jackson they had another chance but let themselves be taken in by cloudy Whig slogans and their own greed. Again in 1896 they contributed to the "final" victory of capital over themselves.[5] Parrington's American hero is a dreamer cozened by sharpers, but it is his own gullibility and obvious yearning to be a sharper himself that deliver him into their hands.

[2] Maxwell Geismar, "Was 'Papa' a Truly Great Writer?" *New York Times Book Review,* July 1, 1962, p. 1.

[3] See Arthur A. Ekirch, Jr., "Parrington and the Decline of American Liberalism," *American Quarterly,* III (Winter, 1951), 295–308.

[4] *Main Currents in American Thought: An Interpretation of American Literature from the Beginnings to 1920,* 3 vols. in 1 (New York, 1930), I, 368.

[5] *Ibid.,* III, xxvii.

A contradiction in terms, an unoptimistic Jeffersonian, Parrington felt that when Jefferson took office in 1800 "the drift was all in the direction he was facing," but that by the time Thoreau came to die, the New Englander was "fortunate in not foreseeing how remote is that future of free men on which his hopes were fixed." [6] In spite of his repugnance toward the Puritans, Parrington shared with the New England Saints a fervently held assumption that America was somehow uniquely exempt from the burden of the past and free to work out a peculiarly original destiny. Whatever its varying formulations the idea of an American destiny has been perhaps the central focus of American self-consciousness. Under the Puritan dispensation a refusal to follow destiny was rebellion against God; for believers in the power of reason it was at least a sad mistake. "Democracy," Parrington gloomily concluded, "may indeed be only a euphemism for the rulership of fools." [7]

Such disillusionment followed logically from Parrington's special definition of the American identity which gave meaning to its history. That there were other ways of defining America Parrington recognized when he cited post–World War I intellectuals as contending that "nobody wants social justice." [8] But an America that did not want social justice was one he could never accept as American. In his idea of America were fused meaning and existence.

Roughly from the Peace of 1815 to the death of Thoreau in 1862, America was engaged in a quest for a definition of self that would give meaning to the American past, present, and future. The questions "What is America?" and "Who are the Americans?" had been asked before, but not with particular urgency. Rarely were they phrased so specifically, and the answers were varied, yet the American essay at self-definition during this period carried

[6] *Ibid.,* I, 397; II, 413.   [7] *Ibid.,* III, 85.   [8] *Ibid.,* III, 412.

a critical significance. First, because the United States became in this time a viable enterprise, beginning to feel the twin forces of technology and urbanism which were to become so characteristic in the future. Second, because of the crucial position of the generation that was attempting to hammer out the meaning of the national self-consciousness. With the passing of the Revolutionary generation that had heard the voices at Sinai, it remained for a generation of Americans born free to discover for themselves in a shifting environment what it meant to be an American and what the destiny of America was.

In tracing the evolution of a tribe of nomads from desert wanderers to the conquerors and masters of a city civilization, the fourteenth-century Arabic historian Ibn Khaldun marked out four stages of what his translator has called "prestige." Roughly, the term refers to a mixture of esprit de corps and efficiency based upon an environmentally fostered realism, essential for both victory and the retention of power. The generation of the founders, Khaldun said, knows the cost of what they have achieved; the following generation knows the founders; the third generation lives by the tradition; and the last, in token of decay, knows the cost of nothing and believes that it has everything coming to it.[9]

This scheme may suggest something about America. James Monroe, President in 1820, was the last incumbent to have been an adult at the time of the Declaration of Independence. Clay, Calhoun, and Webster, men who "knew the Founders," passed from the scene around the middle of the century, having themselves contributed to the formulation of the American idea. Abraham Lincoln, a railroad lawyer born in the nineteenth century, reaffirmed the outlines of a tradition on which he was prepared to stake the existence of the nation. Parrington's own era,

[9] *The Muqaddimah*, trans. Franz Rosenthal (New York, 1958), I, 278–81.

from Grant to Hoover, could perhaps pass without distortion for Khaldun's last stage.

This is a study of certain ideas and attitudes in the years preceding the Civil War, during which Americans attempted to know themselves as a people committed to the idea of freedom. The period has come to present something of a puzzle. Since these were years of booming geographical and economic expansion, it is natural that their interpretation has rested upon the doctrine of progress. But increasingly in the last decade and a half, students have uncovered convincing evidence of widespread nostalgia and regret for the past. Somewhere in this period, it is now fairly clear, a great American body lies buried, whether it is Parrington's agrarian democracy, an Edenic forest paradise, or simply an Adamic condition of moral innocence.[10]

All cultures that undergo social change probably demonstrate some inclination to hold onto the past, so there would seem nothing surprising in this discovery. Yet the American carcass, whatever it may be, can still poison the enjoyment of the present, as Parrington's book demonstrated. The reviewer of a recent work which indicts tech-

[10] Henry Nash Smith, *Virgin Land: The American West as Symbol and Myth* (Cambridge, 1950); Marvin Meyers, *The Jacksonian Persuasion: Politics and Belief* (Palo Alto, Calif., 1957); R. W. B. Lewis, *The American Adam: Innocence, Tragedy, and Tradition in the Nineteenth Century* (Chicago, 1955); Charles L. Sanford, *The Quest for Paradise: Europe and the American Moral Imagination* (Urbana, Ill., 1961); Leo Marx, *The Machine in the Garden: Technology and the Pastoral Ideal in America* (New York, 1964). For a closely reasoned, if involuted and strained, analysis of the philosophical assumptions underlying American attachment to an agrarian past, see Roland Van Zandt, *The Metaphysical Foundations of American History* (The Hague, 1959). Many keen judgments are to be found in Stanley M. Elkins, *Slavery: A Problem in American Institutional and Cultural Life* (Chicago, 1959). The books of Meyers and Lewis have especially informed my understanding of this period.

nology as the killer of the dream goes so far as to say that
"all thought and feeling in this country has been profoundly affected by the rapid transformation of a rather
simple agrarian nation into a highly complex urban civilization." [11] Assuming, as I think we can, that during this
critical period of transformation something important did
happen, and that technology and urbanization had something to do with it, the problem remains to account for
what appears to have been a disproportionate effect.

In the days of Calvin Coolidge, Americans learned from
Will Rogers' newspaper column: "That's one thing about
history, it never has to explain anything. It just gives you
the bare facts and there is no way of cross-examining them
to find out." [12] Rogers could combine cracker-barrel
shrewdness with a devastating naïveté. It would be more
accurate to say that history was all cross-examination with
the aim of eliciting some "not-so-bare facts" from an un-
cooperative context. But fortunately, as in the courtroom,
hostile witnesses may be asked leading questions. Taking
as my point of departure the conclusion of the historian
who has most extensively examined the idea of progress in
America during the pre–Civil War era—"that [it] . . .
was the most popular American philosophy, thoroughly
congenial to the ideas and interests of the age" [13]—I have
directed my own leading questions at the commonest and
most pervasive aspect of this idea: the visible fact of American prosperity. This fact I have seen as the key to the
sense of American selfhood, of America as a free society.

It is my contention that some of the contradictions that
appeared in American life during the first half of the nineteenth century, and that had such lasting cultural effects,

[11] Charles L. Sanford, reviewing Marx' *Machine in the Garden,
American Quarterly*, XVII (Summer, 1965), 276.

[12] *The Will Rogers Book*, ed. Paula McSpadden Love (Indianapolis, 1961), p. 144.

[13] Ekirch, *The Idea of Progress in America, 1815–1860* (New York,
1951), p. 267.

were largely due to an agonizing and finally unsuccessful attempt to retain the esprit of a sacred society, a family brotherhood, within a framework of conceptual and institutional constructs based upon freedom of contract. The somewhat sudden and apparently permanent prosperity brought to sharp realization the divisive and centrifugal tendencies of a social momentum which was in danger of losing vital contact with the still-revered ideals of a past essentially communal. The American response to this realization involved a national reorientation, an assessment of what America had been, what it was, and whither it was bound. A grand opportunity for such reorientation and assessment was provided by the return of Lafayette in 1824–1825, a cultural event of tremendous magnitude which involved all sections of the nation and the participation of Americans in all stations of life. As such, it offered a marvelously unified setting, fully documented, in which to identify and track down a host of fascinating clues, all pointing toward a determined and almost desperate American attempt to justify the present and the future through a time-defying union with the virtuous past. In the historiography of George Bancroft this longing was later to find its classic expression.

That this period of surface optimism should turn out to be shot through with critical tensions is understandable. Until recently no other major society has had to face such wrenching social change within the short space of three or four lifetimes. The resulting ferment is what makes the period so intriguing. It may even be possible that the proliferation of communitarian settlements, a subject that I do not treat, was the most striking testimony on a spatial level to the powerful longing for temporal community which I have tried to understand.

The limitations of this study are obvious, and I pretend no all-inclusive answers. For one thing, except for the subject of Lafayette's tour, I have paid little attention to the South, and with good reason: the South became increasingly involved in its own special identity problem and the categories of its thinking on the subject of American freedom became idiosyncratic and particularist. In thus deserting the banner of universalism under which the rest of the country continued to proclaim "America for the Sake of the World," [14] the South failed to participate in a moral impulse fundamental to the activity I describe.

Again, I have endeavored to follow the dictum of Charles S. Peirce that "it is the belief men *betray* and not that which they *parade* which has to be studied." [15] Such a method of operation is always risky, and may have led me at times into methodological peril. But it was a risk worth taking, and at any rate much of this study rests upon a real enough host of beliefs that *were* paraded.

Finally, because my story deals so largely with public discourse, it might appear that zeal for Peirce's doctrine may have caused me to draw upon an unusual variety of such sources and to range somewhat uncritically through time and space in using them as historical evidence. Recent sophisticated analysis has sharpened our perception of important social, economic, and political alignments during this period, and without question such differentiation was connected with particular attitudes toward slavery, states rights, banks, tariffs, and internal improvements. The kinds of fears and unease with which I am concerned, however, seem to me to have cut across these conventional groupings, and to have represented feelings and attitudes not susceptible of such clear-cut categorization. At any rate, even if many of those who expressed their apprehensions for the fate of the republic turn out to be political Whigs, yet the hundreds of thousands who were terror-stricken at the idea of a secret Masonic or Catholic con-

[14] David D. Riddle, *Our Country for the Sake of the World, a sermon preached in . . . New York and Brooklyn, May, 1851* (New York, 1851).

[15] *Collected Papers of Charles Sanders Peirce,* eds. Charles Hartshorne and Paul Weiss (Cambridge, 1934), V, 297 n.

spiracy, or at the influx of dangerous foreigners, must have reasonably included a fair proportion of those who voted Democratic on the issue of canals or public lands.

An examination of hundreds of addresses, particularly Fourth of July orations, for the period 1815–1860 [16] leads me to conclude that the age had a certain unity of shared public utterance, an utterance which was perhaps representative in a way that has not been the case since. Speeches, orations, sermons, and disputations of all sorts were listened to by large crowds, published, reprinted, anthologized for school reading-books and pored over by lip-moving cabin-dwellers in remote areas. Not only Sangamon County pullulated with budding Websters and Clays, sermonizers, arguers, debaters, and just plain talkers. And it is safe to say that, for the better part of fifty years, the great theme of all this expression, whether in form political, religious, or cultural, was a powerfully held belief in the concept of American freedom.[17] This was pre-eminently the *res Americana,* the *matter of America.* This theme, not always explicit, and sometimes to be found only by indirection, was sufficiently generalized so that one may venture to speak, as I have, of what "Americans" thought and felt about it. To a surprising extent during these years ordinary individuals, not to speak of the prominent, felt themselves deeply implicated in the destiny of a free American society, and put themselves on record in a thousand ways, articulate or otherwise, on the exhilarating subject. It is this record that I have endeavored to decipher.

[16] In addition to various addresses of all sorts in the collections of the Olin Library at Cornell University and the Library of Congress, I have looked at every Fourth of July oration available at the Library of Congress for this period. With few exceptions, however, I have cited only the small fraction of such addresses from which direct quotations have been made.

[17] The evidence makes it apparent that the "idea" united cognitive and emotional elements with a sense of involvement in what William James was later to call "a live option."

CHAPTER ONE

Prosperity the Riddle

In the decades after the War of 1812 Americans reaped the full measure of that prosperity which their pious ancestors had envisioned as the reward of the righteous. When President James Monroe assessed the results of the forty years since the Declaration of Independence in his First Inaugural Address, he could announce that "the United States have flourished beyond example. Their citizens individually have been happy and the nation prosperous." Enumerating some of the causes of this state of affairs, Monroe went on:

Situated within the temperate zone, and extending through many degrees of latitude along the Atlantic, the United States enjoy all the varieties of climate, and every production incident to that portion of the globe. Penetrating internally to the Great Lakes and beyond the sources of the great rivers which communicate through our whole interior, no country was ever happier with respect to its domain. Blessed, too, with a fertile soil, our produce has always been very abundant, leaving, even in years the least favorable, a surplus for the wants of our fellow-men in other countries. Such is our peculiar felicity. . . .

Never did a government commence under auspices so favorable, nor ever was success so complete. If we look to the history of other nations, ancient or modern, we find no example of a growth so rapid, so gigantic, of a people so prosperous and happy. In contemplating what we have still to perform, the heart of every citizen must expand with joy when he reflects how near our Government has approached to perfection; that in respect to it we have no essential improvement to make.[1]

The adjectives "prosperous and happy" were to be the counter words of Monroe's public statements. Prominent in the inaugural address, they reappeared in the opening and closing sentences of his First Annual Message, and even in the midst of the bitter depression which followed soon afterward he did not abandon them. They survived to find place alongside the customary admonition in his valedictory to the American people in the closing days of his second administration.[2] James Monroe belonged to a generation that could visualize the accomplishments of national development as the extended fulfillment of their own life careers. For this veteran of the Revolution, and last President to wear knee-breeches, the eighteenth-century dream of the Founding Fathers had become reality.

A few months after Monroe became President the Tammany Society of New York City had for their Fourth of July orator Mordecai Manuel Noah, a bustling local littérateur, newspaperman, and minor politician. Born in Philadelphia in 1785, Noah was a complete urbanite whose myriad activities and extroverted temperament, coupled with an aggressively second-rate mind, made him completely at home in the social milieu of the rising port

[1] James D. Richardson, ed., *A Compilation of the Messages and Papers of the Presidents, 1787–1897* (Washington, 1901), II, 5, 6, 10.

[2] *Ibid.*, pp. 11, 20, 74, 262. See also the conclusion of the Monroe Doctrine message (*ibid.*, pp. 219–20).

city. No one appreciated more thoroughly the flourishing environment of New York in the first half of the nineteenth century. "We enjoy at this day," he rhapsodized to the Tammany brethren,

more national happiness and individual prosperity than falls to the lot of any people on the face of the globe. A country the most extensive, embracing all the varieties of climate and fertility of soil; a rapidly increasing population, an honourable and just government, a moral and enlightened people, wealth, power, and liberty.

But all that America had accomplished, Noah went on to explain, had been achieved against the experience of history. "Cast your eyes around, fellow citizens," he said, "and you will see how effectually ambition, faction, and tyranny have swept every republic from the face of the earth." The result was that

we stand alone. . . . We have been spared by the hand of time, which sweeps in its course nations and countries—we have been left like a golden column, standing firmly erect, and surrounded by the crumbling fragments of other republics.[3]

As the glittering symbol of American success and exceptionalism the golden column of Mordecai Manuel Noah was singularly appropriate. A piece of classical architecture, it represented the highest achievements of civilization, and was capable of standing for the kind of New World victory over Europe which no indigenous American product could match. That it was of gold and not marble testified to the naturalization of affluence in America and aided in assimilating the column as symbol to the national catalogue of blessings. Yet these blessings, as the "crumbling fragments" of republican rubble littering Noah's tableau testified, were hardly to be enjoyed in a mood of

[3] M. M. Noah, *Oration, delivered . . . before Tammany Society . . . to Celebrate the 41st Anniversary of American Independence* (New York, 1817), pp. 3, 23-4.

careless acceptance. The fact was that the shining emblem of America's "national happiness and individual prosperity" was planted inescapably amid wreckage. Just as inescapably, the meaning of American prosperity within such a context presented itself as a hieroglyph to be deciphered. The greater that prosperity, and the more apparently stable, the more anxious the spirit in which the task was likely to be undertaken.

Whatever the implications to be drawn from it the undoubted fact of American prosperity provided a handy vehicle for years of national self-evaluation. "We cannot open our eyes," said a speaker in 1822, "without beholding the most unequivocal monuments of the general success, which has crowned the industry and economy of our citizens." [4] The expansion of the national territory, the creation of new industries, and the development of a vast transportation network were a few of the "unequivocal monuments" that were to provide unfailing indicia of "the general success" for decades to come. In particular, the growth of American population continued to hold out a promise of ever-increasing greatness. Even in the 1820's it seemed probable that the doubling of the population every twenty-two years or so, the old formula that had been such a source of colonial pride to Benjamin Franklin, would continue for the foreseeable future.[5] The sheer number of Americans was seen as a testimony of divine favor and a plain confirmation of America's moral worth. Into the faces of his European critics the American thrust the good news of each decennial census as a mathematical vindication of his national character.

[4] John C. Gray, *An Oration, pronounced on the Fourth of July, 1822, at . . . Boston . . .* (Boston, 1822), p. 5. Such expressions were common. See also Thomas Whittemore, *An Oration, pronounced on the Fourth of July, 1821 . . . before the Republican Citizens of Milford, Massachusetts . . .* (Boston, 1821), p. 14.

[5] See, for example, Edward Everett, *Orations and Speeches on Various Occasions* (9th ed.; Boston, 1878–1879), I, 34–35.

In a universe of providential order, of course, virtue and prosperity were intertwined. The works of the "Blessed man," the Bay Psalm Book had promised, would "prosper well," and President Washington entered office proclaiming that

there is no truth more thoroughly established than that there exists in the economy and course of nature an indissoluble union between virtue and happiness, between . . . the genuine maxims of an honest and magnanimous policy, and the solid rewards of public prosperity and felicity.[6]

All Americans agreed that the preservation of the republic depended on the maintenance of a high standard of virtue, and much of the public discourse of several generations amounted to florid insistence that such virtue was indeed widely alive. Ritualistic identification with a spiritually heroic past was an obvious resource. Yet, without presuming on the merits of ancestors the nineteenth-century American could turn to the very real prosperity of his own time for some assurance that virtue would not depart from the land.[7]

If it was true that virtue led on to prosperity, it was also good doctrine that there was such a thing as an environment peculiarly conducive to the virtuous life. An old proposition, it had had Thomas Jefferson for its most prominent American exponent. Seventeenth-century New Englanders may have looked upon the obdurate materials of a harsh environment as aids to salvation, but two hundred years later the business-minded Mathew Carey could see scant sweetness in the uses of adversity. Carey was willing to concede that "a little occasional adversity which

[6] Richardson, *Messages and Papers*, I, 53.

[7] A good example of the common association of prosperity, virtue, progress, and increase in population is the speech of Governor DeWitt Clinton at the ground-breaking for the Erie and Ohio Canal, July 4, 1825 (*Niles' Weekly Register*, CXXVIII [July 30, 1825], 346).

checks a man's career of prosperity, but does not wholly
lay him prostrate, may be serviceable in a moral and religious point of view. But," he felt convinced,

with the generality of mankind, the effect of extreme adversity, is, to harden the heart, and curdle the milk of human
kindness in the breast; whereas on the other hand, prosperity
generally expands the heart, and leaves it accessible to the
suggestions of benevolence and beneficence.[8]

The realistic Carey saw Americans as more like Job's wife
than like her saintly husband. It followed that a prosperous America was the best guarantee of felicity both in
this world and in the next.

This question of the influence of prosperity upon "the
heart," so easily disposed of by Carey, often led into a
thicket of unhappy introspection and misgivings. When
Timothy Flint revisited his beloved New England in the
1820's, after ten years in the Ohio Valley, he took immediate note of the quickened economic pulse, improved travel
facilities, and the wide availability of what had formerly
been considered luxuries. Along with these evidences of
progress, he was somewhat disconcerted to find, went "new
modes of reasoning and acting." The "American character," he concluded, "had recently undergone a great
change" in the direction of a rage for money-getting and a
preference for easy living. The careless gaiety of Saratoga
Springs, New York, now a flourishing resort, filled Flint
with a sense of disquiet, a feeling that something unpleas-
ant had happened. Some shock was of course inevitable
when a Congregational conscience tinged with a frontier
psychology encountered for the first time the new American institution of the vacation resort. Yet Flint was no
querulous moralizer, but an observer of unusually equable
temper, and he was genuinely convinced that within the

[8] M. Carey, *Miscellaneous Essays* . . . (Philadelphia, 1830), p.
451.

space of a few years there had been a significant deterioration of the American character. He was objective enough
to record that nobody seemed very worried about it, certainly not at Saratoga Springs; that, in fact, "all affect to
be happy." [9]

The ambiguous blessing of the new age of prosperity
prompted the Reverend Elihu Baldwin of New York to
preach, in 1827, on the text "Rejoice with Trembling."
Internal peace, social mobility, the diffusion of knowledge,
the success of religion, and general prosperity were all reasons for rejoicing. Yet each benefit was counterbalanced by
a corresponding danger. Prosperity was indeed well, but it
certainly magnified the power of men to do evil. "Increasing wealth rolls the tide of fashionable vice over the land,"
Baldwin declared. "Who that reflects, but must tremble
for the consequences?" [10] Baldwin's attitude was traditional
enough; wishing men to avoid sin he regretted that their
capacity to transgress had grown. He knew exactly what it
was he wished men would turn from: the "facilities of
vice." This was a particular area, easily identified. For men
like Baldwin, within the milieu of a ubiquitous prosperity,
the danger zone was clearly defined and more or less
limited.

It remained for Lyman Beecher to become the leading

[9] Timothy Flint, *Recollections of the Last Ten Years* (Boston,
1826), pp. 389–90, 394. Sixty years later, another New Englander
recalled the altered tone of life in that decade. "The enormous increase of wealth without labor which had come to fortunate speculators since the peace of 1815 seemed to make the invocation of
chance almost a legitimate business." He was still able to give examples of fantastic profits in shares of the Charlestown Bridge
Company and Pennsylvania lands which must have shocked the
consciences of older Bostonians (Josiah Quincy, *Figures of the Past,
From the Leaves of Old Journals* [1883] [9th ed.; Boston, 1901],
p. 275).

[10] Elihu W. Baldwin, *Considerations for the American Patriot:
A Sermon delivered on the occasion of the annual Thanksgiving,
December 12, 1827* (New York, 1828), pp. 18 and *passim*.

spokesman of a general theory of prosperity which sensed peril not only in the known avenues of "vice" but in areas of American life usually considered props to virtue, or at least morally neutral. Still smarting from the disestablishment of Connecticut Congregationalism, and alarmed at the decay of the Calvinist Sabbath, Beecher was in no mood to rejoice, with or without trembling. "All which is done to stimulate agriculture, commerce, and the arts," he thundered,

is, therefore, without some self-preserving moral power, but providing fuel for the fire which is destined to consume us. The greater our prosperity the shorter its duration, and the more tremendous our downfall, unless the moral power of the Gospel shall be exerted to arrest those causes which have destroyed other nations.[11]

Much of Beecher's concern came from his fear of social anarchy, the dangers of which seemed greatly increased by the spread of a vigorous population beyond the effective range of organized religious influences. Physical mobility had been seen as an evil so long before as the early years of the Massachusetts Bay Colony, and the theocratic government had intervened to prevent the dispersion of its infant constituency. That had been at a time when the settlement was still young and weak. Now Beecher's argument took an opposite tack—not weakness and indigence, but strength and affluence, were fear-inspiring. "Indeed," he asserted,

our Republic is becoming too prosperous, too powerful, too extended, too numerous, to be governed by any power without the blessed influence of the Gospel. The bayonet, in despotic governments, may for a time be a substitute; but ours must be self-government, or anarchy first, and then despotism.[12]

[11] Lyman Beecher, "The Gospel the Only Security for Eminent and Abiding National Prosperity," *The American National Preacher,* III (March, 1829) , 147.

[12] "Propriety and Importance of Efforts to Evangelize the Nation," *ibid.,* p. 154.

Beecher spoke these words in 1829, and it is not difficult to see in them the apprehensions of a defender of the settled order at the triumph of Jacksonian equalitarianism. Fear of the aroused democracy was a necessary corollary to the orthodox Calvinist position that social institutions had to keep a tight rein on the natural man, who was in a depraved and corrupted state. If men came to believe that they could manage themselves through institutions based upon reason instead of tradition, then the effects of sin and the need for unmerited grace were both in danger of being obviated. Just as clearly, if men were seen to be acting out of an interest which could be organized and directed toward the attainment of happiness—a proposition with which Mathew Carey and his economist son, Henry, would have agreed—the legitimacy of institutions of social control came perilously close to resting solely upon considerations of utility. Thus American Evangelicals like Lyman Beecher fought back after the dissolution of the Federalist party to revive what they called a "lively" sense of sin and to discourage the growing tendency away from traditional inhibitions.

If prosperity brought the danger of physical mobility, many felt that increased opportunities for social mobility, the American drive to rise in the world, carried comparable dangers. In 1844 the Episcopal Bishop of North Carolina lamented the abandonment of agriculture by farmers intent on entering the professions of law and medicine. Far from seeing in this movement the happy evidence of advancing civilization, Bishop L. Silliman Ives was inclined to blame a desire for wealth, and predicted that if it continued the "integrity" of the state's population was bound to decline. Like Beecher, Ives was obsessed with a vision of the disintegration of society. If agriculturists became seized by "the money-getting mania," he feared that the higher classes would no longer be able to impress the masses of the people by their example. "Sympathy between the poor and the rich [will] be destroyed . . . And then, as all history shows, we may . . . inscribe 'Ichabod' upon the fading tablets of our country." [13]

If the simple husbandman was being tempted from the plow in North Carolina it was no wonder, since even scholars were apparently not immune to the allurements of a corrupting prosperity. Only a few years earlier the New York lawyer and writer Gulian Verplanck had warned the boys at Union College that prosperity could be "more fatal" to the scholar than adversity, since the attraction of easy affluence might shake his devotion to learning and tempt him to enter the race for wealth or political office.[14] According to Nathaniel Hawthorne, prosperity could even be blamed for inhibiting the growth of American literature. In a passage later to become famous he complained that the United States provided none of the classic materials for the writing of romances—nothing, in fact, "but a commonplace prosperity, in broad and simple daylight." [15]

Nevertheless, the principal complaint against prosperity was that it had somehow turned a nation of God-fearing, freedom-loving idealists into a grasping horde of mercenary egoists. With a regularity and assurance that argued an unshakeable conviction, visiting Englishmen venomously repeated the charge that Americans were out-and-out materialists, but although the carping of Mrs. Trollope and Charles Dickens was widely resented their remarks on American preoccupation with money were hardly sharper than the charges in the national indictment drawn up by Americans themselves. "Human Nature, in no form of it,

[13] L. Silliman Ives, *The Introductory Address of the Historical Society of the University of North Carolina delivered in the University Chapel, June 5th, 1844* (Raleigh, N.C., 1844), pp. 16–17.

[14] Gulian C. Verplanck, *The Advantages and Dangers of the American Scholar. A discourse delivered . . . at Union College, July 26, 1836* (New York, 1836), pp. 41, 44.

[15] *The Marble Faun . . .* (1860), Riverside ed. (Boston, 1888), Preface, p. 15.

ever could bear Prosperity," John Adams wrote to Jefferson in 1814,[16] and for the next forty years a host of his countrymen were loudly proclaiming that the rule still had no exception. As a sermon topic, denunciation of the unalloyed pursuit of wealth had the advantage of an unambiguous Biblical foundation. At the same time its traditionalism and its generality made it a fairly safe mechanism for discharging resentment without specifically attacking powerful interests. "An overweening estimate of money, and an excessive and unscrupulous eagerness to acquire it," Americans were ready to admit, seemed to be "national characteristics." The bluntness of the Reverend Caleb Stetson, who in 1842 was bold enough to extend his denunciations to slavery, were echoed almost in the same words by many of his more restrained brethren. "The basis of *our* civilization," said Stetson,

is wealth. The love of money is almost the universal passion. The inordinate pursuit of it for the gratification of avarice, vanity, pride, and ambition, has deeply corrupted the principles of the country, and nearly destroyed all generous public feeling.[17]

Stetson was no economic radical, much of his protest being directed against the repudiation of state debts, and his solution advocated merely a personal amendment of character.

Yet if "the love of money" was for Americans a "universal passion," it was also a remarkably joyless one. Despite the scene Timothy Flint witnessed at Saratoga Springs, even ordinary cheerfulness did not seem to be a national characteristic. At the same time that Americans boasted of the superiority of the United States over Great Britain, Emerson noted that in comparison to the English, "young

[16] *The Adams-Jefferson Letters,* ed. Lester J. Cappon (Chapel Hill, N.C., 1959), II, 436.

[17] Caleb Stetson, *A Discourse on the State of the Country . . . on the annual fast, April 7th, 1842* (Boston, 1842), pp. 13–14.

people in this country are much more prone to melancholy." [18] Reflecting on "the times," he asked, "What has checked in this age the animal spirits which gave to our forefathers their bounding pulse?" [19] To the visiting geologist Charles Lyell, a puzzled Bostonian who had returned from Britain remarked, "We ought to *be* happier than the English, although we do not *look* so." While he was also inclined to blame the climate, Lyell ascribed the "careworn and anxious expression in the countenances of New Englanders" at least partly to "their striving and anxious disposition." [20] Sour and embittered as Dickens obviously was, there may thus have been little that was wholly subjective in the novelist's observation of a "prevailing seriousness and melancholy air of business: which was so general and unvarying, that at every new town I came to, I seemed to meet the very same people I had left behind me, at the last." [21]

As might have been expected, the great depression that began in 1837 was welcomed by many of the clergy as a means of redirecting this "prevailing seriousness and melancholy air of business" into higher channels. Natural disasters had of course always been useful as providential examples of divine wrath, but they had the frequent disadvantage of lacking specificity, with the result that their precise signification was not always clear. The collapse of the towering financial structure which men had erected as a stairway to a worldly heaven seemed unambiguously to chastise sinners with the presumptuous work of their own hands. Not surprisingly, many defenders of orthodoxy be-

[18] "Character," *The Complete Works of Ralph Waldo Emerson,* ed. Edward Waldo Emerson, Centenary ed. (Boston and New York, 1903), V, 128.

[19] "Lecture on the Times" (1841), *ibid.,* I, 285.

[20] Sir Charles Lyell, *A Second Visit to North America* (3d ed.; London, 1855), I, 153.

[21] *American Notes for General Circulation* (London, 1850), p. 173.

lieved that "the cause of religion will ultimately be promoted by the present commotions in the commerical world." [22]

Still, the religious mind was not entirely united when it came to assessing the meaning of prosperity for the success of religion in America. Thus, the Wesleyan University professor who reviewed Francis Wayland's *Elements of Political Economy* for the *Methodist Magazine* in 1837 argued that easy circumstances, far from increasing the temptation to vice, actually weakened it. Once men were relieved from the urgent necessity of providing for the present, he continued, "the mind is more at liberty to reflect upon a future world." [23] Such an argument evidenced the felt need to come to terms with a secular condition which promised, despite occasional setbacks, to be a permanent feature of American communal life. American religion would henceforth, it was fairly clear, have to survive in an atmosphere of continuing prosperity.

A standard defense of the commercial spirit emphasized its civilizing function, and the extent to which it was an improvement on the traditional impulse toward war. To Tocqueville the expansion of America's maritime trade displayed the same seagoing bravery associated with the conception of glory. The nobility of the old martial spirit seemed to have found a new channel. The descendant of French aristocrats could say that "Americans show a sort of heroism in their manner of trading." There was an *élan* to the activities of the American merchant which showed that he "does not follow calculation, but an impulse of his na-

[22] George W. Burnap, *The Voice of the Times; a sermon delivered in the First Independent Church of Baltimore, on Sunday, May 14, 1837* (Baltimore, 1837), p. 15. See also a review of four sermons on the hard times by N. L. Frothingham, George Ripley, *et al.,* in "Existing Commercial Embarrassments," *Christian Examiner,* XXII (July, 1837), 392–406.

[23] "The Elements of Political Economy," *Methodist Magazine and Quarterly Review,* XIX (1837), 407.

ture." The immigrant Pole Adam de Gurowski and the Frenchman Michel Chevalier pointed out that money played a different role in the United States than it did in Europe. Furthermore, it was apparent that private capital often carried out what was usually performed in Europe by government action.[24]

Over and over again Americans called attention to the danger which prosperity posed for the safety of free institutions and for the maintenance of republicanism. From the days of Monroe to those of Abraham Lincoln hardly a crisis developed that could not somehow be attributed to too much affluence or luxurious living. "Our Country presents a situation hitherto unparallelled among men," said a Boston public orator in 1833. "We are suffering, not like the nations of Europe, from a debt which bows us to the earth under our vain efforts to discharge it, but from a state of prosperity which is perhaps even worse." [25] That speaker was referring to the nullification crisis, but such expressions had already become a staple of American rhetoric. To cope with the historic conjunction of affluence and civic decline, the more sanguine social prophets sometimes resorted to making a distinction between the American brand of prosperity and the old European variety which purged the local variant of an inherited taint and corruption. Here again, enthusiastic visitors supplied armament for the defense of American affluence. The French officer who served as Lafayette's secretary for an American tour in the 1820's disposed of the question with

[24] Alexis de Tocqueville, *Democracy in America,* ed. Phillips Bradley (New York, 1945), I, 424–425; Michael [sic] Chevalier, *Society, Manners, and Politics in the United States: Letters on North America,* ed. John William Ward, Anchor Books (Garden City, N.Y., 1961), p. 294; Adam G. de Gurowski, *America and Europe* (New York, 1857), pp. 67 ff.

[25] Edward G. Prescott, *An Oration: delivered before the citizens of Boston, on the fifty-eighth* [sic] *anniversary of American Independence* (Boston, 1833), p. 17.

ease. "People who think republican principles incompatible with the enjoyments procurable by wealth," he conceded,

will find the luxury of New York excessive, and may suppose that a people which treads upon the richest English carpets; which profusely pours into gold and crystal, the most delicate wines of France, and runs after pleasure in elegant carriages, cannot long continue their independence.

Apprehension for liberty in the United States would indeed be justified, M. de Levasseur agreed, "if luxury here, like that of our princes and courtiers of Europe, sprung from the oppression and toils of the people." But in America one could say that "this luxury is the offspring of industry, the rich and fruitful daughter of liberty." [26] Thus American affluence was already the sign of an antecedent grace.

In a somewhat similar manner Americans, while quick to condemn the national pursuit of wealth when it seemed to them plainly excessive, felt at the same time that the world of American action rested on a saving principle which was absent in Europe, regardless of superficial similarities. In 1852, George Washington Burnap, who had taken over Jared Sparks's Baltimore pulpit a generation before, delivered an address at Dickinson College on *The Philosophical Tendencies of the American Mind*. In spite of the fact that Americans laid heavy emphasis upon the development of mechanical power, upon the conquest of nature, and upon the accumulation of wealth, Burnap protested, they were still "not a nation of mere utilitarians." Those prototypes of the American as enterpriser and mechanic, Samuel F. B. Morse and Robert Fulton, Burnap reminded the audience, were first artists before they became inventors and entrepreneurs. The American charac-

---

[26] *Lafayette in America in 1824 and 1825 . . .* (Philadelphia, 1829) , I, 127–28.

ter, in other words, involved such a balance of idealism and practicality, intuition and logic, as no other nation had been able to achieve. A simple materialism could never reproduce America's accomplishments. "The philosophy of the American mind," Burnap concluded, ". . . IS THE PHILOSOPHY OF COMMON SENSE." It followed that the nations of the world could copy American prosperity only if they adopted the American philosophy.[27]

In calling attention to the element of artistic creativity in American commercial life, Burnap raised a defense infrequently invoked. By and large, American artists themselves, in the manner of Hawthorne, reacted with hostility to the growth of business and industry. It took Harriet Martineau, sounding the heart of America in the 1830's through a pair of shrewd eyes and an ear trumpet, to realize that "there are other, though not perhaps such lofty ways of pursuing art, than by embodying conceptions in pictures, statues, operas, and buildings." Those who would insist that "the desire of gain" was the central motive of American commerce she invited to

witness the meeting of one kind of American merchant with his supercargo, after a long, distant voyage, hear the questioning and answering, and witness the delight with which new curiosities are examined, and new theories of beauty and civilisation are put forth upon the impulse of the moment.

Could one then "still doubt," she asked, "the existence of a love of art." [28]

[27] George W. Burnap, *The Philosophical Tendencies of the American Mind* . . . (Baltimore, 1852), pp. 24-25, 30. See Philip Freneau's poem "On the Death of Robert Fulton":

> And they, who on our Hudson's waters sail,
> And dread no mischief from the impending gale,
> These, these will say, when passing near your tomb,
> *The world's great Artist sleeps in yonder gloom!—*

The Last Poems of Philip Freneau, ed. Lewis Leary (New Brunswick, N.J., 1945), p. 117.

[28] *Society in America* (2d ed.; London, 1839), II, pp. 361–62.

When Burnap touched upon the relationship between American example and European actuality he raised a point that was crucial to every serious attempt at American self-understanding. The issue of how far Europe was bound to follow American example, or just when America was justified in proclaiming a moral superiority, received almost constant attention. On a famous occasion, during the debate over the Greek Independence question in 1824, Daniel Webster demonstrated the way Americans usually thought about the matter. Unquestionably, he declared, the United States had prospered and grown under a system of representative government, and Americans were opposed to the perpetuation or establishment of anti-democratic regimes. Yet it was not in the interest of a theory that Americans would be propagandists for free government, but "we shall no farther recommend its adoption to other nations, in whole or in part, than it may recommend itself by its visible influence on our own growth and prosperity." [29] The American idea, then, was an idea of success; not merely a successful demonstration of political purity, but a successful prosperity. Without prosperity, Webster was saying, America was without a more general significance.

Such an attitude implied that the American prosperity which did indubitably exist carried a heavy freight of responsibility. When America prospered she did so not only for herself. An experiment in the feasibility of free government, she felt always the consciousness of European judgment. Americans might favor a policy of international nonentanglement, but it was not because they believed that the divergent systems of Europe and America to which the retiring Washington had called attention would permanently coexist. Merely by continuing to flourish, the United States exerted a force upon the trend of political

[29] *The Writings and Speeches of Daniel Webster,* National ed. (Boston, 1903), V, 66.

development in the Old World. This assumption was common enough to be part of the national faith, and along with the notion of prosperity helped to make up the idea of America. On the fiftieth anniversary of the Declaration of Independence, Congressman Edward Everett assured a gathering of patriots that the American idea, the American example of popular government, guaranteed that the whole world would finally settle for nothing less. "It is in this way," he pointed out, "that we are to fulfill our destiny in the world. The greatest engine of moral power, which human nature knows is an organized, prosperous state." [30] America's moral legitimacy was therefore critically related to its secular prosperity. Prosperity was, for Everett, the supreme test of the success of free political institutions. It was the indispensable vehicle in which were embarked the fortunes of America's missionary effort to convert the world to republicanism.

Both Webster and Everett, of course, came out of a Federalist background and were later national figures in the Whig party, but Democrats were hardly less interested in the advancement of prosperity. Propagandists such as George Bancroft did their utmost to fix the labels of materialism and selfishness upon their political opponents alone, and with a certain amount of long-range success. The Whig vision of American society has ever since failed to inspire, has even seemed doubtfully American. The often bald honesty of its appeal could seem repellent. "My desire, and that of the Whig party," proclaimed a fairly typical Clay supporter of the 1840's, "is to see every man rich." [31] And millions of his countrymen were ready to deny with him that such an objective was at all lacking in concern for the higher American destiny. Perhaps the best

[30] "Principle of the American Constitutions," *Orations and Speeches,* I, 129.

[31] Burton Alva Konkle, *The Life and Speeches of Thomas Williams* (Philadelphia, 1905), I, 201.

statement of their case was made by the Illinois Whig Abraham Lincoln, long a follower of Henry Clay, when he came to weigh the merits of the dead leader. "He loved his country," said Lincoln,

partly because it was his own country, but mostly because it was a free country; and he burned with a zeal for its advancement, prosperity and glory, because he saw in such, the advancement, prosperity and glory, of human liberty, human right and human nature. He desired the prosperity of his countrymen partly because they were his countrymen, but chiefly to show to the world that freemen could be prosperous.[32]

Seeing in Clay that balance of idealism and practicality which Burnap identified as the hallmark of the American mind, Lincoln paid him the tribute which the Kentuckian would most have valued: Henry Clay was an authentic American. Thus, within the context of America's moral obligation to be prosperous for the sake of the world, presumably even the duty on hemp performed sanctified service in the larger interests of world history.

If an unsuccessful America was somehow un-American, and prosperity was necessary "to show the world that freemen could be prosperous," it was obviously of critical importance that American growth and affluence be recognized as the fruit of free institutions, and not, as many Europeans continued to insist, as the ordinary result of heavy immigration combined with vast natural resources. The American claim to moral superiority over Europe, and the reiterated invitation which American public speakers extended to the Old World to conform itself to the United States, would lose their point unless America's prosperity was indeed a consequence of its ideology. Thus Malthus' *Essay on Population,* which founded secular felicity on the

[32] "Eulogy on Henry Clay" (July 6, 1852), Roy P. Basler, ed., *The Collected Works of Abraham Lincoln* (New Brunswick, N.J., 1953), II, 126.

maintenance of a favorable ratio between population and arable soil, threatened not only to relieve the monarchies of Europe from responsibility for the condition of their masses of poor, but also to rob the United States of credit for the high level of well-being which her citizens enjoyed. The necessity for an immediate refutation of Malthus' ratios could not, however, appear urgent when so many Americans believed that the supply of land already available for settlement would last for hundreds of years. Thomas Jefferson could see no flaw in the Englishman's reasoning, and had himself acted on grounds more or less Malthusian when he strained Constitutional principle to acquire Louisiana. Whatever its apparent logic, the land-population argument was ignored in American practice. A people engaged in setting up new governments and in writing constitutions could not be bothered with the proposition that its future prosperity was already circumscribed by a mathematical formula.[33]

That measure of acceptance which Malthus found in the United States was attributable, at least in certain measure, to the fact that his *Essay* preached the doctrine of individual responsibility and self-reliance, characteristics upon which Americans traditionally prided themselves. By minimizing the influence of great impersonal forces, and insist-

[33] Timothy Flint's attitude toward Malthus was fairly representative of the age: "The process of doubling population, without Malthus, and without theory, without artificial or natural wants, goes on . . . on the banks of the Ohio as rapidly as anywhere in the world" (*Recollections,* p. 29). Also, "Discussions of the theory of population we conceive to be rather curious than useful. Give the people freedom, good laws and good land, and they will best settle the theory of population in fact, while theorists are dreaming over it in their closets" ("America," *Western Monthly Review,* I [July–August, 1827], 224). See George Johnson Cady, *The Early American Reaction to the Theory of Malthus* (Chicago, 1931), and Joseph Spengler, "Population Doctrines in the United States: I. Anti-Malthusianism; II. Malthusianism," *Journal of Political Economy,* XXXXI (1933), 433–67, 639–72.

ing that America was the place where men could make of themselves what they chose, Americans exalted the role of the free individual and the institutions which he constructed. Both Malthus and westward-moving Americans recognized the primacy of natural law and the necessity for men to conform themselves to its structure. But speaking as he did out of an economy of scarcity, Malthus insisted upon contracting the field for individual activity within a set of narrow natural bounds. The American demand for wider scope reflected the optimism of a nation which was used to manipulating and expanding nature through positive action. In that way an ordinary identification could be made between American national prosperity and the American character. The snug correlation was traced in explicit terms by the speaker who addressed the meeting of the New England Society of New York City in 1846. Associating the admittedly American traits of the Pilgrim Fathers directly with the prosperity he saw around him, Charles Wentworth Upham explained:

The power of character, growing out of this free development of the turn of mind of every individual, and the feeling connected with it, that each one may and must choose his own course, open his own path, and determine his own condition, has made New England impregnable, and covered her comparatively stubborn and sterile soil with abundance. This is the secret magic by which her sons command success and wealth wherever they wander.[34]

While prosperity in itself was an acknowledged good, and its connection with virtue could be demonstrated, much of the foreboding to which it gave rise was concerned with the question of scale. Had not American pros-

---

[34] "The Spirit of the Day and its Lessons," *The New England Society Orations, Addresses, Sermons and Poems delivered before the New England Society in the City of New York, 1820–1885*, Cephas Brainerd and Eveline Warner Brainerd, colls. and eds. (New York, 1901), I, 439.

perity exceeded all safe limits? Writing to the sculptor
Horatio Greenough in 1838, James Fenimore Cooper was
convinced that America was doomed to commonness and
mediocrity. The trouble, he felt, was that "the extraordinary material prosperity of the nation has forced so much
dross to the surface, that it is difficult to get at the pure
ore." [35] Others, like Professor Laurens Perseus Hickok of
Union College some years later, saw America as "endan-
gered by nothing but our prosperity," and in peril "of
death . . . from plethora." A fatal disproportion was
what America had to fear. "Should our grand experiment
of self-government ultimately fail," said Hickok, "it will
doubtless be because our prosperity is greater than our virtue can bear." According to his assessment the problems
arising from too much American prosperity, and with
which American virtue would have to cope, included the
growth of slavery, the influx of "Romanists," the increase
in crime, territorial overexpansion, and even the rabid
sectarianism of the home missionary societies which were
formed to deal with some of the evils.[36] For Ralph Waldo
Emerson the race between virtue and prosperity was already over by 1851. In the acceptance of the Fugitive Slave
Law he saw the fearful extent to which "our prosperity
had hurt us, and that we could not be shocked by crime." [37]

The full realization of America's prosperous condition,
almost apart from any corrupting consequences, was frequently enough to introduce a mood of apprehension.
American prosperity could seem so great that it laid the
nation under an obligation which prevented any simple
enjoyment of the state of well-being. Certainly, the affluent
Amos Lawrence had to be counted as one of the great

[35] *The Letters and Journals of James Fenimore Cooper,* ed.
James Franklin Beard (Cambridge, 1960–1964), III, 330.
[36] *A Nation Saved from its Prosperity only by the Gospel* . . .
(New York, 1853), pp. 8–9 ff.
[37] *Works,* XI, 229.

gainers from economic expansion. Yet just because we obviously owed so much as a people to the help of God, he wrote to his daughter in 1835, the extent to which Americans were prone to be carried away by their prosperity into forgetting this obligation filled him with "mournful forebodings." [38] This line of argument was carried to a conclusion a decade later by the Reverend Thomas Atkinson of Baltimore. Grimly, and without finding occasion for satisfaction, he counted over a long list of national blessings ranging from a tremendous increase in population and the means of subsistence to a decline in the incidence of disease. For him the disproportion between virtue and reward had now become so huge that he abandoned any attempt to find some relation between them. As America's great blessings had very apparently come upon her in spite of her great sins they could mean only one thing: the Almighty had given a sign that he was trying to win back the nation "by the endearments of parental affection." All the more reason, therefore, to tremble before the coming storm, since punishment, having been delayed and stored up, would strike with augmented power.[39]

Thus in the expansive and golden decades before the Civil War an ever-growing prosperity forced Americans to consider the relationship between material progress and America's spiritual duty to remain true to itself. Doubtless the great majority never felt any distinction, certainly no opposition, between the two. At the same time a widespread uneasiness reflected the fear that American success had poisoned the springs of the national spirit. An almost automatic prosperity, unaccompanied by significant moral

[38] *Extracts from the Diary and Correspondence of the Late Amos Lawrence . . .* , ed. William R. Lawrence (Boston, 1856), pp. 133–34.

[39] *National and Ecclesiastical Blessings, A Sermon preached in . . . Baltimore, on . . . the 12th day of December, being the thanksgiving day recommended to be observed by the Governor of Maryland* (Baltimore, 1845), pp. 4–7.

development, would rob the American experiment of its exemplary and missionary character. From this point of view, heralded benefits of progress were not only a sign of decay but an emblem of betrayal by which America confessed her apostasy to the truth of her founding. Feeling the need for a great purgation, intellectuals like Emerson were psychologically prepared to welcome the blood bath of the Civil War as a payment of suffering by which America could reclaim its heritage.

While the debate over the implications of national prosperity provided fuel for orators from college societies to the halls of Congress, it was only the most widespread symptom of a kind of national hypochondria which professed to see fatal dangers in any one of a lengthy catalogue of alleged social evils. Dozens of those "voluntary associations" that Tocqueville and other foreign visitors admired as evidence of democratic initiative were in reality special kinds of defense organizations, armed to carry on battle against a besieging host of malign influences. From all sides, seemingly, America was environed by corrupting forces, each of which, it was claimed, threatened nothing less than the cataclysmic destruction of the entire nation. To dramatize the frightfulness of the impending disaster the leading choristers of catastrophe, who were by no means all clergymen, drew upon the store of terrific weaponry in the vast arsenal of the Old Testament: water, which had furiously cleansed the world of a degenerate pre-Noachic society; fire, which had consumed the vicious cities of the plain; and pestilence, the traditional chastising rod of an angry deity. The composite picture that they put before the minds of millions depicted a smugly complacent America reclining over a heaving volcano of proletarian unrest, while a river of alcoholic fire rolled through the land, the black cloud of slavery darkened the horizon, the "disciples of Loyola" seized control of the West, and the vice and crime of the cities, spreading virulent infection through the institutions of freedom, poisoned the heart of the nation.

Altogether, an impartial observer might have fairly concluded that the United States of America, commonly referred to as the last hope of oppressed humanity, had already fulfilled in every particular the prophecy of Increase Mather in 1697:

I know that there is a blessed day to the visible Church not far off; but it is the Judgment of very Learned men, that in the Glorious Times promised to the Church on Earth, *America* will be Hell. And altho there is a number of the Elect of God yet to be born here, I am verily afraid, that in the process of Time, *New England* will be the wofullest place in all *America,* as some other parts of the World once famous for Religion, are now the dolefullest on the Earth, perfect Emblems and Pictures of Hell.[40]

With the aid of historical hindsight, the discomfort of the conservative temperament in America has always been easy to deprecate. The historic alarms and terrors of the antipopular faction found it difficult even to gain recognition. The pattern was set by Thomas Jefferson himself, as he clung to a single-track definition of what constituted the authentic line of American development. In so doing, he tended blandly to ignore the patently pluralistic character of events and movements in which he had been a prime participant. When he casually mentioned to John Adams, after their epistolary reconciliation, that the "Terrorism" of the 1790's was "felt by one party only," the old New Englander exploded:

Upon this Subject I despair of making myself understood by Posterity, by the present Age, and even by you. . . . I believe You never felt the Terrorism of Gallatins Insurrection in Pensilvania: You certainly never reallized the Terrorism of

[40] Perry Miller and Thomas H. Johnson, eds., *The Puritans* (New York, 1938), p. 347.

Fries's, most outragious Riot and Rescue, as I call it, Treason, Rebellion as the World and great Judges and two Juries pronounced it. You certainly never felt the Terrorism, excited by Genet, in 1793, when ten thousand People in the Streets of Philadelphia, day after day, threatened to drag Washington out of his House, and effect a Revolution. . . . I have no doubt You was fast asleep in philosophical Tranquility, when ten thousand People, and perhaps many more, were parading the Streets of Philadelphia, on the Evening of my Fast Day . . . when some of my Domesticks in Phrenzy, determined to sacrifice their Lives in my defence. . . . What think you of Terrorism, Mr. Jefferson? [41]

Whatever Mr. Jefferson thought of "Terrorism," for the Federalists of Boston and their descendants John Adams' capsule history was only the beginning of a protracted martyrdom. Decades of blooming prosperity served only to intensify their old fear of the mob. To those who profited most from the spectacular commercial and industrial growth of the American economy the possibility of violent revolution always remained a grinning death's head at the rich feast. Concomitant with the rise in value of stocks and bonds, Jeffersonian democracy was succeeded by the Jacksonian brand, accompanied by the rise of workers' organizations and the swarming influx of a foreign proletariat. State Street never had a chance to relax. The presence of suffering and envious masses, declared Lyman Beecher, constituted "a most malignant and terrific physical power," in fact "a magazine . . . under the foundations of all which is valuable to man." Only the "strong arm of the law" prevented an outburst of violence which would level "all which art, and industry and science have reared up." [42]

Underneath Beecher's highly colored imagery lay a mine of very genuine terrors. William Ellery Channing re-

[41] *Adams-Jefferson Letters,* II, 346–47.
[42] "The Perils of Atheism to the Nation," *Lectures on Scepticism* . . . (3d ed.; Cincinnati, 1835), pp. 106–07.

ported from Boston in 1835: "The cry is, 'Property is insecure, law a rope of sand, and the mob sovereign.'" Never an alarmist, Channing was constitutionally inclined toward optimism and had small sympathy with the chronic gloom of Bostonians. After thirty years in the locality he concluded, "We are a city too much given to croaking. I have been told that we were on the brink of ruin ever since I knew the place." [43] Channing knew his Bostonians, yet the feeling in other commercial centers was perhaps not much different. In the 1830's Austrian-born Francis Grund published *Aristocracy in America,* a book that he wrote after extensive conversations with men of business and property in leading eastern cities. After putting his imaginary interviewer to bed in a New York hotel, Grund had him assailed by a nightmare whose demons were obvious projections of the fears he had so often heard expressed:

I imagined myself somewhere near the Hudson or the Delaware, in the midst of a large, flourishing city, besieged, stormed, and finally carried by a victorious Western army, whose gallant leader dictated laws written in blood to the affrighted populace. A deputation of "leading citizens," who had come to offer their riches as a ransom for their lives, he thus apostrophized in a stern and solemn voice:—"Fools that ye were to wish for artificial distinctions! Know that the origin of every aristocracy is the sword, not the purse. . . . You have claimed the purse for yourself, and now the sword shall take it!" [44]

Here was an emotion-laden vision of the West as judge and avenger which rarely found overt expression. It was the capitalist counterpart to the evangelical bogeyman of a Catholic kingdom in the Mississippi Valley.

But for Boston, at least, comparable agonies lay much

[43] *Memoir of William Ellery Channing, with Extracts from his Correspondence and Manuscripts* (London, [1848]), II, 250, 513.

[44] *Aristocracy in America, from the Sketchbook of a German Nobleman* (London, 1839), I, 318–19.

nearer to home. More than a decade after Channing's death a speaker at the Massachusetts Constitutional Convention of 1853, while plainly aiming at political effect, expressed fearful anxieties that must long have gripped many hearts. Distinguishing between the poverty of the countryside and that of Boston, a convention delegate depicted the latter as

rebellious, destructive, exterminating, hopeless, homeless, and Godless. This is the poverty which prowls around our dwellings as wolves around a sheepcote, seeking an unguarded point where they may enter. It is a poverty embittered by the sight of enormous wealth—the luxuries of which it cannot enjoy; it is a poverty which hardens and brutalizes; it suppresses the man and brings out the tiger. This is the poverty that we have to fear.[45]

Such language raises a vision of Boston's great Whig merchants huddling behind the windows of their banks and town houses, while malevolent and ferocious beasts in human form roamed the jungles of Beacon Hill. Channing had noted what was practically a permanent feature of the life of Boston's middle classes. Amid their ease and comfort, they were worried men, and they remained in a state of tension and crisis down to the Civil War.

The essential fragility of civilization and its liability to instantaneous and utter destruction were themes constantly reiterated, as if in a new theology of prosperity. Lyman Beecher's "magazine under the foundation" captured perfectly the widely felt sense that Americans were sitting on a live bomb. In a society where a boundless faith in progress seemed daily more justified by spectacular achievement, the idea of concealed menace introduced a disconcerting element. Even in the golden world of business and

---

[45] *Official Report of the Debates and Proceedings in the State Convention, assembled May 4th, 1853, to revise and amend the Constitution of the Commonwealth of Massachusetts* (Boston, 1853), II, 131.

western expansion things were, after all, perhaps not quite
what they seemed.

To bring home to Americans the contingency of their
situation the image of the volcano was readily available. If
Michael Wigglesworth's "Day of Doom" was no longer
much read, selections from President Dwight's "Conquest
of Canaan," depicting a fiery Judgment Day marked by
quaking, fire-belching mountains, were reprinted in the
Columbian Orator for years after the beginning of the national period.[46] The fateful republican experiment upon
which the nation was to launch itself found conservatives
ready to predict the long-familiar disaster. "A democracy,"
warned Fisher Ames in the Massachusetts Convention of
1788, "is a volcano, which conceals the fiery materials of its
own destruction. These will produce an eruption, and
carry desolation in their wake." [47] Even so enthusiastic a
republican as Joel Barlow, in his bombastically optimistic
Columbiad, prophesied that if slavery were to continue
America would be destroyed in one tremendous explosion.[48]

The idea of a violent breakdown of the social order during an age of prosperity, whether the cataclysm would be
due to slavery or a popular uprising, easily utilized the
metaphor of volcanic eruption. "All may be smooth and
fair on the surface," explained the Reverend Ephraim
Peabody of Boston in 1846,

the sides of the mountain may be covered with verdure, the
shepherd may keep his flocks, and the vineyards may put forth
leaves, and their clusters may ripen in the sun, but the fires of
a volcano are moving beneath the thin crust, and without
warning, in a moment, they may burst through and lay the labors of centuries in ruins.[49]

[46] Caleb Bingham, ed., *The Columbian Orator* . . . (Boston,
1817), pp. 169–170.

[47] *Works of Fisher Ames* . . . (Boston, 1809), p. 24.

[48] *The Columbiad: A Poem* (London, 1809), Bk. VIII, pp. 260–61.

[49] *A Sermon delivered before the Boston Fraternity of Churches,
April 2, 1846* (Boston, 1846), p. 7.

Just as, in Jonathan Edwards' theology, living men hung suspended over the glowing pit of fiery damnation, from which they were withheld merely by the arbitrary will of an incensed deity, so the catastrophic exhorters of a century later pictured American civilization—"all which art, and industry and science have reared up"—as teetering on a rickety base, subject to instantaneous dissolution, and upheld only by a weak and overburdened social power. And as, for Edwards, neither good works nor other outward signs of election were anything but snares only the more horrible for their power to delude, so the national well-being and prosperity served only to camouflage the yawning gulf of national desolation.

Not simply as a matter of rhetoric, but in frightening actuality, Americans seemed strangely able to accept the possibility of violent death on a mass scale. An admirer of American technology, Michel Chevalier noted the frequency of fires and great steamboat disasters in the United States, yet at the same time he saw Americans continuing to smoke casually around heaped-up bales of cotton and stores of gunpowder. Dangers that in Europe would raise an outcry, he concluded, were here accepted as part of the price for quick expansion. Here fast and plentiful means of transportation ranked above an anticipatory saving of human life. It was a case of *Vae Victis!* [50] Still, it was not easy for foreigners to accustom themselves to this attitude. After he had been in the United States one month, Carl Schurz wrote to a German friend: "This nation has a strange indifference to life, which manifests itself in its sports, its races, its wars and also its daily life." To Schurz it appeared that "men who daily win their life anew in sustained effort give it up with reckless indifference." [51]

Such indifference could be seen as an American virtue.

[50] Chevalier, *Society, Manners, and Politics*, pp. 215–16.

[51] *Speeches, Correspondence and Political Papers of Carl Schurz*, ed. Frederic Bancroft (New York and London, 1913), I, 4.

Speaking in the Senate in 1832, Henry Clay observed that immigrants from Ireland were peculiarly adaptable to the New World. Both Irishmen and Americans, Clay thought, shared "the same careless and uncalculating indifference about human life." [52] The connection between a peril-fraught progress and the tradition of a fiery judgment was made explicit in terms of the new technology a few years later by the Reverend John Codman in Boston. "There seems to be an analogy," he remarked, "between the improvements of the age in the mechanical arts and in our moral and religious movements." Commenting on the ease and speed of modern transportation, he went on to point out:

It is true, now and then, a boiler bursts, and a number of precious lives are lost by the explosion; or in some of our western waters, while the majestic steamer is passing on its high pressure, with almost incredible swiftness, its progress is instantly arrested by some concealed and fatal obstruction, and the souls who had committed themselves to its guidance, are precipitated in a moment into eternity.[53]

American as it was, the steamboat was only the most recent embodiment of the elemental power behind the façade of nature. The fate of the republican experiment, of the *S.S. United States,* was perhaps most dramatically prefigured in James Fenimore Cooper's novel *The Crater,* published in 1847. Here Cooper depicted the sudden and complete destruction by volcanic action of a Utopian community, born originally from an earthquake, which had degenerated into demagogic democracy after an initial phase of pure republicanism. Such a sudden death, congruent to a sudden birth, was highly appropriate for

[52] *The Speeches of Henry Clay,* ed. Calvin Colton (New York, 1857), I, 451.

[53] William Allen, *Memoir of John Codman, D. D., with Reminiscences by Joshua Bates* (Boston, 1853), pp. 343–44.

America. A decade earlier, former President John Quincy Adams had described the volcano-like birth of the United States: "The earth was made to bring forth in one day! A Nation was born at once!" [54] So also, Cooper's "earthly Paradise," brought down at the end by those three great prides of American civilization—religion, the law, and the press—had come "into existence in a manner that was most extraordinary, and went out of it in one that was awful." The whole affair, Cooper moralized at the close, was a sign of the eventual death of the universe itself, when our world "will one day be suddenly struck out of its orbit, as it was originally put there, by the Hand that made it." [55] Thus, the old pageant of sin and damnation could present itself to Americans in the mid-nineteenth century in wholly political terms, but the scenario remained the same.

The jeremiads of the seventeenth century, Perry Miller has shown, were a ritual of humiliation that paid tribute for the sins of the times and assuaged the communal feeling of guilt for the mass departure from the old ways.[56] Yet whatever their pragmatic function, the jeremiads stayed close to a rationale that rested upon spiritual categories. Salvation was finally not of this world, and although the national covenant was capable of being dishonored and abrogated the great work of redemption would proceed to the end of time. The Saints were well aware of the value of religion as a means of social control, but its role in that regard was incidental.

In contrast, their nineteenth-century descendants had an earthly republic to preserve, and Lyman Beecher was only one of the loudest voices that never tired of proclaiming

[54] *An Oration delivered before the inhabitants of the Town of Newburyport . . . July 4th, 1837* (Newburyport, [1837]), p. 12.

[55] *The Crater, or Vulcan's Peak,* Mohawk ed. (New York and London, n.d.), Chap. XXX, pp. 481–82.

[56] Perry Miller, *The New England Mind, from Colony to Province* (Cambridge, 1953).

that a populous democracy could only survive by a general recognition of the objectivity of moral distinctions. In practice, so far as Beecher was concerned, this came down to the support of Evangelical Christianity and the fostering in the masses of what he called a sense of "accountability." [57] On this hinged the preservation of civilization and free government, which were themselves commonly associated with private property rights. If a large part of America's urban labor force were to remain, asked the Reverend Orville Dewey, "neglected, scorned, corrupt, debased, and desperate, who is willing to take the risk and the peril of such a coming day?" Dewey's "coming day" was obviously nothing less than the ancient "Day of the Lord," but before a different tribunal and a packed jury. No Beecherite firebrand, Dewey was simply a sober-minded Unitarian with what he regarded as humanitarian instincts. Urging the wealthy to get to know the working class "in kindness and brotherly love," he added plainly, "Better is it for their property . . . that they should." [58]

Inevitably the critical task of preserving the republic pressed into service those old standbys of the redemption drama, the divine judgment and its prophetic revelations. The wrath-drawing sins became whatever appeared to threaten the Protestant and republican character of the United States. The divine judgment came to be interpreted in politico-social terms. In a spirited appeal for missionary funds in 1855, the Reverend Richard Storrs surveyed the dangers then facing the country. Around him he saw the demons of infidelity, vice, crime, slavery, and an onrushing Catholicism whose "disciples of Loyola" swarmed "like locusts in the land." Wheeling up the old volcano artillery, he announced:

[57] *Lectures on Scepticism,* p. 88.
[58] *A Sermon . . . on the Moral Importance of Cities, and the moral means for their reformation . . .* (New York, 1836), pp. 15–16.

If, even now, we be not sleeping on the crater's edge, whose fiery floods threaten an overflow of our civil and religious liberties more terrible than was felt by Pompeii or Herculaneum, the signs of the times and the interpretations of prophecy deceive us! [59]

Not alone for Richard Storrs, by 1855, were the "signs of the times and the interpretations of prophecy" no longer reserved for the annunciation of the coming of the Son of Man in glory. Nothing was by that time more natural than that they should be unquestioningly accepted as having clear relevance for the fate of American "civil and religious liberties."

Somewhat in a parallel manner the temperance movement, as an evangelical enterprise, began as an effort to keep the body sound as a temple for the spirit of God and an essential vehicle for salvation. Gradually the campaign came to emphasize heavily the social consequences of drunkenness and even the ruinous effect of alcohol upon numerous internal organs. In Horace Mann, who was interested in both mental and physical culture, the secularization of the prophetic method and imagery came out clearly. While engaged in attacking the dangers of an uneducated electorate in a Fourth of July oration, he gave the volcano gambit an original twist. "If the country is an active volcano of ignorance and guilt," Mann queried, "why should not Congress be a crater for the outgushing of its lava?" [60] Here was a safety-valve doctrine with a political signification, except that in a democratic country the rushing of the lava could be expected to wipe out the nation in its course.

For Mann sin had become the failure of self-cultivation, of which ignorance was only one facet. With others of his generation he agreed that Americans were not what their

[59] *Home Missions: As Connected with Christ's Dominion* . . . (New York, 1855), p. 21.

[60] *An Oration, delivered before the authorities of the City of Boston, July 4, 1842*, 4th ed. [Boston, 1842?], p. 29.

fathers had been, but instead of railing generally against the decline of virtue he called attention to specific and remediable defects:

The old hearts of oak are gone. Society is suffering under a curvature of the spine. If deterioration holds on, at its present rate, especially in our cities, we shall soon be a bed-rid people. . . . There is a general effeminacy of our modes of life, as compared with the indurating exposures of our ancestors. Our double-windows; our air-tight houses; our heated and unventilated apartments, from nursery to sleeping-room, and church . . . slackening the whole machinery of life.

Through a misguided and fatal humanitarianism, Mann went on, those unfit were being coddled and allowed to survive who previously had perished justifiably.[61] Thus the defense against death itself brought catastrophe nearer.

After all allowances for individual idiosyncrasies, the fact remains that the theme of decline and doom remained a constant one throughout the first half of the nineteenth century. With the establishment of international integrity after the War of 1812, the effective opening of immense territories in the West, the increase of wealth and appurtenances of cvilization, there came also a swarm of grim prophecies for the future of the nation. It was almost as though such forebodings were a necessary exercise, a groping toward the definition of freedom by a generation born clear of traditional entailments. In the concept of national destruction a people devoted to the idea of popular sovereignty sought the defining limits which would give meaning to the national existence.

Laws, divine and human, had historically constituted the rim of formality which gave shape to the substance of freedom. The Founding Fathers who studied their favorite Tully were familiar with his maxim, "We are in bondage to the law that we may be free." It was the "givenness" of

---

[61] *Common School Journal* (1842), excerpted in Merle Curti, ed., *American Issues* (Chicago, 1941), p. 472.

the law that provided the mold within which freedom knew itself. Yet in creating the republic and proclaiming its basis in the sovereignty of the people, Americans had taken from the law its mystical determinant. Its meaning would have to be sought now in the conditions of American experience. In this connection a tableau recorded by the waspish Mrs. Trollope is endlessly revealing. To the persistent attempt to squeeze a large box aboard her already crowded stagecoach, she objected: "No law, sir, can permit such conduct as this."

"Law!" exclaimed a gentleman very particularly drunk; We makes our own laws, and governs our own selves."

"Law!" echoed another gentleman . . . "this is a free country, *we have no laws here,* and we don't want no foreign power to tyrannize over us." [62]

Thus did the authentic voice of a laissez-faire society look upon law as an attempt to contain the special boundlessness of American opportunity, and concluded that it proved itself, by that very token, an agency of the Old World.

The symbol of the volcano, as it represented the assurance of a justice beyond the law of popular will, supplied a background of meaningfulness till the time when a free America should no longer feel the need for it. Meanwhile the volcano was variously useful; first, it was a conclusive end, a real termination point; and second, it had the quality of imminence. Without imminence the loss of contiguity would entail a break in necessary connection. As a final end, the fact of its foreseeability cleared up the present and made a pattern out of what might otherwise appear simply a jungle of circumstance. In thus weaving a web of significance, the idea of cataclysm paradoxically served the function of building a sense of security. However direful the future might appear, it was still intelligible and just, and its intelligibility and justice communicated a sense of themselves to the present.

[62] *Domestic Manners of the Americans* (London, 1832), II, 246.

According to the cultural anthropologist Franz Boas, the more uniform the society, and lacking in class and functional distinctions, the more likely it is that the *concept* of freedom, as apart from the *feeling* of freedom, will present a particular problem. The *feeling* of freedom is present when the agent is in such complete harmony with his culture that obedience to custom and opinion is given without consideration. On the other hand, only the rasp of conflict between the individual and the culture can produce the *concept* of freedom. Thus the cultural homogeneity of a strongly equalitarian society would appear to increase the *feeling* of freedom to the impoverishment of the *concept*.[63]

Yet, unquestionably, the concept of freedom was one of the commonest and probably the most talked about and argued about idea in the United States of the early nineteenth century. And even in Boas' primitive communities it seems that one form of subjection may nevertheless be felt: "the impotence of man against fate, against fate as determined by the forces of nature, by supernatural powers, or by predestination." [64] Though by itself insufficient to create the *concept* of freedom in such a society, the recognition of fate seems at least to assure an ever-present tension between human and extrahuman powers. It would appear plausible, then, that the area of dread between opposing natural and supernatural forces should be the eventual site for the most anxious awareness of man's paradoxical liberty.

In measuring the promise of American life against the possibility of an imminent and catastrophic subversion the prophets of destruction helped to make clear the implications of freedom, and called attention to the fact that true freedom involved the obligation to act against a background of peril and contingency. Such a reminder might

[63] "Liberty among Primitive People," in Ruth Nanda Anshen, ed., *Freedom, Its Meaning* (New York, 1940), p. 376.
[64] *Ibid.*

well appear necessary in a society where a form of naïve, self-willed exploitation was coming increasingly to be identified with the true meaning of the republic. That the concept of fate was bound to be of central importance in a democratic society was suggested by Tocqueville in his famous chapter on the subjects for poetry among democratic peoples. Discarding memories of past orders as clearly unsuitable, he predicted that man's fate alone, now a representative and collective fate, would be democracy's highest theme.[65] The meaning of the new age of democratic freedom would take form by coming up against an edge somewhere. As private destinies merged into the destiny of a democratic nation, the more thrillingly urgent became the contact and collision between America and its fate. The jeremiads of the seventeenth century had testified to New Englanders that the covenant which gave cosmic meaning to their history was still in operation, and that their high destiny had not drifted into the indifferent tide of causal determinism. Similarly, for their nineteenth-century descendants the idea of cataclysmic destruction provided a framework of meaning that could be clung to in an environment of heart-freezing change.

Scholarly attention has recently been drawn to the existence of a significant body of catastrophic fiction in the 1830's and 1840's.[66] The dark themes of Hawthorne and Melville, then, may turn out to have been less exceptional than has been supposed. Even Edgar Allen Poe, it might be argued, far from being the "pure" artist Parrington thought him, may well have been the one writer who responded with exquisite sensitivity to anxieties and fears characteristically American. If we look at the Massachusetts Election Sermon for 1836, a year before the beginning of the great depression, we recognize a typical plaint:

[65] Tocqueville, *Democracy in America,* II, 76.

[66] Curtis Dahl, "The American School of Catastrophe," *American Quarterly,* XI (Fall, 1959) , 380–90.

It is with nations as with individuals, that prosperity. . . . is the parent of vice. . . . In the long festival of peace which has smiled upon us, the very sunshine of our fortunes has hatched out a pernicious brood of evils. The political atmosphere is becoming charged with noxious misasmata, which threaten grievous distempers to society. . . . We see luxury, the fatal bane of all republics, spreading its infection and eating as a gangrene into the vitals of the state.[67]

Six years later a pestilence, ancient sign of divine judgment, invaded the happy palace of the fortunate Prince Prospero (prosperity?) : "And Darkness and Decay and the Red Death held illimitable dominion over all." But whether or not Prospero's downfall was charged with social meaning Poe was obviously fascinated by the destructive possibilities of human nature, when either the will or the intellect grew beyond the bounds of the feelings. This is the theme of many of his tales, and it appears as a background factor in those of his writings which depict the cataclysmic destruction of the world. The United States, Poe pretty clearly suggested in several places, was a nation which had expanded the volitional and intellectual portions of its being to a state of cancerous giantism. Having ruthlessly manhandled the order of nature, through the imbalance of its own development America would finally be destroyed together with the cosmic order it had violated.[68]

[67] Andrew Bigelow, *God's Charge Unto Israel: A Sermon preached before His Honor Samuel T. Armstrong, Lieutenant Governor, The Honorable Council, and the Legislature of Massachusetts, at the Annual Election, on Wednesday, January 6, 1836* (Boston, 1836), pp. 22–25.

[68] "The Masque of the Red Death," "Mellona Tauta," "The Colloquy of Monos and Una," "The Conversation of Eiros and Charmion," in *The Complete Tales and Poems of Edgar Allen Poe,* Modern Library Edition (New York, 1938), pp. 269–73, 384–94, 444–56. On Poe and the will see Allen Tate, "The Angelic Imagination: Poe as God," in *Collected Essays* (Denver, 1959), pp. 432–54. Recently, Edward Fussell has ventured an ingenious interpretation

No group labored the destruction theme harder than the embattled defenders of the Puritan Sabbath. Pleading with a society grown increasingly unhomogeneous and secular, they argued desperately that the nation's survival was organically bound up with the preservation of Sabbath observance. "The dreaded consequences of sabbath-breaking are not left to uncertainty," preached one Brooklyn pastor on the Sunday after the Fourth of July, 1836. "If we, as a nation, pollute the holy sabbath, GOD 'will pour forth his fury' upon us. This may be done by plague, pestilence, or famine, as well as by revolution, rapine, and blood." [69] In 1841 the militant author of a compendium on the Sabbath question as a public issue pointed out that history made clear "how other nations, which have dared to pollute the Sabbath, as we are doing, have been swept as with the besom of destruction, except when prevented by timely repentance and return to duty." [70]

Sometimes, of course, the "besom of destruction" was largely visualized in the form of red ink on the balance sheet: "In general, a nation's prosperity has been and is proportioned to the sacredness with which it keeps the Sabbath." [71] And the textile manufacturer Amos Lawrence could write to his manager: "We must make a good thing out of this establishment, unless you ruin us by working on Sundays." [72] At least as common, however, was the attitude

---

of Poe's "Masque" in social terms. His remarks on the spatial layout of Prospero's palace as related to American historical time and space are highly intriguing, if not convincing. (*Frontier: American Literature and the American West* [Princeton, 1965], pp. 166–69).

[69] Benjamin Cutler, *A Sermon delivered in St. Ann's Church, Brooklyn, on Sunday following the celebration of our national independence, MDCCCXXXVI* (New York, 1836), pp. 13–14.

[70] Harmon Kingsbury, *The Sabbath* . . . (New York, 1841), p. 298.

[71] George B. Cheever, "The Elements of National Greatness" (1842), *New England Society Orations*, I, 303.

[72] *Diary and Correspondence*, p. 202. Entry in 1845.

of Elijah Whitney, Corresponding Secretary of the American Society for the Promotion of Christian Morals. The Sabbath, said Whitney,

is the bulwark of our free institutions . . . the rock on which rests the moral sense of the nation. If this be abandoned, immorality, licentiousness and infidelity will sweep over the land in an irresistible and overwhelming flood of moral desolation.[73]

Wholly aside from the religious issue, in an America baying upon the path of exploitation the Sabbath was a standing rebuke to greed and materialism, an inherited symbol of a cosmic brake on the inordinate desires of men. "The sabbath, considered as an institution either of piety or mercy," explained a Baltimore lecturer,

surpasses any thing that the wisdom of man has ever invented. . . . Proclaiming a truce to the absorbing cares and sordid passions of men, it invites them to hold communion together as fellow pilgrims of time, the heirs of immortality, the children of the skies.[74]

A widely read work on American religion, by the Presbyterian Robert Baird, identified the Sabbath with the state of the New World before the commencement of colonization. At that time, wrote Baird, "the work of God, in all its simplicity and freshness, and grandeur, was seen everywhere; that of man almost nowhere; universal nature rested, and, as it were, kept Sabbath." [75] Thus the Sabbath provided an opportunity of coming into contact once again with the lost Paradise of early America, a world of godlike purity and innocence.

Furthermore, it was clear that since the Sabbath declared that the world was once and for all completed and

[73] "Advertisement," in Harmon Kingsbury, *The Sabbath*, p. iv.

[74] George W. Burnap, *Lectures on the Sphere and Duties of Woman* . . . (Baltimore, 1841), p. 265.

[75] *Religion in America* . . . (New York, 1845), p. 11.

full, its observance was an acknowledgment and acceptance of a divinely instituted order. The abandonment of the Sabbath, then, was the sign of a fatal disruption of harmony, one whose consequences could well appear to reach to the foundations of a universe which was through and through moral. The end could only be total extinction. In the light of such a threat the battle to preserve the Sabbath loses its crotchety character, and the Sabbath itself takes on some of that high serious purpose which its proponents claimed for it: not a day of rest in seven, but a link to the creation of the universe; not a piece of irksomely enforced piety, but a window to freedom from the bondage of matter.

The United States was the first nation to stake its being on the romantic conception of man's nature, to adopt as its conscious aim a limitless expansion and the fulfillment of all desire. "Liberty and the Pursuit of Happiness" dedicated a whole people to the great race. Thoroughly in tune with his environment, the naturalist Constantine Rafinesque, in concluding his memoirs with a list of projects for the future—for others, if not for himself—proposed the establishment of "societies of happiness." [76] It was not from such a simple-hearted faith in the autonomy of human reason and will that a notion such as the Sabbath could be justified. The fundamental beliefs of American society, no less than its booming success, militated against the concept of the Sabbath. What its defenders were doing, at their best, was to call attention to the ineradicable presence of an irrational area of existence, one that it would be tragic to disregard. After all, the theory of popular sovereignty emphasized only that man could act for himself, but nowhere did it supply the assurance that, having acted, he would be able to face the consequences of his acts. The living consciousness of an incalculable *otherness* to the uni-

[76] *A Life of Travels and Researches in North America* . . . (Philadelphia, 1836), p. 148.

verse was the necessary balance weight to the sweep of man's will in the world, and the institution of the Sabbath was its visible token.

If the steamboat with its load of fire was an apt metaphor for American material progress, it was also no accident that both Cooper and Poe thought naturally in terms of comets when expressing their disaffection with what appeared to be a runaway democracy. What they had in mind was well illustrated by the speaker at a New York celebration of the three hundred and thirty-second anniversary of the Pilgrim landing. Defending the Puritan's so-called "austerity," the orator pointed out that such rigorousness was in reality the self-discipline which replaced institutional restraints. As a result, having once gained freedom, the Puritan "was not intoxicated and ruined by it." He was able, therefore, to understand that the problem of freedom was the problem of the internalization of order, and not simply a reliance upon documentary guarantees.

The motive power, the mainspring, the regulator, balance and detent, must be combined in the same mechanism. Give to the comet its centrifugal force alone, and it will burn and destroy, strewing its lawless flight with blazing ruin; but join therewith the centripetal power, and it will be sure to turn at the right point, and shoot along its boundless path, itself a world of fire, yet passing between other worlds without collision or harm, awakening only admiration at the harmony and beauty of the mighty laws it obeys.[77]

Under the best of circumstances, then, democracy was a flaming comet, whose chance of avoiding incineration lay in the development of an internal gyroscope for self-regulating order.

The comet as the image of America's rushing power was placed in the context of American space, America's boundless opportunity, by the poet William Cullen Bryant. An

[77] *New England Society Orations*, II, 189–90.

enthusiastic democrat, he could glory in the excitement of America's wild cosmic ride:

> Here the free spirit of mankind, at length,
> Throws its last fetters off, and who shall place
>   A limit to the giant's unchained strength,
>   Or curb his swiftness in the forward race!
>   Far, like the comet's way through infinite space,
>   Stretches the long untravelled path of light,
>   Into the depths of ages: We may trace,
> Distant, the brightening glory of the flight
> Till the receding rays are lost to human sight.[78]

In the midst of a society which was raising the belief in progress to the status of a national faith, the doubters and the nay-sayers, frequently shrill and grotesquely comic, sounded a note that was far from being merely a disgruntled attack upon democratic and capitalistic values. However wide the orbit of man's freedom, they insisted, the important fact about it was that it was an orbit, that it moved within a field of regulating and restraining invisible forces. To ignore this fact in an excess of exhilaration was to shoot wildly outward to a brilliantly spectacular, but finally no less miserable, death.

[78] "The Ages," *Poems of William Cullen Bryant* . . . (Philadelphia, 1849), p. 30. Recited at the Harvard Commencement in 1821, this poem was thereafter placed at the head of successive editions of Bryant's works.

CHAPTER TWO

Yesterday, Today, and Tomorrow

Periodicity characterized both the Sabbath and the comet. In its weekly recurrence the Sabbath provided a home base for the dynamic of history, a permanent haven for respite and renewal, while the track of the comet, swift yet curved, demonstrated the aberrant possibilities of that dynamic and its vulnerability to the simple attrition of time. For a nineteenth-century America glorying in its progressivism, where lay the safe course between the two poles of Sabbath rest and cometlike motion? What, after all, was the meaning of time for America?

To the "Sovereign-Kings of Vivenza" an anonymous scroll unfolded the destiny of their society according to the decrees of Oro:

Throughout all eternity, the parts of the past are but parts of the future reversed. In the old footprints, up and down, you mortals go, eternally travelling your sierras. And not more unfathomable the ponderings of the Calculating Machine than the deductions from the decimals of history. . . . And

55

though crimson republics may rise in constellations, like fiery Aldebarans, speeding to their culminations; yet, down must they sink at last, and leave the old sultan-sun in the sky; in time, again to be deposed.

Thus, in 1848, did the young Herman Melville lecture his countrymen on time and the American republic. That they desperately needed such lecturing, Melville, shocked and disgusted by the Mexican War, was thoroughly convinced. For as the mysterious scroll declared,

In these boisterous days, the lessons of history are almost discarded, as superseded by present experiences. And that while all Mardi's present has grown out of its past, it is becoming obsolete to refer to what has been. Yet, peradventure, the past is an apostle.[1]

If the past was an apostle, Americans were denying the succession. More than other people they had needed to come to a right understanding with the past, to define the meaning of time for themselves and for the republic, which had not come into existence through the normal course of historical time. The nature of its appearance, as John Quincy Adams pointed out, was in itself remarkable. How conscious Americans were of the importance of this fact in regard to their relation to Europe can be seen in the remarks of a Cincinnati dignitary who greeted the touring Lafayette in 1825. The confrontation was bound to be a dramatic one: Lafayette, when associated with the events of the Revolution, had been young, and now he was old; but the same could not be said for America. The states of Europe, declared the speaker, in what was perhaps an unwitting analogy to his European guest, "have passed from infancy to manhood, and from manhood speedily to old age." On the other hand,

The American government, no less prudent, cautious and circumspect, than those of the old world, like Minerva from the

[1] *Mardi, and a Voyage Thither,* Standard ed. (New York, 1963), II, Chap. LVII, 241–42, 238.

head of Jove, sprung at once into full maturity and symmetry, and armed in sovereign panoply, took her rank among the kingdoms of the earth.[2]

The implication was that America stood athwart history like a discontinuity in the stream of time. In that case, the relevance of the past, so far as it represented the experience of Europe, was perhaps questionable.

It was notable that the delegates to the Constitutional Convention turned for instructive parallels to the classic world rather than to the England of the Commonwealth. A cultural nationalism that rejected England aspired at the same time to identify itself with a universalism that transcended the mere homeland. In the classic, archetypal forms of political life were to be found the rights of man, as distinguished from the rights of Englishmen. Such a point of view argued an American alienation from the grasp of an organic, efficacious past, as though America were itself a kind of rebuke to time. An appeal to the nature of man, rather than to his history, evidenced a faith in something that had emerged unscathed from the gauntlet of historical time. As record, as deposit, the past undoubtedly existed, but Americans contested the extent of its jurisdiction.

The notion of unprecedentedness, of utterly new beginnings, remained for a long time a primitive asssumption of the American mind. The feeling was common, as Charles Pinckney had put it in 1787, that the existence of free land in the West had given rise to "an equality of condition" which made the American situation "unexampled." [3] So long as American history could retain its unexampledness, then, the development of such a sense of the past as Melville saw lacking in his time would of necessity be inhib-

---

[2] *Liberty Hall and Cincinnati Gazette,* May 21, 1825.

[3] Charles C. Tansill, ed., *Documents Illustrative of the Formation of the Union of the American States* (Washington, 1927), pp. 804–05.

ited. It would make of references to the Amphyctyonic
Council in the *Federalist Papers* and appeals to the Grac-
chi during debates on the Homestead Law mere categories
of rhetoric. It was not that Americans refused to recognize
the past; on the contrary, they were always prepared to
salute it, in Whitman's famous words, as a corpse going out
the door.[4] That was, however, but to acknowledge its past-
ness, and not to concede with Herman Melville that "the
parts of the past are but the parts of the future reversed."
Herein lay Melville's cause for annoyance, for if time made
all things new, it guaranteed as well that real newness
should be impossible.

Ambiguity about newness lay at the heart of the American attitude toward time. It was a puzzle America had inherited from the Europeans who had named a *New World*.
To the Old World, America was new because it had not
participated in the moral drama of the European consciousness. Obviously, the land itself, as Emerson said, was
"as old as the Flood."[5] "Time hath endless rareties,"
wrote Sir Thomas Browne in the seventeenth century,
"and shows of all varieties, which reveals old things in
heaven, makes new discoveries in earth, and even earth itself a discovery. That great antiquity America lay buried
for thousands of years."[6] Still, the author of an American
magazine article reported about India in 1837, it was hard
to "believe that America and India belong to the same
world. One appears so new, and the other so old, you
would suppose that there must have been thousands of
years of difference in the date of their creation."[7] Gazing at

[4] "Preface to 1855 Edition of 'Leaves of Grass,'" *Complete Poetry
and Selected Prose*, ed. James E. Miller, Jr., Riverside ed. (Boston,
1959), p. 411.

[5] "The Young American" (1844), *Works*, I, 395.

[6] *The Works of Sir Thomas Browne*, ed. Simon Wilkin, F.L.S.
(London, 1852), III, 7.

[7] "Letters on India—By a Lady," *The Mother's Magazine*, V
(November, 1837), 246–47.

the scored and kneaded Indian soil, this straightforward American found it natural to associate age with the consequential labor of man. But what would be the result of such labors in America? One answer was that given by John Quincy Adams, when he made the long journey in the closing years of his life to address a local scientific society in Cincinnati. Here was a busy area of civilization where in his youth there had been untouched nature. *"We—you— you,"* the old man declared, "have converted the wilderness into a garden, and opened a paradise upon the wild." [8] His hearers could not have missed noticing that Adams considered their progressive labors as having created a primitive refuge exempt from the ravages of time.

Quite another response to this problem, reflecting a difference in generations and temperaments, was that of Henry David Thoreau. With a distaste at least equal to Melville's, he spurned the novelties of progress for the permanent novelty of what was oldest in America, its forest landscape. On the eve of the Civil War he was still pleading, "Let us keep the New World *new,* preserve all the advantages of living in the country." [9] Yet, if Adams aimed at the achievement of an America that was Edenicly sinless, Thoreau's purpose was no less moral. In his journal for 1841 he had noted, "Sin, I am sure, is not in overt acts or indeed, in acts of any kind, but is in proportion to the time which has come behind us and displaced eternity,—that degree to which our elements are mixed with the elements of the world." [10] As an American moralist Thoreau was as much concerned as Adams that time should not "come behind" his countrymen to displace eternity. In sharing this

[8] "Oration delivered before the Cincinnati Astronomical Society, November 10, 1843," Adrienne Koch and William Peden, eds., *The Selected Writings of John and John Quincy Adams* (New York, 1946), p. 406.

[9] *The Writings of Henry David Thoreau,* Walden ed. (Boston and New York, 1906), XVIII, 387. Entry for Oct. 15, 1859.

[10] *Ibid.,* VII, 300.

social aspiration, both men, different as they were, revealed that they partook somewhat of the American hope-
fulness about time which so bothered Melville.

Part of the paradox of growing old while remaining
young came from the idea of the continent itself. Outside
time, of course, on the sidelines of history, America had
grown old in this way—and would continue to do so as
long as time remained for it only a formal concept, empty
of experiential reality. The nonhistorical character of the
land for such a long period lent plausibility to the traditional American belief that it had been foreordained to a
cosmicly important role. Cotton Mather had seen "the
Wicked One . . . like a *Dragon,* keeping a Guard upon
the spacious and mighty *Orchards* of *America*" until the
coming of the proper time.[11] America was thus born into
time, but only into the *right* time, a time that inaugurated
a new era. So powerful and enduring was this idea that
even past the middle of the nineteenth century it was possible for a patriotic orator to launch yet again into the familiar description of

this New World enveloped in the mists of the ocean, its rivers
running silently to the sea, its vast surface waiting for a future
population, its existence altogether unknown, till the aus-
picious moment had arrived, when God's hand lifted the veil
of the sea, and a new continent was revealed as the home of
new men and the theatre for a new act in human history.[12]

The genesis of America, both land and nation, was thus
felt as a providential conspiracy against time, as an attempt
to outwit time by an evasion of the exigencies of temporal
causality; by an appeal, finally, from time to eternity.
America as the site of a "New Heaven and a New Earth,"
America as the first nation ever founded on the principles
of natural rights and justice, was manifestly a spectacular

[11] *Selections from Early American Writers, 1607–1800,* ed. William B. Cairns (New York, 1910), p. 226.
[12] *New England Society Orations,* II, 172–73.

assault against the efficacy of time as history. Europe was doomed to go on in the old way, controlled by prescription and tradition, but America, structuring itself upon first principles, lived now upon her own time, henceforth to be the definitive time. With a glorious exuberance Joel Barlow's *Columbiad* proclaimed that America's function was to

> Mould a fair model for the realms of earth,
> Call moral nature to a second birth,
> Reach, renovate the world's great social plan,
> And here commence the sober sense of man.

As order had primitively come into the universe to supplant the reign of physical chaos, Barlow declared, so the rule of American freedom was a regeneration of the "moral frame" of the world, a return to true order from the chaos of spiritual tyranny.[13]

Barlow's conviction that the pre-American past was chaos robbed time—old time, Europe's time—of its historic quality. And his identification of American freedom with the "moral frame" of the universe assimilated the new nation to a timeless order of the right and the true, immutable and exempt from temporal vicissitude. America, then, by cleaving to the primitively old, to that which had not grown old through the agency of time, gained the possibility of continuing to be always new. The extreme optimism of men like Barlow was not ascribable merely to naïve enthusiasm over the material resources of the continent. They were far from simply denying the importance of the past, but they believed that America had given full scope for the first time to the moral element in history, an element that they were sure would be decisive. Men were still men, and land was still land, yet a new relationship between the two, founded at last on the principles of true right, endowed American destiny with its extratemporal quality.

[13] *Columbiad,* Bk. VIII, pp. 255–56.

The rhetoric of intellectuals and backwoodsmen alike could reflect a common understanding that the genuine idea of America was too vast for secular measuring rods. It came naturally to the urbane and cultivated Caleb Cushing, no holdover from the age of the Founders, when speaking at his native Newburyport on the deaths of John Adams and Thomas Jefferson, to picture the United States as "the centre of the great solar system of civil freedom." [14] While a legendary Kentuckian, asked to give the boundaries of the nation, blandly explained: "Why sir, on the north we are bounded by the Aurora Borealis, on the east we are bounded by the rising sun, on the south we are bounded by the procession of the Equinoxes, and on the west by the Day of Judgment." [15] Terms less than astronomical and apocalyptic would not serve to draw the line upon America. Her definition had to be as ample as the time-measuring and time-creating elements of the cosmos itself.

Having been released from thralldom to the past by a providential dispensation, it was not surprising that Americans should slight the values of that past, even deny its real status, in favor of an ever-present present. Visiting the United States in the 1830's, Tocqueville was shocked when he was casually given original documents in response to his inquiries. It appeared to him that in America "no one cares for what occurred before his time." He saw the newspapers alone, the archrepresentatives of the concern for the immediate and the passing, as the connecting links between past and present. Yet if a daily number was missing, no one bothered about the gap. Such irreverence toward the past puzzled the historically minded Frenchman; there was something uncivil about it. "In America," he noted, "society seems to live from hand to mouth, like an army in the

[14] *A Eulogy on John Adams and Thomas Jefferson, pronounced in Newburyport, July 15, 1826* . . . (Cambridge, 1826), p. 56.

[15] B. A. Botkin, ed., *A Treasury of American Folklore* (New York, 1944), p. 276.

field." Under such conditions, it was to be feared that the passage of another fifty years would make the America that he now saw about him more difficult to reconstruct than the France of the Middle Ages.[16]

Americans were not as uninterested in their own past as Tocqueville believed. They were willing to collect the remains of so much of the past as they felt to be genuinely part of their present, even if they were content to ignore the fact that the present was becoming the past. When Tocqueville was making his notes Jared Sparks was hunting out Revolutionary documents and George Bancroft was preparing the first volume of his lifework on the history of the United States. It was only a question of what past Americans could acknowledge and what meaning they were prepared to assign to it. In 1836, when the town of Dedham, Massachusetts, celebrated the two hundredth anniversary of its founding, the leading speaker delivered "An Historical Address" based on a study of the accumulated town records. Although it was sometimes claimed, the Reverend Samuel F. Haven told the assembly of citizens, that the principles of freedom Americans gloried in were carried over with the Pilgrims from the Old World, that was a mistake, for "all that is peculiar in the nature of our institutions is wholly of American growth." [17] At the same time Bancroft was laboring to stake out as authentically American those areas of colonial history that could be assimilated to the era of Andrew Jackson.

In refusing to recognize the non-American past as an organic tradition, in insisting that what was American was wholly self-made, Americans could claim freedom to judge the past on their own terms. "In a society which has no Past," Michel Chevalier noted thoughtfully, "the Past counts for nothing." [18] Yet Americans were well aware that

---

[16] *Democracy in America*, I, 211–12.

[17] *An Historical Address delivered before the citizens of the Town of Dedham* . . . (Dedham, 1837), p. 23.

[18] Chevalier, *Society, Manners, and Politics*, p. 407.

history seemed to reveal distinct patterns of growth and decay in the life of nations, and that popular governments in particular had indeed followed the course of Melville's "crimson republics," rising in "constellations" and "speeding to their culminations." The fearful possibility that the United States, despite the fortunate circumstances of its environment, was doomed to see its vitality decline, was a specter that had to be exorcised.

However seriously certain segments of the American population may have taken the cyclical theory of history in the late eighteenth century,[19] two generations later its popular acceptance was largely tied to a series of qualifications which allowed America to thumb its nose at history. The traditional American notion of mission, complementary to the notion of providentiality, offered serious-minded patriots a handy method of overcoming, or at least postponing, any fated end. Thus Caleb Cushing, a conservative Whig with a good sense of history, conceded to a Fourth of July audience in 1839 that "it seems to have been the fate of highly civilized states to have a set career before them to run, and then to yield the ascendancy to others." Everybody was acquainted, of course, with the examples of Greece and Rome, yet it was obvious that neither had declined before accomplishing the furthest development of those institutions which it was their respective destinies to perfect. "I consider it the destiny of the United States," was Cushing's conclusion, "to people, cultivate, and civilize this Continent; and I anticipate no end of her power until the appointed work be done." [20] Tied to the completion of such a large task, the date of America's final decline could be effectually placed beyond the edge of a western

[19] See Stow Persons, "The Cyclical Theory of History in Eighteenth Century America," *American Quarterly,* VI (Summer, 1954), 147–63.

[20] *An Oration, on the Material Growth and Territorial Progress of the United States, delivered at Springfield, Mass. on the Fourth of July, 1839* (Springfield, 1839), pp. 24–25.

horizon whose boundaries hardly seemed real. To render the problem practically academic it was merely necessary to invoke the commonly accepted American aims to evangelize and republicanize the whole world. Cushing himself took one of the first official steps in this direction a few years later when he negotiated an American treaty with the Empire of China.

Another Whig conservative, Professor George Tucker of the University of Virginia, took up the question in 1847. In an article entitled "Dangers to be Guarded Against in the Progress of the United States," Tucker was not satisfied to base the security of America's future on the concept of its mission. As a political economist he refused to acknowledge the existence of a law of history by which nations were forced to decline from a position of greatness into a stage corresponding to old age and death. Tucker rejected such a notion as the product of an inapplicable analogy drawn from the animal kingdom. So far as he could see, natural bodies had been confounded with artificial bodies. Utilizing the then standard notion of the fixity of biological species, Tucker proceeded to draw his own analogy from the animal kingdom: "Governments may be more correctly compared with species than with individuals— while the latter flourish for a time and then pass away, the former have the power of perpetual renovation." For Tucker, the reliability of political techniques, and not historical law, would decide the fate of the United States.[21]

As could have been expected, the moral element was uppermost for President Mark Hopkins of Williams College when he tackled the same problem in 1853. Like Tucker, he made use of a biological analogy, but for Hopkins the analogy was simply a handy illustration. Growing at its top in the manner of a tree, society drew sustenance at its roots from material progress, and transmitted energy to the

[21] *The American Review: A Whig Journal* . . . , V (June, 1847), 614.

leaves so they could "expand into the higher air and purer light of beauty, and of moral and religious truth." A reciprocal downward movement would then return to the roots "nutritive power and regulative principles, causing a growth that will defy the touch of time, that time will only strengthen and enlarge." What then had been the reason for the spectacular decay of so many highly developed cultures? "The difficulty with past civilizations," Hopkins explained,

has been that they did not form an adequate top. The products of the physical and intellectual life circulated in and for themselves, and hence plethora, stagnation, debility, spasms, and dissolution. This is the stereotyped round in which families and nations perish through prosperity. But if these products might flow on and up, if the affections might distribute them rather than appetite, benevolence rather than ostentation, and principle rather than fashion and caprice; if they might minister to a pure and spiritual religion, and be controlled and distributed by that, it is not for the imagination to depict the beauty and blessedness that would pervade society.

Particularly do we believe that there would spring from this a higher culture of all that pertains to beauty; and only from this a permanent civil liberty.[22]

Unquestionably, then, Hopkins could regard his work as an educator as a contribution to the moral strategy that would preserve the republic.

Tucker's explicit denial of the cyclical character of history was somewhat unusual. Cushing and Hopkins expressed variants of the standard American reaction to this conundrum of the supposed evidence of the past, a reaction that was in the nature of what common-law lawyers called *confession and avoidance*. That is, the claimed facts —here the law of the past dictating the rise and subsequent decline of civilizations—were admitted, but the proposed

---

[22] "The Central Principle," *New England Society Orations,* II, 222–23.

implication, the attempt to subsume the case of the United States under the general rule, was flatly denied. Thus Pinckney at the Constitutional Convention had relied on the new social and physical environment to exempt the nation from the power of the past, and those aspiring nationalistic bards Timothy Dwight and Joel Barlow, in so many ways at opposite poles from each other, had joined in agreeing that the cyclical procession of history was grinding to a full stop in their own time. As Dwight's epic poem of the 1780's declared:

> Some land, scarce glimmering in the light of fame,
> Scepter'd with arts, and arms (if I divine)
> Some unknown wild, some shore without a name,
> In all thy pomp, shall then majestic shine.

Without equivocation his well-known Revolutionary song proclaimed: "Columbia . . . thy reign is the last, and the noblest of time. . . ." [23] In a like mood the celestial spirit in Barlow's *Columbiad* answered Columbus' fears based on the past decline of all great nations by the argument that the progress of scientific enlightenment in modern times made the old rule obsolete.[24]

Territorial expansion coupled with an extraordinary population growth provided visible encouragement for such hopes. In the increase of population alone many Americans were inclined to see strong evidence of the existence of that moral element so essential for continuing national virility. Even an experienced diplomat like Alexander Hill Everett could view the growth of American population as "a short and decisive answer to the calumnies on the moral character of the citizens of the United States, in which some European writers are accustomed to indulge." Striking back at British attacks, he went on:

When the judicious travellers, and still more judicious critics of the mother country, think proper to gratify their spleen by

[23] Cairns, *Early American Writers,* pp. 418, 410.
[24] *Columbiad,* Book IX.

representing us as an indolent, immoral, and irreligious people, we have only to refer them to the census for a complete mathematical demonstration of the folly and falsehood of their assertions.[25]

Alexander Everett's reliance upon columns of figures to overrule the judgment of the Old World was carried further in 1824 by the author of a statistical survey of American social and economic progress. In place of the traditional record of history this writer put forward the American decennial census report as the only adequate measuring stick for the United States. So crucial was the American freedom from prescriptive tradition, and so unprecedented its geographical base, that only a wholly American standard was applicable: the conditions obtaining thirty years earlier. "In the speculation before us," he explained, "we dismiss the ancient guide, and start with a new one. It is the act of comparing America with America herself; from the recent past, to infer the proximate future." [26] Less baldly, substantially the same point was made by the scholar Gulian Verplanck in 1836 when he told the students at Union College that "the actual state and the probable future prospects of our country, resemble those of no other land, and are without a parallel in past history." [27] The implication had to be that just as an unparalleled present had succeeded an unparalleled past so would the present be succeeded by an unparalleled future.

Such a standard argued that the genuine novelty which America had introduced into the stream of history had

[25] *New Ideas on Population: with Remarks on the Theories of Malthus and Godwin* (Boston, 1823), p. 93.

[26] [Anon.], *A General Outline of the United States of North America, her Resources and Prospects, with a Statistical Comparison* . . . (Philadelphia, 1825), p. 31. This work received a harsh notice in the *North American Review*, XX (April, 1825), 446–48, where the above quotation was especially singled out for ridicule.

[27] Verplanck, *Advantages and Dangers*, p. 5.

vitiated the relevance of all historic analogies, and that, as Melville had complained, "it is becoming obsolete to refer to what has been." America had inaugurated a new time scale, one that brought along with it its own set of values, and these were the sole values by which America would consent to be judged.

When Sir George Templemore ventured to touch upon the subject of "history and tradition" with Aristabulus Bragg, Bragg quickly brushed the whole subject aside:

Why, sir, in the way of history, one meets with but few incumbrances in this country. . . . A nation is much to be pitied that is weighed down by the past, in this manner, since its industry and enterprise are constantly impeded by obstacles that grow out of its recollections. America may, indeed, be termed a happy and free country . . . in this as well as in all other things! [28]

To the past as prescriptive tradition no one assigned less importance than Thomas Jefferson. But at the same time he acknowledged the republican utility of history. In his projected scheme of education for the youth of Virginia he made history the principal study of the great majority of students who were not to go on to higher education. History, Jefferson affirmed, would "qualify them as judges of the actions and designs of men," thus allowing them to recognize and frustrate the first beginnings of ambition and tyranny.[29] Worthless as tradition, history was invaluable as the stored experience of the race. Here Jefferson was assuming that human nature had not changed and would not change, that men would continue to act in the future as they had in the past. Yet he sometimes talked otherwise. Forced to contend with the logic of John

[28] James Fenimore Cooper, *Home As Found,* Mohawk ed. (New York and London, n.d.), Ch. II, p. 23.

[29] "Notes on Virginia," Query XIV, *The Writings of Thomas Jefferson,* eds. A. A. Lipscomb and A. E. Bergh (Washington: Thomas Jefferson Memorial Assoc., 1903), II, 207.

Adams, who could see no reason why class enmity grounded in disparities of wealth and talents should cease to exist merely because America was America, Jefferson answered that "before the establishment of the American states nothing was known to History but the Man of the old world. . . . A government adapted to such men would be one thing; but a very different one that for the Man of these states." [30] Most of the time it was apparent that what Jefferson meant by such statements was only that since America provided so general an opportunity for men to act differently than they had in the past, it could be assumed they would do so.

For Jefferson no less than for John Adams the hope of the United States lay in the maintenance of a social structure based upon accurate knowledge of the historic propensities of men. Much as they might differ about the details of those propensities, or about the relative merits of a decentralized agrarianism or a balance of classes as preservers of republican liberty, both could have approved the remark of the high Federalist John Jay when he observed: "I do not expect that mankind will, before the millennium, be what they ought to be; and therefore, in my opinion, every political theory which does not regard them as being what *they are,* will prove delusive." [31]

But what exactly *was* man in the New World? Jefferson's reluctance to acknowledge the presence of Old World man in a New World setting reflected a grass-roots feeling that Americans matched the uniqueness of their land. Shortly before the Declaration of Independence, Crèvecoeur had expressed the conviction that the American was a "new man" for whom the categories of the Old World were inapplicable.[32] The idea had wide appeal not only for

[30] *Adams-Jefferson Letters,* II, 391 (October 28, 1813).

[31] Jay to Benjamin Vaughn (August 31, 1797), *The Correspondence and Public Papers of John Jay,* ed. Henry P. Johnston (New York and London, 1890–1893), IV, 230–31.

[32] J. Hector St. John de Crèvecoeur, *Letters from an American Farmer,* Everyman's Library (New York, 1926), p. 44.

Americans but for Europeans of a liberal persuasion who
were excited by the vision of a genuine rebirth for European man upon American soil. More than half a century
after Crèvecoeur, his countryman Chevalier, come to investigate the American spirit in Jacksonian times, hailed
the American as "a new political *and physiological* phenomenon, a hitherto unknown variety of the human race
[italics added]." In the manner of a sociological taxono-
mist he proceeded to record the distinguishing characteristics of his find. While lagging behind the Frenchman and
the Englishman "in many respects, particularly in taste
and philosophy," Chevalier's *homo Americanus* was

superior to the rest of the human family by its extraordinary
combination of sagacity, energy of will, and hardy enterprise,
by its admirable aptitude for business, by its untiring devotion
to work, and above all by its recognition and protection of the
rights of the laboring classes, hitherto treated as the off-scour-
ings of society.

To Chevalier it was plain that "this people will become
the founders of a new family." [33]

Almost at the same time as Chevalier was making his
notes Bronson Alcott confided similar sentiments to his
journal. Himself the most untypical of Americans, Alcott
spoke for many others when he wrote that neither the environment nor the men of America were comparable to
their counterparts in Europe. "Physical differences have
moulded us in accordance with their spirit . . . and, despite the foreign associations of our ancestral education,
Nature has assumed her rightful influence and has shaped
us in her moulds." Yet, Alcott insisted, "to us the past *is* of
value." That was not because America could possibly learn
anything from the past but because Americans were in the
position of newborn heirs to a precious fortune, the posses-
sors of the fruits of time without any of its obligations.
"Living on the accumulated treasures of the past in a new
theater of action," said Alcott, "we have monopolized the

[33] Chevalier, *Society, Manners, and Politics,* p. 410.

best of time and space, and stand on a vantage ground to which no people have ever ascended before." [34]

Something of Alcott's sense of unhampered American power, the feeling that Europe's "best of time" had come to Americans as a free possession, had some dozen years before breathed through the lines of a letter from a French scientist to the immigrant naturalist Constantine Rafinesque. "What I hear of the progress of Transylvania University," the Frenchman had written, "is in harmony with the rapid evolution of every thing in the United States of America. Civilization and science have been transplanted there quite grown and perfect, as our Apples and Peaches." With more than a hint of sadness he continued, "In Europe our civilization was created wild and sour as the fruits of our Forests. Time alone has unfolded it, and in its long period of maturity, it is become nearly rotten." [35] The implication was plain enough: what "time alone . . . unfolded," time also spoiled. Only America had succeeded in plundering time and escaping beyond the reach of its retributive justice.

In thus cutting loose from the past, in disengaging themselves from the historical continuum, Americans had no intention of being considered a kind of sport of time, of high individual and particular interest but lacking in more general significance. Abandoning the doomed past to the Old World, Americans were convinced that they had pre-empted for themselves and those who could muster the courage to follow their example the most valuable of all temporal categories, the future. As the books of Daniel and Revelation drew the lineaments of the New Heaven for the Puritans, so for their nineteenth-century descend-

[34] *The Journals of Bronson Alcott,* ed. Odell Shepard (Boston, 1938), pp. 40–41. Entry for April 24, 1834.

[35] *Western Minerva, or American Annals of Knowledge and Literature* (Lexington, Ky., 1821), Reprint ed. (Gloucester, Mass., 1949), I, 70.

ants the volumes of the census reports traced the features of a New Earth. In the controversy between the Old World and the New the Argument from the Past was answered by the Argument from the Future. The same events that drew from Melville words of apprehensive protest caused Walt Whitman, then editor of the *Brooklyn Eagle,* to crow delightedly, "Yankeedoodledom is going ahead with the resistless energy of a sixty-five-hundred-thousand-horsepower steam engine! . . . Let the Old World wag on under its cumbrous load of form and conservatism," Whitman preached; "we are of a newer, fresher race and land. And all we have to say is, to point to fifty years hence and say, Let those laugh who win!" [36]

Across the immense and hardly known forest the American presumed to lay a geometrical grid, bending to an American rationalism an ancient undefined mystery; so over the coming time itself he cast an American framework, to the end that the future should be nothing but American. For the understandably annoyed British it was only another proof of Brother Jonathan's unlimited impudence. Even for William Cobbett, once the scurrilous Peter Porcupine, but grown friendly to American popular liberty in his latter days, America was no more than another England, but without treadmills and game laws.[37] Cobbett looked for reforms at home and acknowledged no immanent spirit in history that directed the movement of civilization with inexorable logic from east to west. Resting in such a faith, Hegel was able to point out America's congruence with the future while he held on to the current perfection of the Prussian state. For him America was as yet only Europe extended, eventually to become itself. America was not, but was to be; as such, it could not be

[36] *The Gathering of the Forces,* eds. C. Rodgers and J. Black (New York, 1920), I, 32–33.
[37] *Rural Rides,* ed. James Paul Cobbett (London, 1853), p. 602. Entry made in 1830.

entered into, but only awaited. Meanwhile it was an emotion. "America," Hegel declared, ". . . is a land of desire
for all those who are weary of the historical lumber-room
of old Europe." [38] America was still dream.

Simply by virtue of its location on the map of the world
America could appear justified in its claim to possess the
future. Speaking before Harvard's Phi Beta Kappa Society
in 1824, shortly before the beginning of his long political
career, Professor Edward Everett quoted with approval the
well-known lines of Bishop Berkeley,

> Westward the course of Empire takes its way;
>   The four first acts are already past,
> A fifth shall close the drama with the day;
>   Time's noblest offspring is the last.

Historically, Everett explained, the West had been the object of longing and aspiration, the great good place where
visions were to be fulfilled. But as west had succeeded to
west, America was now the end of the West, and "farthest
Thule" had at last been reached. Picturing the hopes of
the "seers and sages of the elder world" as bound up with
the success of the New World, Everett exhorted the audience to feel the weight of its responsibility toward those
who had dreamed for ages of a "favoured land beyond the
mountains or seas; a land of equal laws and happy men."
The time was critical, he was convinced, for "there are no
more retreats beyond the sea, no more discoveries, no more
hopes. Here, then, a mighty work is to be performed, or
never, by mortals." [39] The nature of the globe itself had determined that America would have to be time's last frontier.

During his lifetime Everett was the accepted master of
the exaggerated style of public speaking then widely ad-

[38] *Lectures on the Philosophy of History,* trans. J. Sibree, Bohn's
Libraries ed. (London, 1894), p. 90.

[39] "The Circumstances Favorable to the Progress of Literature in
America," *Orations and Addresses,* I, 41–42.

mired. But many sober and thoughtful Europeans were also prepared to recognize an American hegemony over the future. One would have thought that by the 1850's the primitivistic bloom would have had plenty of time to rub off the American dream. By then, cities, slums, crime, industrialism, labor problems, and railroads had gone far to transform the country into an image of industrial Europe. Still, the scholar Philip Schaff, revisiting his homeland to inform the cultured German public of what he had seen in America, could say with calm assurance, "Either humanity has no earthly future and everything is tending to destruction, or this future lies—I say not exclusively, but mainly —in America, according to the victorious march of history, with the sun from east to west." [40] Neither a Puritan nor a spread-eagle expansionist, Schaff saw no impropriety in letting the Old World know that henceforth it was to be America or nothing.

From the "vantage ground" where Americans stood, having "monopolized," according to Bronson Alcott, "the best of time and space," it sometimes appeared that they were beleaguered by importunities from both the past and the future. Called upon by Edward Everett to remember their responsibilities to "the elder world," they were told by George Bancroft that all their obligation was toward the future. Speaking to the New-York Historical Society at its fiftieth anniversary banquet in 1854, Bancroft, by then the most widely read of American historians, expounded a theory of progress that conscripted past and present into the service of the future. Adapting divine providentialism to secular purposes, Bancroft portrayed civilization as an enormous river which gained accretions from tributary streams as it swept onward through time. Since its last state, by containing all the rest, had to be its most comprehensive and best, so also the last philosophy and the last

[40] *America* . . . (1855), ed. Perry Miller (Cambridge, 1961), p. 212.

form of political organization were bound to be the most excellent. From this assumption Bancroft deduced that "it becomes us all to venerate the future. We must be ready to sacrifice ourselves for our successors," he declared, "as they in their turn must live for their posterity." [41]

Although he was one of the most ardent of republicans and had taken part in practical politics, Bancroft remained something of a literary democrat. The scheme of progress which he advanced that day at Niblo's Saloon would presumably have renounced for his own contemporaries their share in the third member of the great American trinity of natural rights. Only some last fortunate generation, apparently, living at the end of time, could be allowed to take its eyes from the future and turn to the legitimate pursuit of its own happiness.

Bancroft's doctrine of sacrifice was largely German and a priori; it was hardly based on any objective consideration of American life. Yet something like it could provide a rationalization for American backwardness in matters of higher culture. The American emphasis upon immediate utility, which was so much criticized by upper-class Europeans, could be justified as a self-limiting preliminary to less desperate days ahead. "The prayer of this young country is, 'God give us this day our daily bread'; and for the other petitions of the Pater Noster it has no time," conceded John Milton Mackie, a Massachusetts man, only a few years before the Civil War. "So must it be for the present," he concluded.

We must be content with little literature, less art, and only nature in perfection. We are to be busy, not happy. For we live for futurity, and are doing the work of two generations yet unborn.[42]

[41] "The Necessity, the Reality, and the Promise of the Progress of the Human Race," *Literary and Historical Miscellanies* (New York, 1855), p. 516.

[42] Warren S. Tryon, comp. and ed., *A Mirror for Americans:*

Present happiness was a genuine possibility for neither Bancroft nor Mackie. But Mackie's observation, unlike Bancroft's, was unsystematic and undoctrinaire, and perhaps the more American for that reason. Relieving time from the perpetual entailment which Bancroft put upon it, Mackie looked forward only a few generations to an age when it would no longer be necessary for Americans to "live for futurity." Yet there was less of voluntary choice in Mackie's formulation. He was describing an unavoidable circumstance, while Bancroft urged the claims of a moral principle.

The feeling of compulsion, the de-emphasis of free will, coupled with the acknowledgment of a prevalent joylessness, were points that had been made even more sharply in Verplanck's Union College address twenty years earlier.

Our past is but brief [Verplanck had said]. We can scarcely be said to have a present—certainly we have none for mere indolent enjoyment. We are all pressing and hastening forward to some better future. No single mind can well resist the general impulse. The momentum of the whole mass of society, composed of myriads of living forces, is upon each individual, and he flies forward with accelerated velocity, without any other power over his own motion than that of the direction of its course. The universal ardor is contagious, and we all rush into the throng of life, and are swept along by its broad, resistless current.[43]

In the activity generated by an expanding society Verplanck saw opportunities for the American scholar to exert that influence upon social and political affairs which the greatest thinkers and artists had done in the past. For him, a present of "indolent enjoyment" was the sign of a stagnant civilization where noble exertion found no reward, and the road to improvement was blocked up. In the

---

Life and Manners in the United States, 1790–1870, as Recorded by American Travelers (Chicago, 1952), III, 612.

[43] Verplanck, *Advantages and Dangers*, p. 10.

vitality of its rushing movement toward the future, Verplanck pinpointed the crucial difference between America and the Old World.

The special relation that obtained between American distinctiveness and the notion of the future was closely connected with the widely popular view of the United States as an unfinished experiment in the validity of republican liberty. In 1825, Charles Stewart Daveis, soon to become prominently known for his long-term connection with the international boundary question, spoke before a rural Maine audience on the hundredth anniversary of a local Indian battle. Daveis utilized the commemoration of an event from the colonial past to explain why it was essential for Americans of his own time to maintain their steady orientation toward the future. For Daveis, America was an argument that had not yet been won. "To test the truth of *our* principles," he asserted, *"we are obliged* to go forward;—to anticipate the progress of time, and the operation of their causes on futurity." A hundred years had passed since the skirmish on a wilderness frontier which was now being memorialized, but another hundred would be required before America could be more than a contention. "To test the truth of our principles, *let us go forward!"* Daveis urged.

Let us advance the space of a single century. When, if we are true to our principles, and those, that shall come after us, shall prove true to our examples, we shall have redeemed ourselves from the reproach, of living in, and for, posterity! [44]

Because Europe no longer had anything to prove, Europe was already itself. But the case of the United States was different. As the embodiment of a principle still unproven, the United States remained an uncompleted essay at free government, and the idea of the future was part of the idea

[44] *An Address delivered on the Commemoration at Fryeburg, May 19, 1825* (Portland, 1825), p. 63.

of America. Only when America had proven herself, Daveis was saying, when America at last existed, would it be possible for her citizens to live for themselves.

Over and over Americans were reminded that they were being trusted to perform an experiment, and one not only for themselves but on behalf of a world whose fate literally depended on American success. "America for the sake of the world" was an axiom largely accepted without question. As a New England politician put it in 1834,

Finally; in connection with the future, let us not magnify ourselves, but our *office*—as Pilots, and Discoverers, in seas which the Ancient world could never navigate; let us bear alway in mind, that on our faithful soundings, and constant watch, the universal weal depends. Our flag, yet flying in advance of the convoy of Nations, is regarded by those who follow, as their light and guide: if shallows, rocks, or mutiny, destroy us, the region of our stranded wreck is one which no political Columbus will dare hereafter to explore.[45]

As bearers of the "flag of the world," [46] Americans were thus a priestly nation. Agents and delegates for mankind, they had been commissioned to the task by the highest authority, for, as the retiring President Jackson assured them, "Providence . . . has chosen you as the guardians of freedom, to preserve it for the benefit of the human race." [47]

With such an assignment, what could be more natural than that they should also have had conferred on them the talents to do the job, and that these talents would be of a prodigious nature. What was needed was a "half horse, half alligator" cosmic amphibian, the master and not the servant of both time and space. These things seemed nowhere

[45] James A. Hillhouse, *An Oration, Pronounced at New Haven . . . August 19, 1834, in commemoration of . . . General Lafayette* (New Haven, 1834), p. 37.

[46] The term is Chesterton's. See Gilbert K. Chesterton, *Orthodoxy* (New York and London, 1909), Ch. V.

[47] Richardson, *Messages and Papers,* III, 308.

to be better understood than in Kentucky, where one W. E. Arthur, on the Fourth of July, 1850, drew the lineaments of the national archetype to the taste of his Covington audience:

The American is the ark of safety, the anointed civilizer, the only visible source of light and heat and repose to the dark and discordant and troubled World, which is heaving and groaning, and livid in convulsions all around him! He is Liberty's chosen apostle: he is a master workman, and universal space is his workshop, and universal perfectibility his hallowed aim. He has present and eternal reward for his exertions, and limitless expanse for his enterprise, his genius, his glory.[48]

The future was then the area in which "the anointed civilizer" would accomplish "his hallowed aim." But that, of course, made the present of critical importance as the preparation for the reign of "universal perfectibility."

> Still, tell me not of years of old,
>   Of ancient heart and clime;
> Ours is the land and age of gold,
>   And ours the hallow'd time! [49]

As much as Americans might refer to themselves in the future tense, it was their obvious concentration upon the here and now that impressed observers most forcefully. Few of his fellow citizens would have denied Melville's accusation that immediate experience seemed to be the measure of all things American. What was more natural in a New World, with the attestations of the past left behind, than that whatever claimed to be right and true should establish its title on present grounds alone. Here again, Bronson Alcott proved himself basically in harmony with

[48] *An Oration delivered on the Fourth of July, 1850, before the Citizens of Covington, Ky.* (Covington, 1850), p. 38.

[49] Grenville Mellen, "The True Glory of America," *The Poets and Poetry of America,* ed. Rufus Griswold (Philadelphia, 1850), p. 236.

the assumptions of a society where he appeared a stranger
and an alien. "History is useful to me," wrote Alcott,

no farther than I am concious of the same facts in my experience. It is in the light of these that I apprehended the facts
of history. I am the highest, and therefore the only authentic,
fact, that can legitimate the facts of all the Past. . . . I become a contemporary of truth, not of men. I am beyond the
range of history. I antedate its records.[50]

On this supposition that an American was himself the
authentic fact which judged the legitimacy of the past, it
could seem only natural for each new generation to hold a
plebiscite over its institutional inheritance. That was to
guarantee that the present would always be a real present,
and not a mere familiar habit. Some self-adjusting social
machinery to help the dial of time point always to the now
was suggested in the plans of Thomas Paine, Thomas Skidmore, and Orestes Brownson for the abolition of the right
of inheritance. Where time made a difference, it was a
tyrant to be overcome.

The assault on time by Skidmore, a leader of the New
York Workingmen's Party in the late 1820's, was un-
matched for boldness. Unequivocally he announced:

Title to property exists for all; and for all alike; not because
others have been; nor because they have *not* been; not because
they had a certain being for a parent, rather than another
being; not because they appear later, or earlier, on the stage of
life, than others; not because of purchase, of conquest, of pre-
occupancy, or what not; but BECAUSE THEY ARE: BE-
CAUSE THEY EXIST. I AM; THEREFORE IS PROP-
ERTY MINE.[51]

In Skidmore's raucous "I AM," existence alone, present-
ness alone, had its claims resoundingly set forth. He filled
in the category of American *being* with positive attributes

[50] *Journals* (1838), p. 106.
[51] Thos. Skidmore, *The Rights of Man to Property* . . . (New
York, 1829), p. 357.

which made a difference against time. The antitraditional premises of radical democracy were here carried onward to their unspoken implications. But unfortunately for Skidmore his own class was less interested in the logic of democracy than in keeping open the doors to capital accumulation. It was never to be workingmen but the Whig merchants who would take Skidmore's type of argument seriously. Logical minds, successful in industry and finance, were always hagridden by the fear that a propertyless electorate would sooner or later move to despoil them of their mills and bank stocks.

Jefferson's faith in the democratic necessity for an ever-recurring American youthfulness was revealed strikingly in the unconscious irony of his attitude toward the city. On the one hand, he believed wholeheartedly that the true virtue which was to preserve the republic could subsist only upon the base of an independent, decentralized agrarianism. As a student of history he knew at the same time that the freedom to which he paid homage, those "natural rights" of the Declaration of Independence, were the rights of the city men, wrested from a feudal overlord by the power of a commerce-based commune. The world history that the Founders debated was city history, the record of civic man. Yet, although Jefferson's antipathy toward the city was pretty clearly not fueled by any belief that the city was the creature of time, that only there was time real, the financial world of the city—one of his principal targets —did rest upon a sense of time which the countryman might find alien and menacing. Divorced from the soil and the rhythm of the seasons, the city's life was bank money, credit money, abstract and hypothetical, lacking the palpable reality of the fruits and metals of the earth. To abandon agriculture for the culture of cities was to trade the timeless for the transitory, to surrender to the power of time. Only the land offered a secure refuge outside time and history.

Much as Jefferson favored the development of science and the diffusion of knowledge, the critical importance of the land lay in its character as a home base from which sallies toward progress could be made with safety. Of that which was subject to the corrosive influences of time the American would be able to say with Whitman,

> But they are not the Me myself.
> Apart from the pulling and hauling stands what I am
>
> .   .   .   .   .
> Both in and out of the game. . . .[52]

For Jefferson the preservation of freedom required the reenactment by each generation of the original drama of republican creation. The maintenance of an "out of the game" area permitted the people to act again as they had in the beginning. In their action together republican liberty would refind its nature, and the irreversibility of time would be denied.

The sense of an ever-present American present found a natural expression in the casual exaggerations of the West. "If such is the youth of the republic, what will be its old age?" a marveling foreigner asked Senator Lewis Cass. "Sir," Cass replied, "it will have no old age." [53] And when Captain Marryat inquired of a Mackinac Islander whether "people lived to a good old age in the island," he received the "quite American" answer: "I guess they do; if people want to die, they can't die here—they're obliged to go elsewhere." [54] More glorious was the prospect opened by a lecturer at Kenyon College in 1849 that if the United States held to its original principles and avoided corruption

[52] "Song of Myself," sec. 4, *Complete Poetry*, p. 27. The foregoing discussion of time and the city has utilized the classic analysis of Oswald Spengler, *The Decline of the West,* trans. Charles Francis Atkinson (New York, 1926–1928), esp. II, 89–103.

[53] Quoted in Merle Curti, *The Roots of American Loyalty* (New York, 1946), p. 64.

[54] Captain Frederick Marryat, *Diary in America* (1837–1838), ed. Jules Zanger (Bloomington, 1960), p. 122.

through an "unjust prosperity" based upon imperial conquest, the nation as a unit might perhaps live forever. The
United States would someday

soar away . . . yet higher and higher, until, like another new-
created star, in her true orbit, about the sun of Righteousness,
she shall wheel her round flight forever, with an unspotted
disk, in a sky of cloudless Immortality.[55]

Despite such apparent concern with the present the daz-
zling speed of American life gave urgent witness that the
present existed only for the purpose of being converted
into the future as rapidly as possible. Returned from
Europe in 1836, the sculptor Horatio Greenough saw in
the American preoccupation with speed the key to the national spirit. "Rail Roads alone seem to be *understood*,"
reported Greenough. "Go ahead! is the order of the day.
The whole continent presents a scene of *scrabbling* and
roars with greedy hurry." [56] While the splenetic Dickens
thought it worthwhile noting that "whenever an Englishman would cry 'All right!' an American cries 'Go ahead!'
which is somewhat expressive of the national character of
the two countries." [57] To the trained engineer Michel
Chevalier, "a locomotive engine or a steamboat" was "the
most suitable emblem" for the American people. Of the
American's "perfect passion for railroads," Chevalier remarked in good Gallic fashion, "he loves them . . . as a
lover loves his mistress." The "speed which annihilates
time and space" constituted the American's "supreme happiness." [58]

[55] Charles Anderson, *An Address on Anglo Saxon Destiny delivered before the Philomathesian Society of Kenyon College . . .
and repeated before the New England Society of Cincinnati, December 20, 1849* (Cincinnati, 1850), p. 48.
[56] Nathalia Wright, *Horatio Greenough, The First American
Sculptor* (Philadelphia, 1963), p. 113.
[57] *American Notes,* p. 91.
[58] Chevalier, *Society, Manners, and Politics,* pp. 60, 297.

To the amazement of foreign visitors the interest of Americans in rapid movement carried over into an apparently inane restlessness which forced them to rock, whittle, or chew even while temporarily at rest. Nonnutritive chewing and the urge to carve something were pastimes equally popular in the halls of Congress and in backwoods cabins, where they testified to an energy which was always in action. As one Englishwoman decided after viewing the furniture factories of Cincinnati in 1854, "Baby-rocking cribs, in which the brains of the youth of America are early habituated to perpetual restlessness, are manufactured here in surprising quantities." [59]

The American propensity for activity was sometimes set down as the effect of an overstimulating climate. But Professor James F. W. Johnston, a British chemist who visited the United States as a Lowell lecturer, was convinced that the cause of American restlessness lay in the digestive diseases with which he believed one half of all Americans were afflicted. According to Johnston, Americans had been nervous Europeans before they emigrated, and their malady had been aggravated by the excitements and "anxieties" of the New World. [60]

Theories such as Johnston's insisted on regarding Americans as though they were still merely visiting Europeans. Yet James Fenimore Cooper's *Notions of the Americans* had earlier tried to explain to the British that time itself needed a new standard of measurement in America. [61] The same contention was made by the German immigrant Francis Lieber a few years after he landed in the United States

[59] [Bishop, Isabella (Bird)], *The Englishwoman in America* (London, 1856), p. 122. See also Chevalier, p. 270; Schaff, *America,* p. 210; Martineau, *Retrospect of Western Travel* (1834–1836) (London and New York, 1838), I, 72.

[60] James F. W. Johnston, *Notes on North America . . .* (Edinburgh and London, 1851), II, 396–97.

[61] *Notions of the Americans: picked up by a Travelling Bachelor* (Phila., 1828), II, 328.

in 1828. "Not distances alone are measured here by a standard different from that of other countries," Lieber presumed to tell his former countrymen; "time, too, receives a different value, but it is measured by a smaller standard than in Europe." To Lieber it was a matter of scale. "Ten years in America," he said, "are like a century in Spain." [62] Both Cooper and Lieber, the American and the European, felt the connection between the New World notion of time and the quality of American life. To say simply that Americans were restless, or infatuated with a rage for speed, was to miss the point. Chevalier's conclusion went deeper than that. "If movement and the quick succession of sensations and ideas constitute life," he reasoned, "here one lives a hundred-fold more than elsewhere." [63]

On these terms, then, the American was one who filled the concept of existence with more content, more live options than the Old World dreamed of. In the manner of Skidmore, Americans were continually discovering new possibilities, analytically and by definition, in the concept of human existence. Here that idea came to mean a growing congeries of claims upon nature and society as the full spectrum of man's powers seemed to be revealing itself in the United States with almost miraculous swiftness. "Why, our people," an American told one astonished traveler, "can turn their hands to a'most anything, from whippin' the universe to stuffin' a mosquito." [64] The vocational versatility that so surprised Tocqueville and Dickens was simple matter of fact to James Fenimore Cooper, who was in other ways more traditional. "As you have now been at school, four months," he wrote to his son in 1839, "I

[63] *Letters to a Gentleman in Germany* . . . (Philadelphia, 1834), p. 287. The book is a literary production, but the opinions seem honest enough.

[63] Chevalier, *Society, Manners, and Politics,* p. 299.

[64] Alexander Mackay, "American Culture and American Prospects," in Allen Nevins, comp. and ed., *American Social History as Recorded by British Travelers* (New York, 1923), p. 347.

suppose you begin to think of a profession. All the arts and sciences are before you. But, perhaps, like a true American, you would choose to attempt them all." [65] Sizing up Horace Greeley in the privacy of his journal, Emerson jotted down: "Greeley surprises by playing all the parts. Only possible in America." [66]

It was not merely that the amplitude of the environment and the American success in dealing with it opened new avenues for meaningful effort, but that Americans assumed easily a broadened foundation for the nature of man himself. When Jefferson's "man of the New World" became the ordinary American citizen the implications were bound to be far-reaching. Even after he had been excoriating American democracy for years, the once hopeful Orestes Brownson still insisted, "It cannot be too often repeated that here man is man, if he chooses." That, very simply, it was the aim of the republic

to make the word *American* mean, not a man born on this soil or on that, but a free and accepted member of the grand republic of men. Such is what has been boasted as the principle and destiny of this New World.[67]

In that case, because Americans had so much genuine life to live, time was at a premium, and their haste was less a heedless rush into the future than a grand effort to live up to the urgent demands of a deeply vital present. An immigrant like Carl Schurz never forgot what those demands were. On the platform of Faneuil Hall in 1859 he recalled his boyhood days in Germany, when neighbors were departing for America. Then many a man had said how he also hoped to go along "to that great and free country,

[65] *Letters and Journals,* III, 373.

[66] *Journals of Ralph Waldo Emerson,* eds., Edward Waldo Emerson and Waldo Emerson Forbes (Boston and New York, 1909), VII, 136.

[67] "Mission of America" (1856) and "Native Americanism" (1844), *The Works of Orestes A. Brownson,* coll. and arranged by Henry F. Brownson (Detroit, 1884), II, 557, 18.

where a man could be himself" [68]—where, in other words, time would be an instrument of human needs and not their determinant.

At ground the American republican faith had always been millennial and apocalyptic. The words of a Jeffersonian orator of the 1790's, as he descanted on the meaning of the French Revolution, were widely reprinted for the benefit of thousands of school children:

The grand POLITICAL MILLENNIUM is at hand; when tyranny shall be buried in ruins; when all nations shall be united in ONE MIGHTY REPUBLIC! when the four angels, that stand on the four corners of the globe, shall, with one accord, lift up their voices to heaven; proclaiming PEACE ON EARTH, GOOD WILL TO ALL MEN.[69]

Melville's quarrel with his countrymen was in substance over the true meaning of the angels' message, over the relationship between time and man in the New World. What he was trying to get them to understand was that time had not come to a stop in America. Through the medium of Mardi's scroll, he informed them bluntly that

the grand error of your nation, sovereign kings! seems this: —the conceit that Mardi is now in the last scene of the last act of her drama; and that all preceding events were ordained to bring about the catastrophe you believe to be at hand,—a universal and permanent Republic.

The trouble with America, thought Melville, was the persistence of an old error: "Each age thinks its own is eternal." [70]

If that were the case, perhaps the absence of monumental ruins, which American writers liked to deplore, involved more than just a few missing stage props for the in-

[68] "True Americanism," *Speeches, Correspondence and Political Papers,* I, 49.

[69] Bingham, *Columbian Orator,* pp. 236–37.

[70] *Mardi,* Chap. LVII, pp. 238, 241.

vention of a romance. Ruins were, after all, the most prominent witnesses to the power of historic time. In a context of progress and material achievement a longing for such ineradicable testimonies to the futility of man's struggle against death could perhaps express itself in an exaggerated concern for ruins. The remark, frequently made, that the United States was after all surrounded by the wreckage of all former attempts at republican government can be seen as a weak attempt to orient America in historical time. All too often, however, such references were becoming conventional gestures, the starting point for a deadly comparison that left no doubt of the American victory over the past. After all, did it not seem plain enough to Americans, as George Washington Burnap put it, that

we are the old age and the maturity of the world, rather than the generations that have preceded us. . . . What could he [Plato] know of the working of a republican government . . . over a territory greater than were in his times the whole domains of civilization, . . . [having] canals and rail roads, and above all enlightened by the emanations of ten thousand printing presses.[71]

The Reverend Burnap can well stand for the America to whom Melville was preaching. Yet both of them were determined to assert in some way the supremacy of man over time: one through the permanent establishment of a time-free present; the other, convinced of the fatuity of such an aim, looked for a spiritual victory of human gallantry over "the power of blackness."

Fundamentally, it was a question of sincerity that Melville was urging, the honesty to admit the efficacy of time, and thereby to take into the American consciousness its most dreaded features: change, death, and the bitter knowledge of the irrevocability of the past. To feel these, to know them, was all the victory men could hope for who were "born with halters round their necks." [72] "Great

[71] *Lectures on the Sphere and Duties of Woman,* pp. 18–20.
[72] *Moby Dick,* Standard ed. (New York, 1963), Chap. LX, p. 357.

men, great nations," Emerson wrote in criticism of his own people, "have not been boasters and buffoons, but perceivers of the terror of life, and have manned themselves to face it." [73] It was no accident that Father Taylor, the real-life model for Melville's nautical "sky-pilot" in *Moby Dick,* prayed in the 1830's that "the members of Congress might be preserved from buffoonery." [74]

Melville was asking his fellow Americans to awake from their unconscious absorption in the present which prevented them from becoming aware of their drifting on the dangerous sea of history. So long as they were not yet "perceivers of the terror of life," that positive threat to their being which history presented, Melville could see only foolishness in the American hope for a triumph over time. Awareness was the first step on the road to being able to say "No! in thunder." And only those who could say that would be able to "cross the frontiers into Eternity." The rest would "never get through the Custom House." [75]

[73] "Fate," *Works,* VI, 5.

[74] Harriet Martineau, *Retrospect of Western Travel,* II, 213.

[75] *The Letters of Herman Melville,* eds. Merrell R. Davis and William H. Gilman (New Haven, 1960), p. 125.

CHAPTER THREE

No Home on the Range

The hope of an American hegemony over time was dependent upon the promise held out by American space, the vision of world enough. If time has historically been America's most valuable resource, space has been its least. From the beginning space was what America had the most of. Filled with holy indignation when a band of Connecticut men seized a disputed portion of Rhode Island, Roger Williams denounced the invasion as the product of

a depraved appetite after the great vanities, dreams and shadows of this vanishing life, great portions of land, land in this wilderness, as if men were in as great necessity and danger for want of great portions of land, as poor, hungry, thirsty seamen have, after a sick and stormy, a long and starving passage. This is one of the gods of New England, which the living and most high Eternal will destroy and famish.[1]

[1] In Miller and Johnson, eds., *The Puritans,* p. 486. On the relationship between space and time in early American history, see Sidney E. Mead, "The American People: Their Space, Time, and Religion," *Journal of Religion,* XXXIV (October 1954), 244–55.

Williams' pious prophecy was to prove wholly unrealistic. The "depraved appetite after . . . great portions of land" was a deity of even wider jurisdiction than Williams recognized in his own time. To Edward Everett, in 1833, the pre-Revolutionary colonists were a timid band whose "thoughts had never wandered beyond the frontier line, marked as it was, in its whole extent, with fire and blood." With the final defeat of the French, however,

the minds of men immediately moved forward into the illimitable space that seemed opening to them. A political miracle was wrought; the mountains sunk, the valleys rose, and the portals of the west were burst asunder.[2]

For much the longest period of American history, space and time, sharing a reciprocal relationship, were almost to be functions of each other in an inverse ratio: the larger the space available for pre-emption and exploitation, the more valuable was time. The immigrant English agriculturist, noted Harriet Martineau, was bound to be hampered so long as he relied upon the experience of an England where men were common and human time was cheap in relation to land. Only after he realizes that "he has got to a place where it answers to spend land to save labor . . . he soon becomes as slovenly a farmer as the American, and begins immediately to grow rich." [3] When towns and states arising out of the wilderness meant the possibility of quick fortune, time became an engine for the envelopment of space, and its worth multiplied in proportion to the magnitude of that promise.

This concept of magnitude, as it attached to the almost inconceivable largeness of American space, carried a special appeal. Looking back forty years at his schooldays in the 1820's, a New Hampshireman recalled: "Our geography was chiefly American, and the United States was

[2] *Orations*, I, 387.   [3] *Society in America*, II, 94.

larger than all the universe beside." [4] "No people in the world," Francis Grund was convinced, "is more fond of magnitude and extension." [5] If this were so, an obvious reason was that largeness in America meant, among other things, room enough. "Fortunate for you, sovereign kings! that you have room enough, wherein to be free," [6] wrote Melville. And the conquests of the Mexican War filled Walt Whitman with enthusiasm for the "enormous untravelled plains and forests." "The mind is lost," he exulted, "in contemplating such incalculable acres." He yearned

that the degraded, starving and ignorant ones of the Old World, whatever and whosoever they are, should be transplanted thither, where their cramped natures may expand, and they do honor to the great humanity they so long have been a blot upon.[7]

For Whitman the magnitude of American space was glorious because it meant elbow-room to uncramp human nature. The free man had to be an uncramped man, and America provided the spaces where he could stretch his spirit and recover the feeling of his own humanity. In contrast to the confining institutional grooves of the Old World, America as space offered a wide zone of multidimensional possibility.

A sharp consciousness of American size lay over the deliberations of the Founding Fathers, and all the arguments and analogies from ancient republics failed before the large fact that America was an immense tract of agricultural land. This was the condition that made inapplicable Montesquieu's observations on the relation between the size of republics and their viability. Here America seemed about

[4] Thomas Low Nichols, *Forty Years of American Life* (London, 1864), I, 62.

[5] *The Americans in their Moral, Social, and Political Relations* (London, 1837), II, 369.

[6] *Mardi,* Chap. LVII, p. 240.

[7] *The Gathering of the Forces,* I, 27.

to reverse the lessons of history. The United States would prove, Jefferson never ceased to believe, that "the larger the extent of country, the more firm its republican structure, if founded, not on conquest, but in principles of compact and equality." The former President admitted that his hope for the future of the nation rested heavily "on the enlargement of the resources of life going hand in hand with the enlargement of territory." [8] In Jefferson's mind the moral superiority of American men and institutions was never disconnected from the assumed reality of a space full of useful possibilities for living. Jeffersonian man was defined in relation to his environment, where he was first of all an operator in space.

The question of the durability of free government, which engrossed Jefferson, was of absorbing interest to Americans and foreigners alike. Considered as a mere phenomenon, American political institutions were bizarre and fascinating enough, fully on a level with the steamboats and painted Indians. Note-taking European travelers who approached America as a curiosity were bound to find the New World exciting indeed but lacking in seriousness. More thoughtful commentators, anxious to communicate to their countrymen whatever sense of genuine novelty they had come across, felt obligated not only to describe and explain but to interpret: was America after all something to be taken into account? To the Swedish Baron Klinkowström the survival of the new nation received a double-sided support from the existence of the western lands. In the book he published in 1824, after his return to Sweden, the liberally inclined aristocrat concluded that "the great uncultivated tracts in the interior," besides being an available stage for the operation of a free society, helped also to guard the older states from the possibility of a conservative counterrevolution. Reflecting, in all prob-

[8] Jefferson to Barbé de Marbois, June 14, 1817 (*Writings*, XV, 130).

ability, ideas that he had heard expressed by some of the more republican Americans with whom he had had contact, the Baron expressed his conviction that

as long as there are vast tracts in the interior where those people can settle who are displeased with possible changes in the Atlantic states, and in the degree these migrations increase they react upon the constitutions of the eastern states; so one need not fear any revolution that could try to install monarchic forms in this part of the world.[9]

Much as Klinkowström saw western space as a fence against the danger of a tyranny from the right, Edward Everett, about ten years later, was ready to attribute to the influence of western space the maintenance of a type of forward-moving equilibrium. "In the old world," said Everett, "society is full." Here, however, there was a wide demand for talent and enterprise, which went along with "the enlargement of the field of action in this country." Of this enlargement the "first and perhaps the main cause" was the abundance of cheap land.

This circumstance alone acts like a safety valve to the great social steam engine. There can be no very great pressure anywhere in a community where, by travelling a few hundred miles into the interior, a man can buy land at the rate of an acre for a day's work. This was the first stimulus brought to bear upon the population of this country, after the revolutionary war, and it is still operating in full force.[10]

Jefferson had been dead only a few years, but in comparison with Everett's vision the interaction between Jeffersonian man and space now appeared almost static. Significantly, where Jefferson's term had been "enlargement of the resources of life," Everett's was "enlargement of the field of action." For the Representative from industrializ-

[9] *Baron Klinkowström's America, 1818–1820,* trans. and ed. Franklin D. Scott (Evanston, Ill., 1952), p. 250.

[10] *Orations,* I, 260. Here may be one of the earliest appearances of the term "safety valve" in this connection.

ing Massachusetts American space was a container for progressive but potentially explosive power. The "great social steam engine" was a phrase that would never have been used by Jefferson.

By the time New England was living through its third straight Democratic administration western space could well appear as the guardian against social upheaval from the opposite end of Baron Klinkowström's political spectrum. In the hands of the shrewd and able Whig Caleb Cushing, the meaning of American space as room took on new urgency as he sought to allay the anxious fears of his constituents over the ominous decline of their own state's importance before the fact of spectacular western growth. Taking the occasion of his Fourth of July oration at Boston in 1839, the congressman freely acknowledged that the power of Massachusetts in the national balance was no longer what it had been in the past, but he pointed to a compensating benefit that had been overlooked:

Emigration to the West is the great safety-valve of our population, and frees us from all the dangers of the poverty, and discontent, and consequent disorders, which always spring up in a community when the number of its inhabitants has outrun its capacity to afford due recompense to honest industry and ambition.[11]

Cushing was of course a politician speaking in an atmosphere of sectional apprehensiveness. Yet the West to which he assigned only the most morally negative of functions was, as he and his audience knew, also being settled by New England sons and brothers. Years before, Yale's cantankerous President Dwight had similarly portrayed the West as a source of peace for the more senior settlements. Where Dwight had dedicated the frontier areas to destruction as the American Cave of Adullam—packed with un-

---

[11] *An Oration, on the Material Growth* . . . , p. 36.

quiet and turbulent spirits [12]—Cushing emphasized the importance of space for the stability of eastern institutions. Dwight, the professional moralist, spoke for the sacred community of Old New England; Cushing's remark was a sign of the extent to which newer problems of urbanism and industrialism were making themselves felt in the ancient stronghold of American Puritanism.

Yet between Dwight and Cushing a more hopeful period for New England's prospects had intervened, and again the spokesman was Edward Everett. Then still a professor, Everett addressed the Phi Beta Kappa Society at Harvard in 1824 on "The Circumstances Favorable to the Progress of Literature in America." Timothy Dwight's censures of the West had been published a few years before, and Everett's words had to be taken as a calculated rebuke to the now-dead Yale man. The western advance, Everett declared, was "not the irruption of wild barbarians, sent to visit the wrath of God on a degenerate empire; it is not the inroad of disciplined banditti. . . . It is the human family, led out by Providence to possess its broad patrimony." In the family interest, which was the development of a national culture, Everett called upon Massachusetts to throw aside all sectional jealousy in an appreciation of the intellectual victory of New England through the coming cultural achievements of America's western space. "What generous mind," he asked,

> would sacrifice to a selfish preservation of local preponderance the delight of beholding civilized nations rising up in the desert; and the language, the manners, the principles in which he has been reared, carried with his household gods to the foot of the Rocky Mountains?

At this point of his career Everett could contemplate with equanimity the renunciation by New England of a spatial

[12] *Travels in New-England and New-York* (London, 1823), II, 440.

hegemony in exchange for an eternally secure hold on a critical segment of American time. "Whithersoever the sons of the thirteen states shall wander," he was certain,

to southern or western climes, they will send back their hearts to the rocky shores, the battlefields, the infant settlements of the Atlantic coast. These are placed beyond the reach of vicissitude. They have already become matter of history, of poetry, of eloquence.[13]

A piety of place, Everett considered, would have to be accepted as compensation for the lost outward thrust into space.

Although space was room and a way beyond, it was also, and had been first of all, a barrier. It was well understood that the benevolent barrier of immense space had protected the American colonies in their infancy and contributed to the attainment of independence. Afterward, however, space appeared a stumbling block to national cohesion, dividing the commonwealth and threatening to fragment the union along geographical lines. Alarmed at the extent of the westward migration after the War of 1812, John Calhoun, then in his nationalist phase, called in 1817 for a federally sponsored network of roads and canals to counteract the influence of sundering space. In contrast to Everett a few years later, Calhoun declared, "Those who understand the human heart best know how powerfully distance tends to break the sympathies of our nature." Showing little confidence in the unifying force of a common culture, Calhoun added, "Nothing, not even dissimilarity of language, tends more to estrange man from man." In the interests of national self-preservation, Calhoun appealed to his fellow congressmen: "Let us conquer space." [14]

The barrier of space that so disturbed Calhoun in 1817

[13] *Orations,* I, 38.
[14] *The Works of John C. Calhoun,* ed. Richard K. Crallé (Charleston, S.C., and New York, 1854–1860) , II, 190.

was capable of working in two directions. If it was effective
to estrange, it could as well foster cohesion. It was this aspect of space as barrier which Henry Clay urged fifteen
years later in an attempt to repel the contention that the
maintenance of a high price for government land, a policy
that was part of his American System, was responsible for
retarding settlement. Quite aside from the "moral, physical, pecuniary obstacles" involved, Clay asserted, "space itself, mountains, and seas, and rivers, are impediments."
And in characteristically high-flown oratory he proceeded
to describe the human costs of westward migration to the
individual emigrant, the anguish of being

separated, forever, from the roof under which the companions
of his childhood were sheltered, from the trees which have
shaded him from summer's heats, the spring from whose gush-
ing fountain he has drunk in his youth, the tombs that hold
the precious relics of his venerated ancestors! [15]

Here in one sentence Clay set reverberating all the popular banalities of sentiment that were beginning to cluster
around the parochial pieties of American place. Familiar
since 1818 with Samuel Woodworth's tender celebration
of

   . . . every loved spot which my infancy knew!
The wide-spreading pond, and the mill that stood by it,

Americans by the thousands were soon to begin singing of
their longing for

   The old oaken bucket, the iron-bound bucket,
   The moss-covered bucket which hung in the well.

And a few years later the country would resound with fervent appeals of

       Woodman, spare that tree!
       Touch not a single bough!

[15] *The Speeches of Henry Clay*, ed. Calvin Colton (New York,
1857), I, 509.

> In youth it sheltered me,
> And I'll protect it now.[16]

Yet, far from testifying to any profound American attachment to place, it seems more plausible that the success of such themes dramatized a prevalent mood of self-conscious and self-indulgent pathos, a form of what W. Lloyd Warner has called "the exaggerated guilt of a mobile man." [17] In the lyrics of Stephen Foster the pathos of nostalgia, set to music, became a favorite entertainment for a mobile people who couldn't be persuaded to stay at home.

Quite plainly, space was no barrier for the constituents of that southern congressman who lamented to Harriet Martineau that "there was no character of permanence in anything," that only the Pacific Ocean would stop the numbers "who were quitting their homes and civilised life, and carrying their brides 'as bondwomen' into the wilderness, because fine land was cheap there." [18] While to the economist Henry C. Carey, who favored the build-up of a compact population on an industrial base, and who estimated grandiosely in 1848 that the "already organized" portion of the United States could support six hundred and forty million people, the unchecked flight to the West was not only economic foolishness but an assault on human nature. "The natural tendency of man," he contended,

is to hold in regard old places and old churches, mellowed by time and sanctified by the recollection of those who had before inhabited them. . . . Why is it that men are everywhere seen flying from their fellow men: from those destined by the Deity to be their helpmates: from parents and relations: from old houses, and old churches, and old schoolhouses . . . ? [19]

[16] Both poems, along with "Home, Sweet Home" (1823), are to be found in Kendall B. Taft, *Minor Knickerbockers* (New York, 1947), pp. 56, 263–64, 148–49.

[17] *The Living and the Dead, A Study of the Symbolic Life of Americans,* Yankee City Series, Vol. 5 (New Haven, 1959), p. 301.

[18] *Society in America,* II, 85.

[19] H. C. Carey, *The Past, the Present, and the Future* (Philadelphia, 1848), pp. 429–32.

Whatever "the natural tendency of man," Americans, when thinking seriously about themselves, had frequently admitted to being a nation of rovers. In bitter opposition to the annexation of Texas during the 1830's, William Ellery Channing had averred: "Perhaps there is no people on earth on whom the ties of local attachment sit so loosely. . . . To this spirit we have sacrificed justice and humanity." [20] But it took the strictures of the English novelist Frederick Marryat, well known in America for *Mr. Midshipman Easy,* to bring the moral question of American irreverence for place into the international forum. In American disregard for what Carey later denominated "old places," Marryat saw simply a greed-motivated spirit of exploitation. While he was touring Rhode Island in 1837 he was shocked to note that the railroad ran through a cemetery, with "the sleepers of the railway laid over the sleepers in death." No English engineers, the prickly novelist was certain, could have been guilty of such a callous solution to the right-of-way problem. Apparently, he was now in a place where "they grind down the bones of their ancestors for the sake of gain, and consecrated earth is desecrated by the iron wheels, loaded with Mammon-seeking mortals." Marryat's conclusion was that "in America everything is sacrificed to time; for time is money." [21]

The following year, James Fenimore Cooper, who agreed thoroughly with Marryat on this point, took up the same question in *Home as Found.* To his English guest, the American landed gentleman Mr. John Effingham remarks:

I have been told, Sir George Templemore, that in England, there are difficulties in running highways and streets through homesteads and dwellings; and that even a railroad or a canal is obliged to make a curve to avoid a churchyard or a tombstone?

[20] *Works,* pp. 629–30.
[21] Marryat, *Diary in America,* pp. 73–74.

On this subject the comment of Aristabulus Bragg, Cooper's caricature of the American as ruthless violator of space, is:

I am for the end of the road at least, and must say that I rejoice in being a native of a country in which as few impediments as possible exist to onward impulses.[22]

There was enough truth in these jabs to rankle, and in 1841 the speaker at the annual dinner of the New England Society in New York City felt obliged to take up the defense. For Charles Brickett Haddock, nephew of Daniel Webster, professor at Dartmouth, and later representative of the United States in Portugal, Americans were distinguished by a *"love of home."* He conceded that

to superficial observers, the more intelligent even, as Marryat and Chevalier, the spirit of enterprise, so prevalent among us, seems inconsistent with strong domestic attachments. That young men and young women should be true lovers of home, and yet fly from it, in their teens, to the ends of the land, and the solitudes of the desert, seems a paradox, and yet how true! . . . I need not tell you how all your tenderest sensibilities cling around the spot of your birth, with more and more tenacity, the farther, in place or time, you are removed from it. . . . The heart wants visible memorials to fasten upon. It requires a centre to revolve about.

So the result was, according to Haddock, that "when the enterprises of ambition are concluded, and the energies of life are exhausted," the wandering sons of New England returned home to die.[23] The curious conclusion of Haddock's oration in praise of New England seemed to indicate that the descendants of the Pilgrims were willing to attest their loyalty to home ground in any way except by actually remaining there.

[22] *Home as Found,* Chap. II, p. 24. See also *Letters and Journals,* IV, 16.

[23] *New England Society Orations,* I, 282–83. The name is there misspelled as Hadduck.

As a traveler in the United States during the 1830's who intended to write a book about it for home consumption, Captain Marryat could fairly be taken as the typical representative of his nation and class. For him, therefore, it was just as natural and necessary to pronounce continual moral judgment on the American character as it would have been unthinkable to admit the possibility that the set of values and logical apparatus used for that purpose might need to be reexamined in the light of an American context. Certainly, it was largely true that the Americans treated both hearth and homestead, those objects of ancient veneration for the European consciousness, as fit, even prime, subjects for barter and profit. No matter what an apologist such as Haddock might say, once having built and planted, Americans were inclined to sell and move on, as Orestes Brownson put it, "strangers even in the land of our birth . . . adventurers, restrained by few ties or associations of early home." [24] An admirer of much that was American, Michel Chevalier could nevertheless report matter of factly:

All that he [the American] has, all that he sees, is merchandise in his eyes. The poetical associations which invest particular spots or objects with a character of sanctity have no place in his mind. . . . To him a waterfall is simply water power for his machinery; an old building is a quarry of bricks. . . . The Yankee will sell his father's house, like old clothes, old rags.[25]

Yet, it was superficial for Professor Haddock to bracket Chevalier with Marryat. Having pointed out the instrumental character in America of objects that the European regarded as values in themselves, the Frenchman, unlike Marryat, delivered no condemnatory moral judgment from the standpoint of European ideas of propriety. Keenly on the watch for elements of novelty in the American situation, Chevalier had already traced be-

[24] *Works,* XVII, 97.
[25] Chevalier, *Society, Manners, and Politics,* pp. 283–84.

tween the American and his spaces a relationship less
European and sedentary than Asiatic and nomadic: "The
full-blooded American has this in common with the Tar-
tar, that he is *encamped,* not established, on the soil he
treads upon." [26] And being thus encamped, he could not
afford to maintain for its own sake alone any merely static
relationship. It was simply a matter of efficiency. An American was a man with a mission to perform in space. "As
pioneer," Chevalier acknowledged, "it is his duty to attach
himself to nothing, to no place, edifice, object, or person." [27] The American destiny, as Cushing had outlined it
earlier, was to people a continent, and to that destiny
Americans were steadily loyal.

Still, if Americans lightheartedly cut loose from the ties
of familiar places upon hearing the siren song of higher
destiny, the lyrics sang of sweet cash profits. Chevalier
could recognize that "at bottom, then, of all that an American does is money; behind every word, money." [28] But
where Captain Marryat saw a case of ordinary greed, extraordinary only in its intensity, Chevalier, near the close of
an entire chapter devoted to the subject of money, came to
the firm conclusion that Molière's miser, Harpagon, was
no American. Himself an ardent Saint-Simonian and be-
liever in the future of technology, Chevalier analyzed the
function of money in the United States and denied that
the Americans pursued wealth in the classic European fashion at all. "The American is devoured with a passion for
money," he contended, "not because he finds pleasure in
hoarding it up, but because wealth is power, because it is
the lever by which he governs nature." [29] In actuality, the
American who, unlike the European, demanded no dowry
when he married, demonstrated unequivocally his distaste

[26] *Ibid.,* p. 130.

[27] *Ibid.,* p. 284. Chevalier did recognize an exception here in favor
of the American wife.

[28] *Ibid.*   [29] *Ibid.,* p. 294.

for the transmutation of nonmaterial values into cash. On the other hand, Chevalier hinted, to transmute possessions and labor into the impersonal symbolic standard of money was a key process in the articulation of the American brand of freedom. With money, it was clear, one paid "once and for all," and one was free to move on unencumbered by any functionally ill defined and potentially limitless demands of sentiment.[30] It seemed, then, that the requirements of the pioneer ethic itself hung the "For Sale" sign on the beloved American farm and mill, bucket and well.

As Americans modified the English common law of land to facilitate ease of transfer they moved away from the idea of land as some sort of ultimate value, but they were never wholly successful in displacing the Old World conception entirely. Through the common law, which many Jeffersonians argued was the product of a historical experience inapplicable to America, part of the reverence grounded in the English soil was imported to the New World. Land, the judges said, unlike its fruits, was always unique: no mere sum of money could be an equivalent compensation for the failure to convey a particular tract. Yet, by extinguishing primogeniture and entail, by severing the quasi-organic linkage between designated land and designated human generations, Americans were affirming the freedom of man's agency over what was after all merely a segment of the natural world. Even the forms of American legal draftsmanship could reflect the dominance of abstract function over material substance. As the law partner of the famous William M. Evarts pointed out,

An English deed for an hundred acres is engrossed on parchment, with the letters of the alphabet tortured into a thousand useless shapes, that ancient forms may be preserved. A New England deed, in one brief page, contains all the elements of a

---

[30] *Ibid.*, p. 284.

perfect contract between the parties, with a direct assurance of title.[31]

In like manner, Americans rejected the English legal doctrine of Ancient Lights, which recognized a prescriptive right in particular tracts to the maintenance of circumjacent open space. Both cases emphasized the freedom and effectiveness of human action over the inert and traditional.

The asserted legal uniqueness of the American land was bound to remain a technicality, for in America the whole economy rested on a consensus that the land, and much else besides, must and did have a price. If American Negro slavery, in its disregard for the ties of family relationship, was denounced by abolitionists as a moral abomination, strictly as a labor system it was based on the popular American principle of convertibility. Convertibility in both lands and men was an American axiom whose natural sense appealed to a people who were almost continually traders and electors. Whether in the cotton fields or in the highest offices of the state, nothing was unique or incompensable. Eli Whitney's interchangeability of parts extended equally to the plantation and the legislature. Fatal as it might be to the genius of art, it was the genuine reflection of a republic that was becoming a democracy.

So long as America remained undifferentiated space it would lack, as so many aspiring writers complained, the kind of particular places which could gather round themselves the strands of legend needed for romantic creation. In the absence of more relevant material, poets like Freneau and Bryant, when they turned to contemplate the high themes of time and mortality, pressed into service the colorless and ambiguous Indian mounds which seemed to lend at least a weakly human element to the otherwise contentless landscape. In an analogous quest for history Joseph Smith, the Mormon prophet, also used the mounds,

[31] *New England Society Orations,* II, 46.

and wrote of baffling pursuits into the wilderness after nebulous "records." [32] Obviously, a country that shocked cultivated Europeans by running a railroad through a cemetery had as yet no very strong feeling for what Mircea Eliade has denominated the idea of a Sacred Place, a place which from undifferentiation and consequent unbeing had taken on differentiation and reality as the site of some thrilling contact with a transcendent value.[33] Even in the 1840's it was possible for Congressman George Perkins Marsh of Vermont to say that material did not exist for the creation of an American feeling based on the piety of place. Here lay a danger, Marsh felt, since

doctrines tied to no forms, connected with no localities, relying upon no authority but individual reason, attaching no sacredness to aught cognizable by the senses, are more easily overthrown, than when they assume the shape of belief, entrenched behind the bulwarks of form, prejudice and opinion. In Europe, where every rock has its name, every landscape its history, the love of country and its institutions, is at once strengthened by thousands of venerable associations, and narrowed to the humble shape rather of attachment to localties, than of enlightenment and expanded patriotism. But with us, who have no dim traditions, no hoary fables, to give, not individuality only, but almost life, to plain and mountain, and rock and river, patriotism, though a larger, nobler, and more intellectual sentiment, is yet a less tenacious impulse.[34]

Marsh was calling implicitly for a campaign to give meaning to the American landscape, to make it, in fact, American. But at the time he spoke such a campaign had long been in progress. In the search to recover and establish an authentic national past, characterized in the 1820's by the document-collecting labors of Jared Sparks, Ameri-

[32] *The Book of Mormon, translated by Joseph Smith, Jr.,* Authorized ed. (Independence, Mo., 1948), 1 Nephi, Ch. 3 and *passim.*
[33] *Myth of the Eternal Return,* trans. Willard R. Trask (London, 1955), p. 4.
[34] *New England Society Orations,* I, 413.

cans had begun to overcome at some points the pervasive anonymity of American space. Even earlier the process had begun of establishing historical sites.

On December 22, 1820, on the ground of the Pilgrim landing two hundred years before, Daniel Webster delivered a commemorative address to a crowd assembled at the invitation of the newly formed Plymouth Society. Webster began by carrying his audience first backward and then forward in time, as he alternately identified them with their progenitors in the one direction and their descendants in the other. In fact, Webster explained, they could well consider themselves

as interested and connected with our whole race, through all time; allied to our ancestors; allied to our posterity; closely compacted on all sides with others; ourselves being but links in the great chain of being, which begins with the origin of our race, runs onward through its successive generations, binding together the past, the present, and the future.

Once he had established this network of rapport in time, the speaker reached out to draw into its web of significance another dimension, the dimension of space. "There is a local feeling," Webster continued,

connected with this occasion, too strong to be resisted; a sort of *genius of the place,* which inspires and awes us. We feel that we are on the spot where the first scene of our history was laid. . . . We look around us, and behold the hills and promontories where the anxious eyes of our fathers first saw the places of habitation and of rest. . . . Beneath us is the Rock, on which New England received the feet of the Pilgrims.

Working upon the talismanic appeal of the Rock, the shore, and the soil, Webster then called up and paraded a panoramic vision of the heroic band in the wilderness, beset by vicissitudes but sustained and strengthened by a catalogue of formidable virtues. All these virtues, Webster solemnly declared, "seem to belong to this place, and to be present upon this occasion, to fill us with reverence and admiration." [35]

Five years later Webster was present at the demarcation of another special area of space, when the returned Lafayette laid the cornerstone of the Bunker Hill Monument. And in 1842, before a crowd estimated at one hundred thousand people, Webster dedicated the finally completed shaft. The shape of the stone, an obelisk, had been proposed in a rejected design by Horatio Greenough. That early design, a product of the nineteen-year-old Greenough's esthetic sensibility and deeply felt patriotism, intended through the form of the Bunker Hill shaft to express a profoundly significant meaning. For an

obelisk has to my eye a singular aptitude, in its form and character, to call attention to a spot memorable in history. It says but one word, but it speaks loud. If I understand its voice, it says, Here! It says no more.[36]

As time went on there would be more reasons to say with particularity, Here! And Brigham Young's "This is the place!" would be only one of several efforts to impress a mark on the vacant face of the American landscape. But Greenough's own spontaneous response to the land after long years in Europe suggested that it would be uphill work to make Americans whittle down their inheritance by specification and circumscription. From a brief holiday in Delaware, a dozen years before *Leaves of Grass*, which he seems to anticipate in spirit, the sculptor wrote to his brother: "How lovely are the plains of this region, the verdure, the quiet, the up-going and down-floating sloops and

[35] *Works*, I, 182–84.
[36] "Aesthetics at Washington," in Henry T. Tuckerman, ed., *A Memorial of Horatio Greenough . . .* (New York, 1853), p. 82. The most profound treatment of Greenough is in F. O. Matthiessen's *American Renaissance* (New York, 1941).

brigs without number! My heart will always yearn after America." [37]

Alongside the controlled emotion of Greenough's mussical cadences, the expression of a private sentiment, Webster's official thunder resounds somewhat rattlingly. Historical markers were important and necessary signposts in their limited way for developing that sense of America which Haddock had called for. But in Greenough one can still hear the echoes of words hopefully spoken long before there was anything especially American to commemorate: "Know that this is the place where the Lord will create a new Heaven, and a new Earth in, new Churches, and a new Common-wealth together." [38] The Puritan chronicler's "Know that this is the place!" served notice that America was not to be just another place. "Every continent," D. H. Lawrence was to assert when writing about America, "has its own great spirit of place . . . call it what you like. But the spirit of place is a great reality." [39] The *Wonder-Working Providence of Sion's Saviour in New England* expressed what was well understood from the beginning, that in America space and divine purpose were to be bound in a conjoint destiny.

But in this partnership of matter and spirit what were to be the proportions of the respective ingredients? Not long after Daniel Webster's second oration at Bunker Hill the New-York Historical Society appointed a three-man "Committee on a National Name," to recommend a replacement for "The United States of America." The committee was composed of the lawyer David Dudley Field, the ethnologist Henry Schoolcraft, and the littérateur Charles Fenno Hoffman. They urged the adoption of a *"distinctive"*

[37] Nathalia Wright, *Horatio Greenough,* p. 226.

[38] [Captain Edward Johnson], *Wonder-Working Providence of Sions Savior in New England,* ed. William Frederick Poole (Andover, 1867), p. 3.

[39] *Studies in Classic American Literature,* Anchor Book ed. (Garden City, N.Y., n.d.), p. 16.

name, one that would express the American *"nationality."*
"What we want," they explained, "is a sign of our identity.
We want utterance for our nationality. We want a watch-
word more national than that of states, more powerful
than that of party." Their report, published by the Society
in 1845, followed a suggestion by Washington Irving and
recommended the name of "Allegania,"—"The Republic
of Allegania." [40]

Unquestionably, the committee's easy abandonment of
"The United States" was partly an attempt to eliminate or
to smooth over the growing estrangement between North
and South. The Alleghanies were a rugged cord roping together both sections. Just as plainly, the committee's own
choice evinced a desire to ground the nation in the earth,
to fix it to a site, even if that site was a large one. No one
could escape the observation that "Allegania" was a natural fact, while "United States" denoted an abstraction resting on the idea of a social compact. Where the Declaration
of Independence had proclaimed the American congruence to "the laws of Nature and of Nature's God," conjur-
ing up a vision of cosmic order in the Newtonian universe,
"Allegania" was an indication that some not unrepresenta-
tive Americans were willing to contract the national pretensions to a local habitation and name. Thus, what had
been largely a moral imperative would, in a sense, be
brought to ground. It was about this time, as Albert K.
Weinberg's *Manifest Destiny* has demonstrated, that the
American messianic dream of converting the world to republicanism by the power of example came to be interpreted in terms of the physical extension of American territory.[41]

[40] *Report of the Committee of the New-York Historical Society,
on a National Name, March 31, 1845* (New York, 1845), pp. 3, 6,
8.

[41] *Manifest Destiny, A Study of Nationalist Expansionism in
American History* (Baltimore, 1935), Chap. IV.

On such a scale American attachment to place could not be justifiably compared to the earth-love common in Old Europe. Americans could sing songs about the old homestead, but Samuel Lorenzo Knapp boasted in 1829 of his beloved New Englanders:

They never cherished, however far removed from home, any of that home-sickness of an exiled peasant, who mourns over what he has left, incapable of finding resources within himself for happiness, or of devising plans in which the past could, in a measure, be absorbed in the future.

The distinguishing mark of these migrants, he went on, was that "wherever they may be" they demonstrate that "they were educated for no particular place, but belong to society and mankind." [42]

If the idea of America meant anything, then it meant first of all that man was here to be cut loose from his historic fetters, that it was at last to be acknowledged that he was man and not earth, man and not thing. It was true that in the New World agricultural man had been preceded in regular order by the hunter and the grazer, repeating what was equivalent, as Jefferson observed, "to a survey, in time, of the progress of man from the infancy of creation to the present day." [43] But there the analogy to Europe's experience stopped. To Old World man, with the origin of his relationship to the glebe he tilled lost in a mysterious past, might come a sense of nature's beneficent concern for him. Nature could be Mother Nature and earth Mother Earth. Americans knew exactly when they had come to the land, as they remarked so many times, and that was bound to make a difference. They had not sprung from the soil, but had taken it and were still taking it, as Channing protested, in a somewhat rough manner. Land whose title had been acquired by forcible rape could never become Mother Earth. Its soil was a machine for the building of a democratic society, for the establishment of a social independence which was to be the guarantee of freedom. Such was the Jeffersonian ideal, and however it was to be distorted, land in America failed to inspire even that modest degree of reverence that would have solaced a Fenimore Cooper.

The morally functional role thrust upon American space had laid heavy obligations on the land as well as its inhabitants. If to the Puritan of New England there had to be something extraordinary about the site divinely appointed for the development of the great work of redemption, something of that same spirit, rationalized and secularized of course, is discernible in the deliberations of a mind so calmly untheological as that of Thomas Jefferson. What is the impression he presents in his famous refutation of Buffon's unfortunate speculations about the lessened potency of nature in the New World? It is not that of a dispassionate observer who seeks only to add a page to the accumulating record of natural history. A satisfaction more than scientific seems to infuse Jefferson's statement that the fossil remains of the American mammoth prove that "it has been the largest of all terrestrial beings." However gratifying in an international game of zoological one-upmanship these indubitably American bones might be, they meant so much to Jefferson because the mammoth provided the evidence "to have rescued the earth it inhabited, and the atmosphere it breathed, from the imputation of impotence in the conception and nourishment of animal life on a large scale." [44] If one did not know Jefferson so well one might conclude from this remark that he had been reading Jonathan Edwards, and had decided that, just as unregenerate man had needed to be *rescued* by divine grace from the *imputation* of Original Sin before he could play his proper role in the cosmic drama, so the reve-

[44] "Notes on Virginia," Query VI, *Writings,* II, 60.

lations of science justified the character of the American environment which had such a critical role to play in the molding of the New World's democratic man.

That Jefferson chose to make such a spirited defense over an issue of physical size, as distinct from utility or some other value, is not wholly as surprising as it seems. Something more than a naïve kind of dimensional patriotism was involved here, for scale alone figured dynamically in the Jeffersonian scheme of moral environmentalism. It was part of the system of ideas with which he habitually worked. So cosmopolitan a thinker as Thomas Paine told Europe seriously in his *Rights of Man:*

As America was the only spot in the political world where the principles of universal reformation could begin, so also was it the best in the natural world. An assemblage of circumstances conspired not only to give birth, but to add gigantic maturity to its principles. The scene which that country presents to the eye of a spectator has something in its which generates and encourages great ideas. Nature appears to him in magnitude. The mighty objects he beholds act upon his mind by enlarging it, and he partakes of the greatness he contemplates.[45]

As Paine's use of the terms "gigantic," "great," "magnitude," and "mighty" demonstrates, the spread-eagle stump speakers of the age of manifest destiny were drawing upon an authentic tradition. Of central importance, here, is his final sentence: "The mighty objects he beholds act upon his mind by enlarging it, and he partakes of the greatness he contemplates." Where Paine was ready to posit a bald, almost mechanical correspondence between landscape and ideas, the belief that the scale of the American natural scene was charged with heavy moral significance became one of the most public of American assumptions. Borrowing from their godly ancestors, Americans agreed that Providence had made ready on their continent a theater

[45] *The Rights of Man,* Everyman's Library (London and New York, 1935), p. 152. For an analysis of the Jeffersonian frame of mind see Daniel J. Boorstin, *The Lost World of Thomas Jefferson* (New York, 1948).

suitable for the performance of the drama of liberal government. And for an experiment so fraught with portentous consequences to the whole world no narrower stage would have been appropriate. As the grandeur of the theme seemed to demand nothing but America, the spectacular dimensions of American land-forms came to be seen as emblems of the weighty responsibility under which both nation and people lay.

Under such circumstances it became part of the problem of being American to avoid the shame of a disproportion between man and the American environment. Americans were constantly being urged to live up to the obligations of their surroundings. Orators looking for a spur to accomplishment got in the habit of pointing to the scenery. In the preface to *Leaves of Grass* Walt Whitman stated the connection very simply: "The largeness of nature or the nation were monstrous without a corresponding largeness and generosity of the spirit of the citizen." [46] The adjective "monstrous" suggests disease, and the "Song of Myself" which follows that observation can perhaps be best understood as incantatory thaumaturgy, designed to raise up, through a celebration of the "largeness of nature or the nation," the desired "corresponding largeness and generosity of the spirit of the citizen." Much of Whitman's Americanness lay in his devotion to the idea of such a "correspondence," a uniting tie between American man and his spatial context. Standing at Niagara, an artist of less democratic instincts, Francis Parkman, marked the moral disproportion between the falls and his fellow tourists by a contemptuous entry in his notebook.[47] Man and nature were obviously twain, and it was clear on which side Parkman's sympathies lay.

But although they were sometimes in doubt as to the details of the connecting mechanism, Americans generally

---

[46] *Complete Poetry and Selected Prose,* p. 412.
[47] *The Journals of Francis Parkman,* ed. Mason Wade (London, [n.d.]) , I, 312. Entry in 1845.

remained sure that America had to mean some sort of congruence between spiritual and material factors. Reviewing a book entitled *American Facts* for Horace Greeley's *New York Tribune,* Margaret Fuller was plunged into a dark fit of Transcendentalist gloom; she was now sure America had proved so false "to the scheme made out at her nativity" that it was no longer clear what the American destiny was. Significantly, the only thing she was still certain of was that it must be something "great." When she pondered the "real character" of America she could only conclude: "One thing is certain; we live in a large place, no less morally than physically: woe to him who lives meanly here, and knows the exhibitions of selfishness and vanity as the only American facts." [48]

Emerson was as capable of judging his fellow Americans by the magnificence of the scenery as Margaret Fuller or Parkman, but without crankiness or primness. Much of the time he owned to "a presentiment that here shall laws and institutions exist on some scale of proportion to the majesty of nature." It seemed plausible to him that "to men legislating for the area betwixt the two oceans, betwixt the snows and the tropics, something of the gravity of nature will infuse itself into the code." For if men had to measure up to the land, it was no less certain that the land helped them to do so.

The land [wrote Emerson] is the appointed remedy for whatever is false and fantastic in our culture. The continent we inhabit is to be physic and food for our mind, as well as our body. The land, with its tranquillizing, sanative influences, is to repair the errors of a scholastic and traditional education, and bring us into just relations with men and things.[49]

Here, as in so many places, Emerson sounds the representative American—but at one remove from the marketplace.

[48] *Life Without and Life Within,* ed. Arthur B. Fuller (New York, 1869), pp. 108–09.
[49] "The Young American," *Works,* I, 365–66.

In the 1830's Harriet Martineau had come away from the
United States convinced that "the possession of land" was
there considered "the cure for all social evils." "If a man is
disappointed in politics or love," she noted, "he goes and
buys land." [50] Where Emerson saw the land as strong
moral medicine, his countrymen, who had also discovered
its "tranquillizing, sanative influences," had long been ap-
plying land-therapy to themselves for less exalted purposes.
The brand of Emersonianism heard on the floor of Congress was perhaps typified by an Ohio Representative during an 1852 debate on a homestead bill. "By the passage of
this bill," claimed Joseph Cable,

how many would be drawn away from your cities, towns, and
villages . . . who, by a removal to a forest life, would . . . .
become ornaments to society, the bulwark of government, and
finally take their places with the patriarchs of old, in a world
of happified and glorified spirits? [51]

What better definition of American space could there be
than to call it a forcing ground for the creation of a "world
of happified . . . spirits."

The fact that Americans lived in "a large place," however perilous for those who lived "meanly," could also be a
promise that when they should finally start to exploit the
environment for artistic purposes they would have that
much of a head start on their less favored rivals for literary glory. That America would surpass the achievements of
the ancient world was taken for granted by Samuel Lorenzo Knapp when he delivered his *Lectures on American
Literature* in 1829. "What are the Tibers and Scamanders,
measured by the Missouri and the Amazon?" asked Knapp.
Calling for a flowering of native American culture, he announced grandly, "Whenever a nation wills it, prodigies
are born." According to Knapp's calculation America had
already produced one prodigy in the person of Daniel

[50] *Society in America*, II, 30–31.
[51] *Congressional Globe*, XXV, 298.

Boone, whose feats depended on the immense distances of American space he had ranged over. The scale of Boone's wanderings, Knapp was sure, outstripped "the travels of Theseus, and the labours of Hercules." In fact, he gloated, "the whole country which these demigods of antiquity traversed, did not extend so far as one of Boone's hunting excursions." [52]

In choosing Daniel Boone as his proto-American, Knapp was saying something about the meaning of space for Americans which it is easy to overlook. Boone was widely recognized as the first white man to have entered whole areas of the West. Yet his carelessness in perfecting land titles finally cost him all his discoveries and forced him to wander again in his old age. Also, his hairbreadth encounters with Indians, known to every schoolchild, revealed an agility and wiliness more akin to the spirit of artful play than any calculated effort to clear the territory of impediments to getting rich. Almost alone in this respect—even the noble Washington had gone west as an advance man for a syndicate of speculators—Boone resembled indeed an ancient god whose antics were performed for the mere joy of doing.[53] In his other aspects, of course, as Knapp's moralism prevented him from realizing, the arch-American would be—and again here he would resemble the gods—the sharper, the horse swapper, the traveling confidence man. All these were natural entertainers, sometimes clowns. An American was some kind of fool in space.[54]

[52] *Lectures on American Literature, with remarks on some passages of American History* (1829), reprinted as *American Cultural History, 1607–1829,* Intro. and index by Richard Beale Davis and Ben Harris McClary (Gainesville, Fla., 1961), pp. 188–89, 260–63.

[53] I refer here, obviously, to the legendary, not the historic, Boone. For the development of the legend see Arthur K. Moore, *The Frontier Mind, A Cultural Analysis of the Kentucky Frontiersman* ([Lexington, Ky.], 1957), esp. Chaps. 5 and 9.

[54] See R. W. B. Lewis, *The American Adam,* Chap. 5. Lewis perhaps overstresses the "Adamic" quality of the American man in space.

One of the few explicit recognitions of the connection between American space as play area and the nature of a free society was made by the lawyer Charles Jared Ingersoll during the course of a Fourth of July oration at Philadelphia in 1832. He was concerned first of all to deny that free society was by nature wholly somber. Although the United States had fewer festivals than other places, freedom did not "diminish amusements," but in fact multiplied them. The United States, asserted Ingersoll,

abounds with pastimes. A free press, universal suffrage, elections of perpetual recurrence, multifarious legislation, open courts of justice, numberless voluntary associations—while they change the character of enjoyment, are nevertheless inexhaustible funds of it; and church or state need not ordain holy days for the recreation of a people with such resources of diversion.

Furthermore, he went on,

the itinerant habits and facilities of Americans, annihilating the magnificent distances of this extensive empire, are both physical and moral entertainment. The miracles of steam boats, already undergoing eclipse by steam carriages, afford to those middling classes, who, in Europe seldom see any thing twenty miles from home, tours of pleasure in the United States which are continual means of animation and improvement.[55]

Yet, the tricky relationship between the American and his space could provide a handy source of ammunition for critics of the American character. Foreigners were quick to make use of a standard that Americans themselves appealed to. By extension from the natural to the artificial environment it was also possible to praise American technological accomplishments while at the same time denigrating the contrivers as unworthy of their own contrivances. This was the style of Thomas Colley Grattan, one-time British consul at Boston, in his account of life in the

[55] *An Oration delivered before the Philadelphia Association . . . July 4, 1832* (Philadelphia, 1832), p. 5.

United States. After working the theme of a "disproportion between inanimate and human nature in America," he went on to say:

The mechanical arts are of necessity in constant progress, energy and ingenuity have ample scope, but the moral greatness of man is nearly undeveloped; and all this is in keeping with the scheme of American progress.

Even worse than this, it seemed that Americans had the erroneous impression that "because their country is vast, their destiny requires them to do great things in a grand style; and an inflated imitation of England is the result." [56] In contradiction, therefore, to those Americans who for several generations had been demanding the creation of an indigenous culture to match the scale of the native environment, Grattan suggested that it was the overpowering nature of that environment which was itself to blame for American cultural mediocrity.

To such strictures many Americans would have replied that an environment which set what was, from an English standpoint, an unrealistic standard did not present the same difficulties to the American. "One thing is plain for all men of common sense and common conscience," Emerson insisted, "that here, here in America, is the home of man." [57] Similarly, much of the power of virtue which resided in Crèvecoeur's "new man" was traceable to his residence in "every person's country." [58] The least that such assertions implied was that Americans, like Antaeus, could draw upon a kind of home strength not available elsewhere. And the evidence of history showed that when Americans had been most themselves, in concerting to establish the reign of liberty in the Revolution, the moral performance of the New World had by common acclaim outsoared ordinary yardsticks of measurement.

[56] Allan Nevins, ed., *American Social History*, pp. 248–49.
[57] "The Young American," *Works*, I, 391.
[58] Crèvecoeur, *Letters from an American Farmer*, p. 56.

Here, too, the open character of American space made a difference. Addressing a public that included numbers who had had some contemporaneous contact with the Founders, William Ellery Channing refused to grant even to Washington the unique status of a Europe-style hero. In the sense that the French Revolution knew the term, said Channing, there were no "great men" in the American Revolution. The opportunities for individuals to "determine a nation's fate" through their own spectacular deeds and personalities did not exist in America because "there was too much greatness in the American people to admit this overshadowing greatness of leaders." Washington, therefore, could not be a "saviour." Instead, his was the distinction "of being the brightest manifestation of the spirit which reigned in his country; and in this way he became a source of energy, a bond of union, the centre of an enlightened people's confidence."

This Revolutionary "greatness" of the American people, Channing went on, just as it refused to localize itself in particular individuals, was spatially coextensive with the colonies as a whole. There was an important reason why the American struggle never developed a centralized hub of activity such as Paris became in the French Revolution, a force to send "forth its influences like 'a mighty heart' through dependent and subservient provinces." The spirit of the American Revolution, Channing declared, was too widely diffused to create such an agency, since "the country was all heart." [59] A concentrated moral homogeneity, Channing was saying, of a uniformly high order, marked not only the men of the Revolution but also the loci of events. At a time when it counted most, therefore, Americans were able to demonstrate so great a spatial diffusion of virtue as to make particular sites important only in their representative capacity. In unfavorably contrasting the French Revolution, one that had failed to establish liberty,

[59] *Works*, pp. 430–31.

to the triumphant struggle of the country that had been "all heart," Channing was pointing to the necessity of maintaining a spatial dimension to virtue as the guarantee of American freedom. As other voices were also proclaiming, a democracy which rested on the virtue of the people could survive its heroic age under no other circumstances.

Channing's reluctance to differentiate space from space carried the high demand that Americans accept the total challenge of their tremendous site and live up to all of it. Toward the attainment of this ideal, so far as it included a determination to have space retain its open-free character, Americans had traditionally demonstrated a strong allegiance. At least their advance from the seacoast was sufficiently marked by a cavalier attitude toward prior claimants of the soil, whether these happened to be Indians, legitimate freeholders, or the federal government. Even closer to home they frequently appeared uninterested in securing to themselves an enclave safe from encroachment. When she toured the model dormitories at the Lowell Mills, Miss Martineau was astonished to discover a degree of crowding that in England was considered the lot of only the most miserable class. "In America," she commented,

where space is of far less consequence, where the factory girls can build churches, and buy libraries, and educate brothers for learned professions, these same girls have no private apartments, and sometimes sleep six or eight in a room, and even three in a bed. This is very bad. It shows a want of inclination for solitude; an absence of that need of it which every healthy mind must feel, in a greater or less degree.

Her advice was that "these gregarious habits should be broken through" by the immediate sectioning-off of separate apartments.[60]

At about the same time, adding to his other troubles, Captain Marryat was encountering extreme frustration in his efforts to get any time to himself at American inns.

[60] *Society in America,* II, 357–58.

Nobody, it seems, would leave him alone. "They even pre-
fer a double bed to a single one," he noted, "and I have
often had the offer to sleep with me made out of real kindness." [61] Fifty years earlier both Chastellux and Moreau
de Saint-Méry had reported much the same thing, and the
latter had declared his rebellion "at the nonsensical belief
that such customs are a proof of liberty." [62] What Americans meant by this could be seen in the long-lived report
that "the Duke of Saxe Weimar narrowly escaped a beating
in the western country for presuming to hire a whole stagecoach for himself and his valet." [63] The disallowance of
privacy was the denial of enclosed, closed-off space as a barrier to the maximum sharing of concurrent experience. If,
as Channing would have it, the maintenance of freedom
depended on a high level of general responsiveness, the ordinary rejection of privacy could be seen as a move to preserve and enlarge the sphere of common experience upon
which that response depended.

At any rate, no matter how necessary a technique for liv-

[61] *Diary in America*, p. 81.

[62] Marquis de Chastellux, *Travels in North America in the Years
1780, 1781, and 1782*, rev. trans. by Howard C. Rice, Jr. (Chapel
Hill, 1963), II, 441, and note 11, p. 603. While the Marquis wrote
of three or four persons in the same room, his original translator
volunteered testimony about plural occupancy of beds (*Moreau de
St. Méry's American Journey* [1793–1798], trans. and ed. Kenneth
and Anna M. Roberts [Garden City, N.Y., 1947], p. 121).

[63] Grund, *Aristocracy in America*, I, 65. Since Grund was hearing
this tale some ten years after the Duke's tour it must have become
something of a *cause célèbre*. The Duke himself barely mentions
the occurrence, and indicates that it was simply a case of trying to
load on another fare; but Mrs. Trollope, a few years afterward,
reprints an extended and lurid newspaper item, the source, doubtless, of the story Grund heard. (Bernhard, Duke of Saxe-Weimar
Eisenach, *Travels Through North America, during the Years 1825
and 1826* [Philadelphia, 1825], II, 18; *Domestic Manners*, II, 115–
18). What is important is that Americans apparently enjoyed telling the story as an assault upon aristocracy and privacy.

ing the enforcement of privacy might seem in a small, densely populated country, even there it was a species of upper-class luxury, and admittedly not for the poverty-stricken masses. Illuminating on this point is the reaction of John James Audubon when he visited England in 1826. Himself the classic American man in space, Audubon at an English country house mourned that it was impossible to roam through the woods as he did at home. "Is it not shocking," he noted,

that while in England all is hospitality *within,* all is so different *without?* No one dare *trespass,* as it is called. Signs of *large dogs* are put up; steel traps and spring guns are set up, and even *eyes* are kept out by high walls.[64]

In the classless society of America, with freedom for every man to rise as far as he was able, the demand for privacy could seem mere finicky snobbishness or even calculated arrogance. Here, again, Marryat put his finger on the heart of the case when he observed that "Americans . . . cannot bear anything like a secret" because "that's *unconstitutional.*" [65] Still, American inquisitiveness could be a welcome relief from the inquisitorial tyranny of European officialdom. Where the police in Europe, Baron Klinkowström reported, "investigate *how one thinks,* and in Sweden *what one says* . . . in America they only ask *what one does.*" [66] This piece of information, however, was one that Americans were strongly inclined to insist upon. The truth of the Baron's observation was to be strikingly demonstrated soon afterward when Revolutionary veterans repeatedly asked the visiting Lafayette, "What do you do for a living?" and even "What was your father's business?" [67] No wonder then that the innkeeper's registry

[64] *Audubon and His Journals,* eds. Maria R. Audubon and Elliott Coues (London, 1898), I, 114.

[65] *Diary in America,* p. 78.

[66] *Baron Klinkowström's America,* p. 76.

[67] Josiah Quincy, *Figures of the Past,* p. 151.

book was not to be bypassed, whether or not a statute com-
pelled its use.[68] Apparently, in an activist and equalitarian society where there was normally no telling from dress
or manners who was who, the display of occupational cre-
dentials was an obligation of civility.

To Marryat it seemed likely that, as Americans told
him, they were a people naturally curious, used to investigate, dismantle, and manipulate. They were notably tol-
erant of religious diversity, yet how could one explain the
destruction of the Ursuline Convent by a Boston mob in
1834? Rather obviously reluctant to admit the possibility
of a simple fear of the unknown, a Bostonian solemnly assured Marryat that the outrage was nothing more than the
expression of an overmastering urge to see what was concealed only because it was concealed.[69]

But an animus against the private and self-contained
strong enough to break out in acts of compulsive violence
could suggest the presence of some latent insecurity. In a
sense the ordinary American intrusiveness in social relations was only a similar, if less forcible, assault against personal and inward defenses. The readiness to believe in the
potency of unseen malignant forces seemed to argue less of
a mechanically oriented curosity than of an irrational
anxiety. Here an old ambiguity chewed at the heart of the
American problem of space against civilization. On one
side lay the anarchic and unorganized space of the wilderness, with Samuel Knapp's solitary frontiersman, Daniel
Boone, its representative spirit. At the same time America's mission was to upbuild the waste places and abolish
the great solitudes.

Between the dream and the reality of the American
West two visions of freedom contended for supremacy.
American college men knew that according to Aristotle
"man is by nature a political animal. And he who by nature and not by mere accident is without a state, is either

[68] Marryat, *Diary in America*, p. 102.   [69] *Ibid.*, p. 78.

a bad man or above humanity." [70] Timothy Dwight's beast was thus Samuel Knapp's demigod. In their enshrinement of Boone's literary apotheosis, Natty Bumppo, Americans paid homage to the ancient gods of solitude, while at the same time they went right on laying out the town lots and bringing in the railroad.

By its nature the town was a greedy invasion of space, a daring effort to spike it down and destroy its anonymous character. Through the efficacious grace of what Michel Chevalier saw as an American trinity—the church, the bank, and the school [71]—the pagan wilderness was to be converted and baptized into the reality of historical time. The timeless biological regeneration of the forest was succeeded by the visible mortality of the town with its old section and new, the being-demolished and the being-constructed. The mandala of the Town Plat elaborated the conception of the *projected,* and called attention to the contrast between what was and what was going to be.[72] As Boone was the hero of the wilderness, the authentic hero of the town, the arranger upon its anonymous soil of that longed-for meeting between higher and lower, may from the beginning have been the land promoter.

Although the American town introduced a certain amount of distinction and singularity to undifferentiated space, the result was not a clear assimilation of the American idea to a category of Old Europe. The European city had begun as an enclosure that was both physical and abstract. The wall corresponded to the defensive hedge of rights which the town possessed in its corporative capacity. The traveling freeman and the escaped serf found shelter in the penumbra of the town's privileges, while the privi-

[70] *Politics,* Bk. I, Ch. 2, 1253ª. B. Jowett's trans.

[71] "I return to the triple emblem of the church, the school with the printing press, and the bank" (Chevalier, *Society, Manners, and Politics,* p. 171).

[72] Lewis Mumford, *The Culture of Cities* (New York, 1938), p. 4.

leges themselves were fixed and nonambulatory. In contrast, the rights of an American were personal and inherent. When it was moved in the Massachusetts Constitutional Convention of 1853 to replace the historic representation of towns by a system of districts based on population, the victorious proponents of the change upheld the contention that towns in themselves had never been represented. For, it was argued, "the right belongs not to the locality but to the man, as such." Yet even if it had been otherwise in the colonial past, one delegate announced, with the Revolution "old things passed away, and all things became new." [73] Whatever the case in Europe, in America the man and not the town was truly primitive. It was the sovereign people who condescended to endow the town with a specious life upon sufferance.

Instead of looking inward to a hermetic realm of refuge, then, the American town naturally scanned the horizon with an exaggerated ambition bordering on the fantastic.[74] In the heated imaginations of their promoters hardly a hamlet failed of world significance, with its dimensions hopefully aligned to the framework of the globe itself. From a St. Louis newspaper Timothy Flint copied the following parody:

The name was "Ne plus ultra." The streets were laid out a mile in width; the squares were to be sections, each containing six hundred and forty acres. The mall was a vast standing forest. In the centre of this modern Babylon, roads were to cross each other in a meridional line at right angles, one from

[73] *Official Report of the Debates . . . in the State Convention, assembled May 4th, 1853 . . .* , II, 139, 400.

[74] "The rectangular street and block system, projectable indefinitely toward the horizon, was the universal expression of capitalist fancies" (*Culture of Cities*, p. 188). In a recent interview that longtime American resident Igor Stravinsky remarked on "those Midwestern parallelogram cities designed to be passed straight through" ("Music and the Statistical Age, An Interview," *Commentary*, Vol. 42 [September, 1966], p. 51).

the south pole to Symmes's hole in the north, and another from Pekin to Jerusalem.[75]

What could be more natural than for Flint to come across a bearded old "visionary" who "was descending the Mississippi, as he said, to the *real* Jerusalem in Asia."[76] If not always on such a grandiose plan, the opening up of transportation and communication, the bridging and demolition of distance, were rooted predicates in the establishment of an American town. To Edward Everett, in 1829, the westward movement rushed on like a planet, while the town it left behind was simply "a monument to mark its way through the vacant regions of space."[77]

So precipitous did the actual physical movement appear that it took on the character of a mass flight. When Henry Carey was calling attention to the abandonment of "old places," he used the terms "flight," "fly," and "flying" eighteen times in the space of a few pages.[78] To Philip Hone, that sophisticated New Yorker, everything was going too fast: "Improvements, Politics, Reform, Religion—all fly. . . . Flying is dangerous."[79] But it was the flight to the West, especially, into an area which afforded an effectually limitless sphere for the operation of the will, that caused eastern Evangelicals to raise the frightened cry "Barbarism the First Danger." "Ere long," Horace Bushnell warned,

there is reason to fear they will be scouring in populous bands over the vast territories of Oregon and California, to be known as the pasturing tribes—the wild hunters and robber clans of the western hemisphere—American Moabites, Arabs, and Edomites![80]

[75] *Recollections*, pp. 187–88.   [76] *Ibid.*, p. 280.
[77] *Orations*, I, 210.
[78] H. C. Carey, *Miscellaneous Essays* . . . , pp. 429–36.
[79] *The Diary of Philip Hone, 1828–1851*, ed. Allan Nevins (New York, 1927), II, 722. Entry for Nov. 28, 1844.
[80] *American National Preacher*, XXI (September, 1847), 212.

Bushnell feared that these Moabites, unlike the earlier New England emigrants, carried no culture as an ark before them to the western wilderness. They were under the spell of that enchantment which Timothy Flint saw resting upon the streams of westward rovers:

There is more of the material of poetry than we imagine, [wrote Flint] diffused through all the classes of the community. And upon this part of the character it is, that the disposition to emigration operates, and brings in aid the influence of its imperceptible but magic power. Very few . . . emigrate simply to find better and cheaper lands. The notion of new and more beautiful woods and streams, of a milder climate, deer, fish, fowl, game, and all those delightful images of enjoyment, that so readily associate with the idea of the wild and boundless license of new regions; all that restless hope of finding in a new country, and in new views and combinations of things, something that we crave but have not.[81]

Thus, while New England saw the West as a site for already operative and acknowledged values, thousands fanned outward urged by "the idea of the wild and boundless license of new regions." For these the space of the West was amplitude for the range of the will and the imagination. Strolling casts, they would play over and over again dramas on the single theme, "something we crave but have not."

A strong consciousness of space, a lively awareness of its demands and possibilities, was an inevitable accompaniment to the effort of mid-nineteenth-century Americans to understand themselves. The heritage of Jeffersonian liberty itself was a function of space relations, for he who died repeating, "Divide the counties into wards!" had first taken care to gather in "an empire for liberty." Liberty in America had to make a difference in space, and it was to be the task of the pre–Civil War generation to try to work out

[81] *Recollections*, p. 241. See also Oswald Spengler, *Decline of the West*, I, 335–36; II, 85 *et seq.*

for itself what that difference was. Even for a nation rac-
ing

      Far, like the comet's way through infinite space,

some fear and trembling was not an inappropriate attitude. Flying, as Hone said, was still dangerous.

CHAPTER FOUR

"The Greatest Man in the World"

"Behave pretty now, Charley," said the driver of LaFayette's coach, to one of his horses, "behave pretty, Charley—you are going to carry the greatest man in the world."

In August, 1824, at the invitation of President James Monroe and the Congress of the United States, the Marquis de Lafayette, former major-general in the Continental Army, took advantage of a lull in French politics to revisit America after an absence of forty years. For thirteen months as "The Nation's Guest" he traveled by stagecoach and steamboat into every state of the Union, where he was hailed and feted by tens of thousands of Americans to whom he had long been an almost legendary figure of the immortal Revolutionary history.[1] In an age which knew

[1] Lafayette's itinerary, with references to local newspapers and other sources, is found in J. Bennett Nolan, *Lafayette in America, Day by Day* (Baltimore, 1934). The secretary who accompanied Lafayette published an account of the tour: A. Levasseur, *Lafayette*

nothing of Presidential campaign trips, the extent and duration of Lafayette's great tour would alone have made it something of a phenomenon. Never before had so many Americans over so extended an area had the opportunity to see and hear a single national celebrity. In addition, wherever Lafayette went he moved in an atmosphere of high drama. The affecting nature of his pilgrimages to Revolutionary battlefields, the poignancy of his reunions with aged comrades, and the spectacular series of entertainments arranged for him captured the imagination of the entire country and made it certain that the memory of the day Lafayette came to town would long stay alive in the land. A new expression, "to be Lafayetted," survived for years as a token of the extreme adulation heaped upon the old warrior.[2] Hundreds of eulogistic poems filled the newspapers, including a *"Sonetto"* by Lorenzo da Ponte, Mozart's sometime librettist and now a resident of the

---

en Amérique en 1824 et 1825 . . . , 2 vols. (Paris, 1829), which appeared in English in one form as *Lafayette in America in 1824 and 1825* . . . , trans. John D. Godman, 2 vols. (Philadelphia, 1829). A man of feeling rather than an exact chronicler, Levasseur requires corroboration. A contemporary Boston Scrapbook in the Rare Book Room of the Library of Congress contains useful, though often unidentified, newspaper clippings relating to Lafayette's activities. Most valuable to me has been the mass of newspaper sources collected and reprinted in Edgar Ewing Brandon, *A Pilgrimage of Liberty* (Athens, Ohio, 1944) and *Lafayette, Guest of the Nation*, 3 vols. (Athens, Ohio, 1950–1957), hereafter cited as *Pilgrimage* and *Guest*. Brandon sometimes makes useful comments on his material. When Brandon's sources have been readily accessible, however, I have cited from them directly. Since the themes of this chapter might be adequately illustrated from almost any one or two of the major Lafayette receptions, cumulative references have generally been avoided. The quotation at the head of the chapter is from the Boston *Evening Gazette*, September 4, 1824.

[2] See *Harriet Martineau's Autobiography*, ed. Maria Weston Chapman (Boston, 1877), I, 356.

United States.[3] Samuel F. B. Morse was commissioned to paint the full-length portrait which hangs in New York City Hall,[4] while Asher B. Durand's engraved miniature head of the hero was "stamped on watch ribbons, ladies' belts, gloves, etc." [5] There were *"La Fayette* boots—*La Fayette* hats—*La Fayette* wine—and *La Fayette* everything." [6] Walt Whitman, then six years old, never forgot how he had been picked up and kissed by the great man in Brooklyn.[7] Even a quarter-century later a sermon by the Universalist patriarch Hosea Ballou used Lafayette's reception as an illustration of "the workings of the law of love," [8] and Margaret Fuller still remembered how the crowds had thrown flowers in front of his steps.[9] Popular opinion agreed with the Fourth of July orator of the 1830's for whom Lafayette's progress through the states exceeded "all that this world has ever known before of glory." [10] And one of the rare occasions when the poetry of William Cullen Bryant expressed the mood of a generation came as he reminisced:

[3] *New-York American,* August 16 and 18, 1824. (Name misspelled.)

[4] Carleton Mabee, *The American Leonardo, A Life of Samuel F. B. Morse* (New York, 1943), pp. 96–100.

[5] Pictures of Lafayette flasks, plates, and other items appear in a pamphlet of the Henry Francis Dupont Winterthur Museum, *Lafayette[,] The Nation's Guest* (Winterthur, Delaware, 1957), where the reference to Durand is on p. 3.

[6] Gilbert J. Hunt, *The Tour of General La Fayette through the U. States . . .* (New York, 1825), p. 6.

[7] Walt Whitman, *Lafayette in Brooklyn,* with an intro. by John Burroughs (New York, 1905). Lafayette kissed many children during the tour. See Josiah Quincy, *Figures of the Past,* pp. 147–48, 150.

[8] Maturin M. Ballou, *Biography of Rev. Hosea Ballou* (Boston, 1853), pp. 357–58.

[9] Margaret Fuller Ossoli, *At Home and Abroad . . . ,* ed. Arthur B. Fuller (Boston and London, 1856), p. 387.

[10] Jarvis Gregg, *Eulogy on Lafayette, delivered in the chapel of Dartmouth College, July 4, 1834* (Hanover, N.H., 1834), p. 22.

I pause to state,
That I too have seen, greatness—even I—
Shook hands with Adams—stared at Lafayette,
When barehead, in the hot noon of July,
He would not let the umbrella be held o'er him,
For which three cheers burst from the mob before him.[11]

So unrestrained was the public enthusiasm that Heze-kiah Niles, perhaps the best-known newspaper editor in the nation, was at one point stirred to issue a rebuke. When he heard that overzealous patriots in New York had attempted to unhitch the horses and pull Lafayette's carriage up Broadway themselves he exploded at the insult to the guest "when he sees the sovereigns of this great and glorious country, aiming at the most magnificent destinies, converted into asses or other beasts of burthen." Outlining for his countrymen the true guidelines of democratic devotion, Niles cautioned:

Let the trumpet to the cannon speak, the cannon to the heavens, and the ardent prayers of free millions ascend to the throne of the OMNIPOTENT, that blessings may be heaped upon him; but, in all this, let us remember that we are *men* like unto himself, and *republicans*.[12]

For Niles to recall Americans to themselves by reminding them of their republicanism was in this case a work of supererogation. For it was largely because Americans were so conscious of their status as republicans that they strove so hard to magnify the splendor of Lafayette's reception. Greeting him in the capacity of republicans, they were trying out the possibilities of a role still new to them. Of course, the return of a Revolutionary hero at a time

[11] "A Meditation on Rhode-Island Coal," *Poems,* p. 160. The term "mob" did not yet, *per se,* carry a derogatory meaning. When Lafayette was in Boston a local paper wrote: "He had on this occasion [a] fine sample of a Boston mob; a collection of intelligent, rational and independent freemen." Scrapbook, p. 23.

[12] *Niles' Weekly Register,* XXVI (August 28, 1824), 426.

coinciding with the half-century anniversary of the War of
Independence would alone have been cause for lavish celebration. But the career of Lafayette demanded more than
the conventional homage due a brave soldier for his youthful exploits. As the steadfast proponent of constitutional
government through all the excesses of the French Revolution, the despotism of Napoleon, and the Bourbon reaction, Lafayette, in the years since he had left America, had
won recognition as Europe's best-known defender of liberalism. The embodiment of the life lived for liberty, Lafayette stood forth on the individual level as the counterpart to the United States on the world scene. In his own
person he had demonstrated the reality and validity of
ideals that it was the task of the United States to uphold in
the form of free political and social institutions. The glory
of his return, therefore, had more than one aspect; it was a
glory that was both his and America's. And as the year-long
Lafayette festival proceeded to hold up for reverent consideration every facet of the General's life and character it
became ever clearer that in praising Lafayette a generation
of Americans were explaining themselves to one another
and to the world.

The special implications of Lafayette's return were al-
ready being recognized before his landing at Staten Island.
All Americans could share the feelings of the venerable
Philip Freneau when he wrote:

> Of the great actors on our stage,
> Of warrior, patriot, statesman, sage,
> How few remain, how few remain!
> Among the first, you claim esteem,
> The historian's and the poet's theme.
>
> .　　.　　.　　.　　.
>
> Approach! appear that welcome day,
> That sees the *Marquis* on his way. . . .[13]

[13] "General De la Fayette On His Expected Visit to America,"
Last Poems, pp. 118–19.

Himself an almost forgotten relic of the early republican years, Freneau welcomed Lafayette as a living return of the heroic past. In this sense, that of a patriotic curiosity, there was to be no question of Lafayette's strong appeal. More complex were the emotions of the committee appointed by the Corporation of the City of New York to arrange for Lafayette's civic entertainment. Rejecting "pomp," "parade," and "ostentatious ceremonies," as inappropriate for the "illustrious visitor" and "opposed to our republican habits," the committee went on to declare:

There are occasions, however, where the American people choose to pour forth their feelings in acts of unrestrained hospitality, munificence, and even profusion. Such will be the case when the Marquis arrives in our City—*In him we will recognise, at once all that appeals most powerfully to us as a free & independent nation* [italics added].[14]

These men of affairs, who included among them New York's next mayor, Philip Hone, could be expected more fully to reflect the temper of their times than the aged poet. Freneau was, after all, essentially an epigone. The full meaning of Lafayette's visit, the committee realized, could not be contained within the verge of his own accomplishments alone, but would involve to a profound degree the character of the American response to his presence. That response, Americans were concerned to emphasize, was not to be considered solely as the "sudden burst of an extatic moment." [15] It was to become over a period of thirteen months something in the nature of a communal pageant, enacted over and over on numerous stages, in which *all that appealed most powerfully* to the American people of the mid-1820's in their still self-conscious role of free men in a free society was to be brought forward and paraded.

[14] *Minutes of the Common Council of the City of New York 1784–1831,* XIII (New York, 1917), 794.

[15] Hunt, *Tour,* p. 6.

From the American point of view, perhaps the leading theme of Lafayette's whole tour centered on the nation's *gratitude* to him for his Revolutionary services. Here Lafayette, as the worthy recipient of national gratitude, provided a grand occasion for the collective display of a prestigious virtue that Americans were eager to claim for themselves. As men with a classical orientation, the founding generation had been uncomfortably aware of the historic charge that republics were notoriously ungrateful to their benefactors. The imputation was part of the general argument that popular rule meant control by the mean-spirited, and that the magnanimous virtues belonged only to an aristocracy. When he closed his pioneer account of the American Revolution with the establishment of the Constitutional government, the historian David Ramsay thought it necessary to exhort his fellow citizens to "cherish and reward" those men who left their private concerns to labor for the public interest, in order to "rescue citizens and rulers of republics, from the common and too often merited charge of ingratitude." [16] In like manner, *The Columbian Orator,* that highly popular school handbook of rhetoric from which a generation of early-nineteenth-century American boys imbibed draughts of civic idealism, reprinted in numerous editions the fervent plea of a patriotic speaker: "Let it never be said of us, as of Rome and of Athens, that ingratitude is the common vice of republics." [17] Apart, therefore, from their lively personal interest in the old hero, Americans were fully primed to welcome Lafayette's reappearance as a heaven-sent opportunity for such a clear-cut display of national gratitude as would vindicate republican government from an ancient aspersion.

No time was lost in making it unequivocally clear to the distinguished guest that his visit was expected to accom-

[16] *History of the American Revolution* (Philadelphia, 1789), II, 355.

[17] *Columbian Orator,* p. 235.

plish such a purpose. Having led a flotilla of six steamboats to the Battery, and ridden to city hall through a crowd estimated at fifty thousand, Lafayette experienced his first official reception on American soil. "The people of the United States look up to you as one of their most honored Parents—the country cherishes you as one of the most beloved of her sons," the Mayor greeted him. "I hope and trust, sir," His Honor continued,

that not only the present, but the future conduct of my countrymen, to the latest period of time, will, among other slanders, refute the unjust imputation, that Republics are always ungrateful to their benefactors.[18]

Proceeding up the Hudson after a quick trip to New England, Lafayette was assured as he debarked at a river town that "the sovereign people of these United States are . . . giving you, sir, and the world the most indubitable evidence that the noxious weed of ingratitude has no root in the American soil." [19] In case any doubt remained, the emblazoned motto on the triumphal arch under which he passed at Albany announced boldly: "One republic not ungrateful." [20] By the time he reached Philadelphia some ten days later the *Evening Post,* having defied "Rome, in her proudest day, to produce a parallel" to the "never-to-be-forgotten day" of Lafayette's reception, concluded that the description of the scene would

be handed down from father to son, as a rich legacy, to show posterity that all Republics have not been ungrateful to those who stepped forward in the hour of adversity to shield a brave people from the talons of tyranny and oppression.[21]

The *Post*'s reference to Rome was far from being merely casual. A follower of Lafayette's itinerary might well have

[18] *New-York American,* August 17 and 18, 1824.
[19] *Niles' Weekly Register* XXVII (September 27, 1824), 60.
[20] *Albany Daily Advertiser,* September 20, 1824.
[21] *Guest,* II, 68.

concluded that Rome was America's principal rival and
competitor in a contest of public gratitude. At the same
time, the dominant motif of the Lafayette celebrations was
heavily Roman. Despite the occasional introduction of
steamboats, it was apparent that Americans lacked a style
of their own for the entertainment of a republican hero.
Wreathes and classical arches proliferated across the country. In such an atmosphere an anti-Rome theme served to
focus attention upon the reality of the national identity
and to prevent its confusion with the appearances of the
ceremonies. Roman trappings provided excellent occasions
for assertions of American superiority. Standing with Lafayette before the tomb at Mount Vernon, George Washington Custis solemnly observed that the national tour
bore "the splendor of a triumph greater than Roman consul ever had." [22] A comparison of this type was very commonly made in order to elaborate an invidious distinction
between the two "triumphs" in which Rome invariably
came out second best. Typical was this comment in South
Carolina:

The triumphal entries of Pompey and of Caesar were but the
adulations of a conquered city; followed by victims, gladiators,
and spoils. But the voluntary burst of gratitude and admiration, which twenty-four free states—which a whole continent
of freedom express [*sic*] for the friend of Washington and the
rights of man, is without a parallel in the history of mankind.[23]

But Americans were not content to garner easy moral
victories over Pompey and Caesar; their real target was the

[22] *Niles' Weekly Register,* XXVII (November 6, 1824), 157.
[23] Charleston *City Gazette,* March 19, 1825. The Roman theme
received its most unusual twist from a Masonic Grand Master in
Baltimore, as he toasted: "Our Republic—never more glorious
than when presenting, like the Roman daughter, 'the full breasts
of her youthful exuberance' to the lips of a venerated father."
With hometown pride Hezekiah Niles reported: "The force of this
toast was electric" (*Niles' Weekly Register,* XXVII [January 1,
1825], 275).

Europe of their own time. Rome was the magnified stalk-
ing-horse for an attack upon the rulers who had persecuted
Lafayette, and whose swollen international pretensions
had lately received President Monroe's well-merited coun-
tercheck. Reporting the Lafayette reception at Worcester,
the *Massachusetts Spy* asked, "What in the history of kings
and emperors can vie with it in interest?" And, after the
customary thrust at "a Roman triumph," proclaimed:
"Thus shall it be done to the man whom the PEOPLE delight to honour." [24] Such a happy conversion of the
famous verse in the Book of Esther from royal to republican uses sprang naturally to the minds of Lafayette's hosts
in many places. Monarchy in general was under assault.
"What a triumph is this day for rational freedom!" exclaimed New Jersey's Attorney General Theodore Frey-
linghuysen as the Lafayette cortege arrived at Newark.
"What are the heartless pageantry, and pomp, and grandeur of titled potentates, to the grateful throb of ten millions of hearts!" [25] Such barbs were sometimes aimed with
greater specificity, as when one newspaper pointed out that
the greeting received by George IV at Leith, Scotland, in
1822, while superficially comparable to Lafayette's American reception, actually was not at all the same. "No ful-
some adulation was here extorted by the power or splen-
dour of royalty, but every feeling and every movement
were the spontaneous bursts of admiration and gratitude." [26]

Here the key word was *spontaneous*. As Americans engaged in the task of discriminating their own brand of *republican* gratitude from the conventional gratitude of aris-

[24] *Massachusetts Spy,* September 9, 1824. Americans quite obviously
enjoyed outdoing the royal Ahasuerus, who "made a feast. . . .
When he shewed the riches of his glorious kingdom and the
honour of his excellent majesty many days, *even* an hundred and
fourscore days" (Esther 1:3-4).

[25] Trenton *True American,* October 1, 1824.   [26] *Guest,* I, 42.

tocratic Europe no word was used more often than *spontaneous*. Hardly an orator let pass the opportunity of making a contrast between the presumably stereotyped, mechanical, even unwilling homage of Europe's subjects and the "spontaneous and voluntary" character of the American response to Lafayette. Neither were his hosts backward in letting Lafayette know the value of the honor he was receiving. "The Nation's Guest," ran the Governor's toast at the Baltimore dinner, "we offer him what treasure could not buy, nor power extort—the spontaneous homage of a free people." [27] A stanza of poetry that greeted Lafayette at Washington epitomized American thinking on the subject;

> The gifts that Kings to servile men assign,
> Let parasites, obsequious deem divine,
> Fit baubles for the empty, mean, or proud,
> Gilt toys and tinsel to deceive the crowd,
> But nought that despots grant, or can withhold,
> No title, badge, barbaric pearl, or gold,
> Can ever gratify true glory's thirst
> Like grateful tears that from a Nation burst,
> Tribute that happy millions now impart,
> That swells spontaneous from each throbbing heart.[28]

Despite numerous assertions that "gold" was no match for "grateful tears" when it came to "gratify true glory's thirst," national pride swelled when it became known that Congress had decided to add a more substantial dimension to American gratitude. In recognition of his large personal expenditures during the Revolution, the aging General, now somewhat threadbare and in financial straits, was to receive two hundred thousand dollars and a township of federal land. By this act, a celebrant in North Carolina was now certain, Congress had "blotted out forever from the

[27] *Niles' Weekly Register,* XXVII (October 23, 1824), 120.
[28] *Washington Gazette,* October 14, 1824.

page of the history of Republics, the charge of *ingratitude.*" [29] The accuracy of an earlier New Jersey toast—
"The American People.—They have no statute of limita-
tion for a debt of gratitude" [30]—seemed vindicated. And a
contemporary chronicler was moved to speak of the "lasting benefit" that Congressmen had conferred "on their
country" through the performance of "a great moral
duty," which had "substantially proved to the world that
republics are not always ungrateful." [31]

As this writer clearly saw, American gratitude was a
duality, with both an inner and an outer nature. As a
moral demonstration it conferred a "benefit" upon the nation itself through its intrinsic rightness, and at the same
time it could be expected to have a more extended effect
upon "the world." To Americans it was hard to say which
aspect was the more important. The exemplary character
of the Lafayette proceedings was a theme that accompanied Lafayette wherever he went. For many of his hosts
it was almost as if the tour had been expressly arranged in
order to transmit salutary instruction to an ideologically
backward Europe. With the fervor normally used in pray-
ing for those who dwelt in darkness, speakers expressed
their simple faith in the saving efficacy of the national performance. "As Americans, as philanthropists," one cried,

we can have but one wish:—Might the Potentates of Europe
but behold this Republican spectacle in America! They would
then feel that the blaze of loyalty cannot warm like the ardour

[29] *Raleigh Register,* March 8, 1825.

[30] *New-Jersey Eagle,* October 1, 1824.

[31] Robert Waln, Jr., *Life of the Marquis de La Fayette; . . .*
(Philadelphia, 1825), p. 504 n. A rare sour note was sounded by
one editor who called attention to several notorious cases of "heartless neglect which the nation has exhibited to its early protectors
and benefactors. In fact," he pointed out, "the reception and treatment of Fayette, furnish the single solitary instance of national
gratitude" (*New-York Literary Gazette,* I [September 17, 1825],
30).

of Patriotism; and realize how much less dear to the heart is the exacted homage of subjects, than the spontaneous gratitude of freemen.[32]

Such active concern for the moral regeneration of "Potentates" lent seriousness to even the most "spontaneous" displays of gratitude by introducing international considerations. The country stood behind a Virginia toast which drank to: "Our gratitude; may it prove worthy of ourselves, and the admiration of all the world." [33] Similarly, a Savannah newspaper, reflecting on the brief glories of Lafayette's passage through the city, could feel sincerely that "the eyes of Europe were upon us, and the conduct pursued by our country, towards an early volunteer in the cause of freedom, will obtain new proselytes to our principles, and respect for the people who practise them." [34] For Americans, there was in this sentiment from a provincial town no lack of proportion, no hint of egoism, but merely the reflection of a traditional national interest in converting the Old World to political righteousness with the gospel of republican truth.[35]

Along with this missionary impulse and its tacit assumption of superiority, however, went an obvious craving for the accolade of foreign approval. Repeated references to the "admiration of the world" and the "respect" that the treatment of Lafayette would gain for America expressed a yearning for the recognition, as it were, of the long-denied moral legitimacy of the republic. Even the good behavior of the crowds, the absence of rioting and crime, was pressed into service in the American contest with Europe. "One good effect of his visit," claimed a newspaper,

[32] *Providence Gazette,* August 25, 1824.   [33] *Guest,* III, 112.
[34] *Savannah Georgian,* March 25, 1825.
[35] The *United States Gazette,* for example, expected the cordial reception of Lafayette in America to terrify the "Royal Brigands" and "trembling tyrants" of Europe into "relinquish[ing] a part of their grasp" (*Guest,* II, 104).

will . . . be to satisfy him, Europe, and the world, what we are in our most extravagant moments—that we have nothing, or at least very little in this country, which corresponds with the *rabble* or *mobs* in older and less favoured nations.[36]

The continual emphasis upon the edifying character of American gratitude to Lafayette was a demand that the nation be at last accepted by others at its own valuation. To Americans themselves the justification for such acceptance was now overwhelmingly clear. No unseemly self-praise was involved, therefore, as they admitted with satisfaction that by honoring the merits of Lafayette they were simultaneously "perpetuating . . . memorials of our own love of virtue and of truth." [37] The matter was a fact that called for rejoicing. It testified, in the words of the Washington poet, that America was a

> Thrice happy land! where gratitude so pure
> Makes Virtue lov'd, and Liberty secure;
>
> .   .   .   .   .
>
> Where public spirit, luminous as free,
> Stirs millions by one suffrage, to decree
> Immortal garlands (borrow'd from no throne,)
> To cherish and exalt good deeds alone! [38]

Understandably, in the excitement of "perpetuating memorials" to America's own sterling qualities it some-

[36] Scrapbook, p. 15. Pride in the good conduct of American crowds became a common theme in the newspapers. One of the first to make such an observation was James Fenimore Cooper, who reported the great Castle Garden fete in the *New-York American,* September 15, 1824 (*Letters and Journals* I, 114–19). At issue was the touchy question whether social order could be maintained under republican government. Nevertheless, reports of rampant pickpocketing began very early (*Salem Gazette,* September 7, 1824). No section of the country seemed exempt, but a southern editorial headed "Hold on to Your Pockets" would admit only that "a set of pick-pockets seem to have followed gen. LAFAYETTE from Boston" (Alexandria *Herald,* October 13, 1824).

[37] *Virginia Herald,* November 27, 1824.

[38] *Washington Gazette,* October 14, 1824.

times happened that the living Lafayette disappeared entirely behind the multiple façade of his social meanings. Thus he became, at Salem, a trinity of what he and the people of the United States could share in common: "A living monument of Royal perfidy, Imperial tyranny and Republican gratitude." [39] Perhaps the most extreme adaptation of the man and his merits to the service of his hosts took place at a dinner in Alexandria, Virginia, soon after Lafayette's arrival at Washington. Before a company that included Secretary of State John Quincy Adams, a naval officer offered the toast:

General Lafayette: The uniform tenor of his conduct in the cause of virtue and freedom, afford to the world, the most happy *illustration that the people of the U[nited] States of America, know how to appreciate worth like his* [italics added].[40]

That Lafayette's true significance lay less in himself than in the response which he evoked and in the appreciation of that response by Europeans was thus often asserted. The very frequency of its repetition suggested some anxiety lest America's republican message to "the world" be misinterpreted. The sort of thing that could happen despite all precautions was illustrated by an article from a London paper which was reprinted in New York and widely copied. As if to demonstrate the perverse obduracy of the aristocratic mind, it seemed that the English writer was determined to see in Lafayette's reception nothing but "how little essential difference there is between republican and monarchical honors." In America, it appeared, there was only "the same flattery; the same pomp; the same ceremony; the same parade; but more servility, and infinitely more of burlesque self-importance." The whole affair was marked by "idle pretensions" engendered by the "thing miscalled equality." Here was a republican moral

[39] *Salem Gazette,* August 31, 1824.
[40] *Richmond Enquirer,* October 24, 1824.

drawn with a vengeance! While with regard to the elaborate compliments exchanged by Lafayette and his hosts, the foreign paper observed maliciously that

> your democrats, and your levellers, of all descriptions, are so profuse of mutual civilities: hence they so be-praise and so be-daub each other; and hence, though differing, perhaps, upon all other subjects, they are so cordially unanimous upon their own superlative merits. General La Fayette, for example, says, whatever he may think, that the Americans are the most exalted people in the world; and the Americans cannot say less in return, whatever they may think too, than that there never was such a man as La Fayette. And so they go on, keeping their countenances all the while, as if the rest of the world were not looking on with scorn and derision at their fooleries.[41]

Foreign jibes could never shake Americans in their confidence that by turning out to cheer Lafayette they were actors in a drama whose "moral sublimity . . . [had] nothing like it in the history of man." [42] If this were not the case there would be nothing serious in republicanism, and no special meaning in the deep-rooted concept of an American destiny. Nevertheless, the quite evident contrast between the loud public professions of "republican simplicity" [43] and the flamboyant and protracted veneration accorded "the greatest man in the world" was bothersome enough to seem to call for a more thoughtful resolution of the apparent paradox than was to be found in toasts or occasional poetry. By the early summer of 1825, when Lafayette got around to Transylvania University in Kentucky,

[41] *Niles' Weekly Register*, XXVII (October 30, 1824), 135–36. Niles used five and a half columns of his next issue to justify the American reception of Lafayette against English sneers, capping his argument with a heavily pro-American extract from another London paper (*ibid.*, November 6, 1824, pp. 145–47).

[42] *Pilgrimage*, p. 424.

[43] This was the term regularly used to describe Lafayette proceedings. For an example see the *Charleston Courier*, March 16, 1825.

President Horace Holley, the foremost educator in the West, was ready to resolve the contradiction on Lockean psychological and linguistic grounds.

Speaking before Lafayette and the convocation, Holley located the basis of European misunderstanding of American motives in the different signification that the same terms were bound to bear in Europe and America. The context and atmosphere of American freedom, he asserted, had an effect upon the meaning of words. Since words drew their strength from the vividness of the impressions for which they stood, the more energetic the experiences represented by particular terms, the more powerful the thoughts to which they would give rise. Therefore, he continued, "our condition gives the force and definiteness of daily practice to the whole vocabulary of liberty, rights, reciprocal advantages, the dignity of our nature, and the common welfare." Words in America, it followed, meant action, and took color from the exigencies of a "government of checks and balances" where everyone bore responsibility for the common polity. This was what made American language *"in earnest,"* and gave it a self-correcting quality based on constant experiment and "the *consent* of those who are deeply interested to maintain its truth and significancy."

Conversely, according to Holley, language in Europe lacked such an intimate interaction with reality, and was instead subordinated to the service of political ends, such as the bulwarking of traditional authority. "It is on this account," Holley explained, "that the best expositions of our state of society, and the most manly sentiments of our great speakers and writers, cannot be fully and fairly translated in Europe."

Having thus prepared the groundwork, Holley then took up the special problem posed by the national reception of his distinguished guest. Turning to Lafayette, Holley reaffirmed popular beliefs as he assured him, "It is then the *moral and political grandeur,* connected with your visit to us, upon which our minds delight to dwell. A mere pageant is unworthy of both parties." As for criticisms from Europe, they were based upon an environmental contrast that led inevitably to a failure of communication. "When foreign presses fling back upon us our homage to you, as inconsistent with our republican principles and manners," said Holley,

they prove the truth of what has been already said, that they *do not,* and *cannot* understand us. They look at all this stripped of its associations, *individualized* and exclusively devoted to *the man,* after the manner of the homage paid to a king or an emperor. But we identify YOU, as we do WASHINGTON, with the cause, the sentiments, the institutions, the blessings, which the recollection, and still more the sight of you can never fail to embody and present with paramount interest and force to our minds. . . . YOUR PRESENCE IS THE JUBILEE OF LIBERTY.[44]

In hailing Lafayette, therefore, said Holley, Americans were in no way fostering a "cult of personality," but were simply honoring the universal ideal of liberty, for which they themselves also stood, in the particular soldier and hero. Such a defense was doubly necessary in a society devoted to the equality that the London paper had disparaged, and where any unusual display of devotion to an individual not only raised fears among competitors but seemed also to denigrate the popular wisdom and competence. Yet, in the praise of Lafayette, Americans could afford to let down their guard and relax all republican inhibitions. A safe hero, he was somebody from out of the game; appearing for a moment, he would soon depart again. As the Boston *Gazette* informed "Europe" in the first month of Lafayette's visit, Americans were convinced that

[44] *Kentucky Reporter,* May 30, 1825.

forty thousand La Fayettes could not affect, if so disposed, the
march of our principles, or make us turn to the right hand or
left in our course of justice and honour. There is no danger
from him: for, in a foreign land, his own native home, he has
kept on in the tract [*sic*] of liberty, *pari pasu* [*sic*], with us;
and if there be any difference, he is on the lead. Such a man is
as full of magnanimity as zeal, and there can be no apprehensions from him.[45]

In fact, many, including the feeble Jefferson, were in
hopes that the tour would exercise a calming influence on
the political pot, which was beginning to boil ominously
after years of consensus government.[46] At a time when the
seeds of irreconcilable party divisions were germinating
everybody could sincerely join in celebrating Lafayette's
return to the fields of his Revolutionary gallantry.

The expectation that the tour of an aged politician from
another country might have such an effect rested entirely
upon the unique character that the *Lafayette idea* carried
in the United States of the 1820's. If the interaction between the American people and "The Nation's Guest" involved on the one side a virtuous expression of national
gratitude, the form of the expression was shaped by the
identification of Lafayette—as Horace Holley indicated—
with the most potent father image in American history:
George Washington. Such an identification had been carefully fostered by Lafayette himself even during the Revolution, and since then had become part of the Lafayette legend. Now he referred to himself easily as *"Washington's
adopted son."*[47] His public relationship to Washington

---

[45] Scrapbook, p. 154.   [46] *Writings*, XVI, 78–79.

[47] Lafayette used this expression at Camden, S.C. (*Pilgrimage*,
p. 48); his hosts used it everywhere. Washington had actually once
said, "I love him as my own son." The development of Lafayette's
"sonship" to Washington is traced in Louis Gottschalk, *Lafayette
Joins the American Army* (Chicago, 1937), p. 39; *Lafayette and the
Close of the American Revolution* (Chicago, 1942), pp. 80–81, 421

was thus twofold: not merely was he hailed as "the friend
and companion of our beloved father . . . Washington," [48] but the claimed tie of special affection provided
the basis for the type of sentiment displayed on a box at
the gala ball in Charleston: "WASHINGTON, our Common Father—*you* his favorite *son*." [49] Appropriately, the
"choir of female singers" greeting him at Newark "chaunted
. . . to the tune 'See the conquering hero comes':

> Welcome! Freedom's favorite son,
> Welcome! friend of Washington;
> For though his sun in glory's set,
> His spirit welcomes La Fayette.[50]

The tandem sense of the Washington-Lafayette figure, as
expounded in a hundred speeches and toasts, was compacted in the lines of an obscure poet who wrote:

> As his bosom companion, advisor, and friend,
>   By the side of our country's great Father he shone,
> Sought his own with that Chieftain's high virtues to blend,
>   And was lov'd and distinguished as Washington's son! [51]

To an important degree, the similarity of the response
that Lafayette evoked in all sections of the Union, whether
part of the original colonies or not, was traceable to his
close association in the popular mind with the revered
memory of Washington. In the merits of Washington and
the Revolution he had led all Americans claimed a share.
If Bunker Hill and Yorktown were on the Atlantic, settlers
beyond the mountains could still say, with Judge James
Hall at Shawneetown, Illinois, "We are the descendants of

(Washington's remark is quoted on p. 81); and *Lafayette between
the American and the French Revolution* (Chicago, 1950), pp. 130,
131, 141, 163.
   [48] *Niles' Weekly Register,* XXVII (October 23, 1824), 120.
   [49] *Charleston Courier,* March 18, 1825.   [50] *Guest,* II, 23.
   [51] Daniel Bryan, "The Greeting," *The Lay of Gratitude . . .*
(Philadelphia, 1826), Stanza XIV, p. 14.

those who fought by your side—we have imbibed their love of freedom—we inherit their affection for *La Fayette.*" [52] Obviously, Washington's identification with a time of patriotic war, a time when geographical, political, and social differences came closest to being submerged under a sense of national unity, attached itself to his former subordinate. Yet here Lafayette was able to benefit from his association with Washington in a manner unavailable to American survivors of the same era, particularly if they were politically prominent. Whereas Washington, in his years as President, became the center of much bitterness and rancor, a figure around whom, in fact, clustered the primal sources of division in American politics, Lafayette retained his place in Washington's earlier, noncontroversial, and wholly heroic period. More than Lafayette's well-known Masonic affiliation led the Grand Master of New Jersey's Washington Lodge to announce as he presented the visiting "Brother" with a gold medal, "LA FAYETTE, a living monument of greatness, virtue and faithfulness still exists—a second Washington is now among us." [53]

The second coming of Washington, it was to be expected, would be accompanied by significant signs and portents. As much as their ancestors, Americans liked to look for and discover "remarkable providences." Appropriately, the rainbow, emblem of a divine promise and symbol of beneficent reconciliation, figured prominently at both Lafayette's entry and departure from the country. To avoid landing in New York on the Sabbath, Lafayette passed the day on Staten Island with Vice-President Daniel D. Tompkins. Then, according to the *Commercial Advertiser,* "a curious circumstance occurred in the elements . . . which, in a superstitious age and country, might have

[52] *Illinois Gazette,* May 14, 1825. I have corrected a slight typographical error here.

[53] *Guest,* II, 26. Of course, this was prior to the beginning of the anti-Masonic agitation.

been regarded as a happy omen." When heavy rain began in the afternoon, and

the thick black cloud passed over Staten Island, it separated, and while the rain descended in torrents in this city, and south of the Quarantine Ground, the sun shone upon the seat of the Vice-President, in all its brightness.

Afterward, "an iris, as perfect, bright and beautiful as ever was seen, appeared in the east," spanning New York harbor from the Battery to the Narrows.[54]

Thirteen months later, on a "boisterous and rainy" day, even as Lafayette had come into the United States under a rainbow so did he go out. After the last farewells and speeches in September 1825, "The Nation's Guest" rode down the Potomac past Mount Vernon to board the new warship that was to carry him home to France. At a point where the Maryland and Virginia shores were seven miles apart, the *Brandywine,* named for the battle where Lafayette had received his wound, lay at anchor. When the time came for the vessel to sail, "the sun burst forth . . . and formed a magnificent arch, reaching from shore to shore, the barque which bears the venerable chief being immediately in the centre." Commented an observer, "It was destined to be the last arch under which he was to pass in his beloved America." [55]

All in all, however, the high point of the entire trip was bound to be the visit to Mount Vernon. There, amid an atmosphere of profound emotion, Lafayette descended into the tomb of Washington to kiss the lead coffin and commune with the man whose life he had tried to make the model for his own.[56] So deeply moving was the occasion that words seemed inadequate for its description:

[54] New York *Commercial Advertiser,* August 17, 1824.
[55] *Niles' Weekly Register, XXIX* (September 17, 1825), 44; Scrapbook, p. 139.
[56] *Niles' Weekly Register,* XXVII (November 6, 1824), 158.

Ah, who may tell the converse sweet,
    Unheard by mortal ear,
When two such godlike spirits meet,
    Each in a different sphere!

Time, thou shalt ne'r again behold
    A scene so fraught with bliss;
No, not till Nature's knell is knolled,
    Behold a scene like this.[57]

With the prevailing tension and excitement, Lafayette "received a contusion on the forehead . . . by striking against some part of the tomb," and the "unruly" behavior of his carriage horses made it necessary for him to walk all the way back to the riverside.[58]

The return of the past in the form of a Washington surrogate was an event all the more thrilling because of Lafayette's long absence from America. He now seemed "like one arisen from the dead." [59] As *Niles' Register* explained,

The volumes of history furnish no parallel—no one like LaFayette has ever *re-appeared* in any country. To us he is like a venerated father, returned from the grave, to bless and receive the blessings of a mightily increased and joyous posterity.[60]

In terms that found wide popular acceptance Speaker Henry Clay, before the joint session of Congress honoring Lafayette, dramatized the same theme. "The vain wish has been sometimes indulged," said Clay,

that Providence would allow the patriot, after death, to return to his country, and to contemplate the intermediate changes which had taken place—to view the forest felled, the cities built, the mountains levelled, the canals cut, the highways

[57] Robert S. Coffin, "Lafayette at the Tomb of Washington," *Oriental Harp. Poems of the Boston Bard* (Providence, R.I., 1826), p. 96.

[58] Alexandria *Herald,* October 20, 1824.

[59] *Nashville Whig,* May 7, 1825.

[60] *Niles' Weekly Register,* XXVII (November 6, 1824), 145.

constructed, the progress of the arts, the advancement of learning, and the increase of population. General, your present
visit to the United States is a realization of the consoling object of that wish. You are in the midst of posterity.

Himself a man of the new age that he was describing, Clay
appealed on behalf of the bustling present for the approv-
ing judgment of a simpler past. Recognizing this fact with
a sure sense of the occasion, Lafayette replied with characteristic gallantry:

No, Mr. Speaker, posterity has not begun for me, since, in the
sons of my companions and friends, I find the same public
feelings . . . in my behalf, which I have had the happiness to
experience in their fathers.[61]

Clay's triumphant recital belonged to a class of paeans to
the advance of American civilization that constituted an
invariable item on the agenda of every Lafayette reception. As Lafayette returned to New York City from the
West for the Fourth of July celebration of 1825, the Lieutenant Governor of the state greeted him with a catalogue
of American achievements intended to make clear to him
the significance of his ten months' experience. "Your recent tour throughout this country has enabled you," the
Lieutenant Governor told Lafayette,

to witness the progress of improvement; and to contrast in
your recollection our present with our past condition. The relative condition of a people enslaved, or a people in the full
enjoyment of freedom, is here strongly exemplified. The wilderness has vanished before the arm of independent industry.
The ignorance of *subjects* has given way to the intelligence of
freemen. Plenty has taken the place of want. Prosperity and
strength have been substituted for poverty and weakness. The
two millions and a half of *subjects,* whom you came to enfran-
chise, and to aid in the day of their adversity, now count
about eleven millions of hardy freemen.

Lafayette's answer was by this time almost a ritual formula
of confirmation and approval, utilizing the same concepts

[61] *Ibid.* (December 18, 1824), 252.

that had been presented to him. "At every step of my visit through the twenty four United States," Lafayette assured his audience,

. . . I have had to admire wonders of creation and improvement. No where can they be more conspicuous than in the state of New York, in the prodigious progress of this city. Those western parts, which I had left a wilderness, I have found covered with flourishing towns, highly cultivated farms, active factories, and intersected by the admirable canal . . . all in consequence of independence, freedom, and a republican spirit.[62]

At the same time that he told Americans what they wanted to hear, Lafayette was testifying to the fulfillment of his own sanguine hopes of 1784, when he had concluded a much-publicized farewell to the Continental Congress with the wish that "these happy United States attain that complete splendor and prosperity which will illustrate the blessings of their government, and for ages to come rejoice the departed souls of its founders!" [63] Now that he was back as a returned founder himself, he stepped naturally into the role that Hezekiah Niles had outlined for him, "to bless and receive the blessings of a mightily increased and joyous posterity."

The long list of American accomplishments was usually introduced by a reference to the supposed feelings of the distinguished guest. As the *"Address of the Citizens of Philadelphia in their collective capacity"* put it, "Although it is not for us to extol the progressive prosperity of our happy and highly favored Nation, we cannot refuse ourselves the pleasure of adverting to the enjoyment which you must derive." [64] The Pennsylvania Cincinnati told their most distinguished member that America's "unrivalled prosperity must impart the most pleasing sensations

[62] *New-York American,* July 6, 1825.

[63] Gottschalk, *Lafayette between the American and the French Revolution,* p. 136.

[64] *National Gazette,* September 30, 1824.

to your sympathetic breast." [65] The existence of such a "pleasing sensation" would of course be most satisfying evidence of the purity of America's material advance, its authentic derivation from the past of the Founding Fathers. As Albert Gallatin, always a good reflector of grass-roots feeling, said to Lafayette at Uniontown after enumerating the nation's gains, "This magnificent specticle [*sic*] affords the highest reward to your labours, above all because that prosperity, those blessings which we are permitted to enjoy[,] are the result of our free institutions." [66]

No one was so qualified as " 'our Father,' the good Lafayette," [67] to assimilate the Americans of the 1820's and their material achievements to the values of those who had formulated the original meaning of the republic. Again and again "the companion and disciple of Washington" [68] was informed that he stood among "a new generation inheriting the virtue and valour of their fathers." [69] For Gallatin, "The prosperity, the long peace they had enjoyed . . . [had] not enervated the Americans." If Bunker Hill was the glory of an earlier age, New Orleans proved the spirit of the present one.[70] Just as Lafayette was accorded the homage due the great Washington, by a kind of symmetry of feeling Americans assumed, as the Mayor of Trenton said to him, "that your heart still beats with the same warm affection to this People, as when in the attitude of the youthful warrior, you flung your shield before our infant republic." [71] This assumption of Lafayette's immutability was reinforced by the often-recounted story of his unshakable devotion to freedom through years marked by the buffetings of a turbulent continental history,

[65] *Guest,* II, p. 76.   [66] *Pilgrimage,* p. 370.

[67] *Virginia Herald,* November 27, 1824.

[68] *New-York American,* August 20, 1824. The speaker here was Philip Hone, then an assistant alderman.

[69] *Georgia Journal,* April 5, 1825.   [70] *Pilgrimage,* p. 370.

[71] *New-Jersey Eagle,* October 1, 1824.

political proscription, and even imprisonment in an Austrian dungeon.[72]

As a triumph over time, and as a symbolic restoration of the era of acknowledged republican virtue, Lafayette's benison was that of the dead Washington. Yet Lafayette was able to provide an important dimension of approval even beyond that of the first President. "Fortunate, fortunate man!" said Daniel Webster to Lafayette at the Bunker Hill commemoration, "with what measure of devotion will you not thank God for the circumstances of your extraordinary life! You are connected with both hemispheres and with two generations." [73] Lafayette's unique status as the "benefactor of two worlds" had been proclaimed by Condorcet in 1786,[74] and more glamorously a few years later when Thomas Paine dedicated the first part of *The Rights of Man* to Washington and the second to Lafayette. Lafayette, therefore, bore a character of otherness not shared by Washington, which made him in American eyes, as a foreigner and especially as a high-born aristocrat and member of the court nobility, capable of standing for that quintessential European quality against which Americans were constantly matching themselves. If nothing more, Lafayette's return visit provided ammunition for a new volley of international comparisons by which Americans sought to bolster the feeling of their own individuality and worth. In the words of an anonymous rhymester,

> The old world's night he leaves behind;
> The morn of the New is before him— . . .[75]

[72] *Niles' Weekly Register*, XXVII (January 8, 1825), 291; *Life and Letters of Catherine M. Sedgwick,* ed. Mary E. Dewey (New York, 1871), p. 170.

[73] *Works,* I, 246.

[74] Gottschalk, *Lafayette between the American and the French Revolution,* p. 225.

[75] Poem, "On the Visit of Gen. La Fayette to America," Scrapbook, p. 8.

At the same time that Americans were denouncing the "night" of the Old World they devoured with fascination descriptions of the exotic life that Lafayette had left behind in order to join the American Revolutionary forces. In numerous biographical compilations issued to satisfy public curiosity about every detail of his career, Lafayette was seen as "the Hero and Patriot, who abandoned his home, his family, his rank, and a princely fortune, for the sake of fighting in the cause of American Liberty." [76] From the beginning Americans had been impressed with what Lafayette had given up in order to assist the Revolutionary cause. When Lafayette first joined the army of General Nathanael Greene as a volunteer, Greene reported to his wife with obvious relish that the young French officer had "left a young wife and a fine fortune of fourteen thousand pounds sterling per annum to come and engage in the cause of liberty." [77] After forty years the splendor of this magnificent renunciation, with all its accompanying details, still exerted a powerful fascination in America. The following lines were a by no means untypical example of the standard terms in which the moral heroism of this initial decision was portrayed:

> With the golden dominion of wealth at command,
>   And arrayed in the honours of title and birth;
> In the ecstatic endearments of wedlock's sweet band
>   United with loveliness, beauty, and worth;
> A favourite of Gallia's magnificent court,
>   And entwined with his fancy's tenderest ties,
> He heard, with a bosom all fame, the report
>   Of the ravaging storm that enveloped our skies.
>
>   .   .   .   .   .
>
> From his temples their peace-woven chaplets he tore,
>   And consigned the loved tokens to beauty's soft hand;

[76] Subtitle of [Anon.], *Sketch of the Life and Military Services of Gen. La Fayette* . . . (New York, 1824). This is typical of what Americans were reading about Lafayette.

[77] Quoted in Gottschalk, *Lafayette Joins the American Army*, p. 80.

He cast from his limbs the rich vestments they wore,
  And, transformed as if touched by a magical wand,
The courtly young noble, in armour arrayed,
  The glittering pageants of Monarchy spurned,
And to wield for Columbia his virginal blade
  His magnanimous spirit impatiently burned.[78]

Europe, in the form of the court, the castle, and luxury,
is rejected in favor of the hardships of America. One to
whom Europe offers the best that she has flees instead to
the purer satisfactions of the American struggle for freedom. The imagined delights of Lafayette's pre-American
existence were recounted to add savor to the tale of his sacrifice. "Oh! Our distinguished adopted citizen of Maryland!" he was told at Frederick, "We owe you much—for
much you adventured for us. What pleasure did you
forego! . . . In the springtime of your life, when everything was gay, you left the fascinations of a splendid court,
for our western wilds." [79] We "see you," said the mayor of
a Virginia town to Lafayette, "in youth, in affluence, and
in the possession of whatever this world could afford to
make you happy; tearing yourself from France, from luxury and from ease." [80] In the ideological defection of Lafayette, America's triumph over Europe was complete. No
wonder so many of his hosts insisted on emphasizing his
origin by calling him "Marquis" in spite of Hezekiah
Niles's reminder that such titles were inapproprate between fellow republicans.[81]

In fact, the Marquis who turned his face from Europe
represented an even older American tradition than republicanism. Like the early Puritan Fathers he had rejected

---

[78] Daniel Bryan, *Lay of Gratitude,* Stanzas V, IX; pp. 9, 11.

[79] *Guest,* III, 222.

[80] *Richmond Enquirer,* November 5, 1824.

[81] *Niles' Weekly Register,* XXVI (June 26, 1824), 267–68. On
this point it was reported that previous to his landing Lafayette
had declared: "I am an AMERICAN GENERAL" (*New-York
American,* August 24, 1824).

the frivolity and inutilitarianism of Europe to seek the genuine and real in America. But his choice was harder than theirs. Exposed from birth to every sort of bad example, Lafayette was a moral champion who had resisted "the easy paths of self-gratification," in order to flee from the "corruption" of aristocratic society. Charmed with this vision of beleaguered innocence, one enthusiastic eulogist pictured the eighteen-year-old youth "soberly placed at the head of a family; and for this noble disavowal of public licentiousness receiving the taunts and jeers of his convivial companions—who were reveling in dissipation and debauchery." [82] What could be more American than such an exercise of self-denial and proven victory over the passions? It was an antecedent purification that qualified the emissary from the Old World's night "to wield for Columbia his virginal blade." To the music of "Hail to the Chief," a song by Samuel Woodworth declared:

> Lo! From the East, with a mystic resplendence,
>   Rose the bright star which enlightened the gloom;
> Led by its ray, and our loved *Independence*,
>   Came the young *knight*, with his lily-white plume.
>
> .   .   .   .   .
>
> Then gallant Washington
> Hail'd Gallia's godlike son! [83]

The importance of the numerous sacrifices made by Lafayette when he threw in his lot with the rebelling colonies lay not only in the implied depreciation of Europe but perhaps even more significantly in the proofs that they afforded of his freedom from the taint of self-interest. "It must be acknowledged, however," said one of the swarm of Lafayette "Memoirs" that American publishers rushed

[82] [Anon.], *Historical Sketches Illustrative of the Life of M. DE LAFAYETTE; and the Leading Events of the American Revolution. By an American* (New York, 1824), p. 6.

[83] Scrapbook, p. 43. The term "godlike" was standard Lafayette rhetoric.

into print, "that there was a *peculiar* disinterestedness in the services and sacrifices of the Marquis LaFayette in defence of American independence." [84] As "spontaneous" was the word most frequently used to express the nature of America's gratitude, "disinterested" was the term almost unfailingly attached to the description of Lafayette's action. In the hierarchy of Lafayette's virtues "disinterest" easily came first, while military achievement was often not even second. The approved ranking seemed to be that of Cadwallader Colden, himself the son and grandson of prominent New York Loyalists, for whom the order of value was "the enviable fame of the disinterested Patriot, the consistent Politician, and the gallant Soldier." [85] And the whole company at the Grand Civic Ball in Philadelphia joined at midnight, "with an enthusiasm proportioned to its truth," in a toast to *"Disinterested Valor: Its fruits, unenvied Glory and unbounded Gratitude."* [86] Although Americans were apparently somewhat unclear on the minor question whether or not their guest had outsoared the possibility of envy, their consensus was not in doubt. Nothing could be plainer than the remarks of the Governor of Pennsylvania as he met Lafayette at the state line with "an escort of two hundred and fifty cavalry." "The eventful scenes of your useful life," said the Governor,

are engraven on our hearts. . . . With ardent pleasure we have ever observed your strenuous exertions as the friend of man; and whilst your great services, rendered in the cause of humanity, have commanded our admiration, the purity of

[84] [Samuel L. Knapp], *Memoirs of General Lafayette, with an Account of his visit to America* . . . (Boston, 1824), p. 14.

[85] *New-Hampshire Gazette,* September 7, 1824. In the following discussion of the role of disinterested virtue during this period I have benefited from William R. Taylor, *Cavalier and Yankee* (New York, 1961), esp. Chap. II.

[86] *Guest,* II, 97.

your motives has insured the love and affection of Americans.[87]

So rigorous could the emphasis upon "purity of motives" become that sometimes it seemed as though no native American patriot would be able to pass the test. The ethical verge to which the search for purity could lead was illustrated in the address of a local dignitary when Lafayette came to Fayetteville, North Carolina. Carried away with fervor in the presence of the hero from whom the town took its name, the speaker did not shrink from pressing a mercilessly logical argument to its ironclad conclusion. Lafayette occupied a lonely and unshared height when it was "remembered that Washington and Hamilton fought for country and for home; Lafayette for liberty alone." [88]

Rigorous as such a judgment might be, it could not be dismissed as the exaggeration of a backwoods axiologist. Before Lafayette had been in the United States one month he had heard the same idea elaborated at Portsmouth, New Hampshire, in a section of the country where almost two hundred years of Calvinist sermonizing had sharpened the minds of the population for the close discrimination of fine moral distinctions. Confronted with Lafayette, the chairman of Portsmouth's board of selectmen had no difficulty with his ethical categories. Beginning with praise for the general class of Revolutionary heroes, the chairman declared,

Enjoying, as we do, the happiness of a free government, we cannot but feel grateful to all by whose exertions it was obtained. Those intrepid men among ourselves, who in the hour of danger stood forth in defence of their country's rights, have a lasting claim upon our regard.

Having thus satisfied the most ordinary patriotic proprieties of the occasion, he went on to make his distinction.

[87] Philadelphia *Evening Post,* October 2, 1824.
[88] *Pilgrimage,* p. 33.

"But in contending for the liberty of their country," he pointed out,

they were striving to secure their own happiness and the prosperity of their children. *They* found a motive for exertion in their own interest—which, while it derogates nothing from the value of their services, places in a strong light the pure zeal and contempt of private advantage, which led *you* to our aid, from the shores of a foreign land. *Their* love of liberty was necessarily the sentiment of patriotism; *yours* was an ardent desire for the general welfare of mankind.[89]

Such unequivocal denigration of the "sentiment of patriotism" in favor of a "love of liberty" sparked only by "an ardent desire for the general welfare of mankind" carried overtones of New England's most uncompromising moral theology. It savored of the self-denying standards of those who followed Jonathan Edwards and Samuel Hopkins in branding as egoistic anything short of a complete readiness to "be damned for the glory of God." With standards set so high, if Lafayette could be deemed to have satisfied the demands of America's national ideal he could well be hailed afterward in upstate New York as "the only Man now living, to deserve, as he has earned, the epithets of truly *good* and truly *Great*." [90] In fact, the Mayor of Albany very early attributed to "The Nation's Guest" the quasi-divine "disinterested benevolence" that, along with "love of Being in general," constituted the goal of Calvinism's most ambitious virtuosos of the spirit.[91]

Yet even this second element was supplied when Lafa-

<hr />

[80] *Guest,* I, 149.   [90] *Pilgrimage,* p. 410.

[91] *Niles' Weekly Register,* XXVII (October 2, 1824), 70. See Joseph Haroutunian, *Piety Versus Moralism* (New York, 1932), pp. 82 ff. A pamphlet using Lafayette's life as a model of *disinterestedness* for the moral instruction of children was published the following year: *LAFAYETTE, or Disinterested Benevolence* (Boston, 1825). A copy is in the collection of the American Friends of Lafayette, at Lafayette College, Easton, Pa.

yette stopped at Emma Willard's Troy Female Seminary, and the "instructress of music," accompanied by the chorus of the entire student body, sang for him the principal's own composition "And Art Thou, Then, Dear Hero Come?" After a stanza conventionally devoted to Lafayette's wartime deeds, Mrs. Willard turned to the elucidation of higher matters:

> But was't our country's rights alone
> Impell'd Fayette to Freedom's van?
> No! 'twas the love of human kind—
> It was the sacred cause of man—
> It was benevolence sublime,
> Like that which sways the Eternal mind!
> And, benefactor of the world,
> He shed his blood for all mankind! [92]

The messianic theme implicit here was expressed openly elsewhere. Having seemingly come back "from the tomb," Lafayette was greeted at Camden, South Carolina, as "one, who redeemed me while yet I was not; and who is the redeemer of posterities which are not." [93] Such language, by no means unique, argued a degree of sincerity in even the kind of obvious bombast to which Lafayette was subjected at the Masonic dinner in Savannah. "Our illustrious Brother General Lafayette," ran the toast of one participant; "He rose like the Sun of Masonry in the *East*, shed his lustre upon us at his *Meridian*, in his decline he has emerged from the clouds which enveloped him, and millions in the *West* are worshiping his declining rays." [94]

The Carolina orator who spoke of Lafayette as "the redeemer of posterities which are not" showed his apprecia-

[92] *Troy Sentinel,* September 21, 1824.

[93] *Pilgrimage,* p. 47. In referring to Lafayette's sacrifices the Mayor of Baltimore, a Catholic city, had used the words "his precious blood" (*Niles' Weekly Register,* XXVI [July 24, 1824], 340.

[94] *Savannah Georgian,* March 22, 1825.

tion for the long-range significance of Lafayette's tour. As the "STAR of the East" [95] wound his way through the country his effect upon the younger generation was a popular subject among his hosts. Having grown up in an age of open self-interest, and never having had contact with the Founders, the young people were expected to benefit most from this "most signal recurrence to *'first principles'* " [96] that Lafayette symbolized. In the opinion of the Governor of Illinois, the appearance of the old soldier not only would spread knowledge of Revolutionary times among those who themselves had no direct memories to draw upon, but the example of Lafayette, "by exhibiting so perfect a model, [would] render more attractive and impress more forcibly on their recollections, the republican principles, and the pure and ennobling virtues of that period." [97] In this respect the problems of a raw frontier environment without Revolutionary associations were little different from those of New England. Discussing a batch of Lafayette "Memoirs" in the *North American Review*, George Ticknor saw Lafayette as "one of the great actors, from this most solemn passage in our national destinies." His return, thought Ticknor, gave Americans the chance "to transmit yet one generation further onward, a sensible impression of the times of our fathers. . . . with all the[ir] highminded patriotism and self-denying virtues." [98] Both Ticknor and the Illinois governor would have agreed with the exuberant newspaper editor who predicted that Lafayette would "have a most salutary influence on the minds and the hearts of the rising

[95] *Charleston Courier,* March 17, 1825. Celestial imagery was sometimes inconsistent. At Newburgh, New York, Lafayette had been "Columbia's bright Occidental Star" (New York *Commercial Advertiser,* September 17, 1824).

[96] *Cahawba Press,* April 9, 1825. Address by the Governor of Alabama.

[97] *Illinois Gazette,* May 21, 1825.

[98] *North American Review,* XX (January, 1825), 62–63.

generation, holding up a high and finished exemplar for imitation . . . enkindling the noblest emulation." [99]

But while Americans were calling the nineteenth-century generation to a life of high moral commitment, the immoderation of their praise for Lafayette tended to heighten the contrast between his example and what could be expected from ordinary humanity. The conduct of "Gallia's godlike son" presented an *"enigma"* [100] of motivation that could only be *"solved"* by ascribing to Lafayette a degree of virtue more susceptible of passive adoration than emulation. "At nineteen years of age to leave his home!" marveled an enthusiast, "—his country—his honors—his rank—his intrepid and interesting wife!—his wealth—nay, to *bring his wealth with him,* to give it to our naked and bleeding fore-fathers!—Sacred philanthropy! how few are thy children!" [101] Analogies to the Moses who had also left a "royal court" to lead a people to freedom sprang easily to mind,[102] and a Christ-Lafayette identification became obvious enough to be discussed openly. Quoting a "Dr. M.," one paper reported the opinion of a "respectable minister" who was supposed to have said that the unprecedented honors accorded Lafayette failed to give religious offense since Lafayette's self-sacrifice came "nearer the comparison with the Saviour, in relation to America, than any other man of whom we had any account." [103] Whether such a remark was actually made is less important than the fact of its publication amid a heavy atmosphere of Christian piety. Yet even the Reverend Henry Ware, Jr., Professor of Theology at Harvard Divinity School, pastor of the renowned Second Church of Boston, and an acknowledged figure of the orthodox Unitarian establishment, contributed an ode to the local Lafayette festivities which purported to relate the genuine

[99] Scrapbook, p. 15.
[101] Scrapbook, p. 49.
[103] Scrapbook, p. 9.

[100] *Pilgrimage,* p. 46.
[102] *Pilgrimage,* pp. 395–96.

dream vision of a "gentleman in Massachusetts" in 1794. Nearing "a temple of wonderful magnificence and beauty," the dreamer had looked up at the sound of a bell "with an uncommonly musical tone" to see "in golden letters the name of FAYETTE." [104] In this way, amid a national chorus of voices asseverating the grand fact of American "republican simplicity," "The Nation's Guest" underwent something close to apotheosis.

As an element in a kind of republican worship of Lafayette such fantasies served two functions, apparently contradictory, but actually complementary. On the one hand, stress upon the transcendent nature of the hero's morality played up his glorious isolation and remoteness, qualities that tended to nullify the much-vaunted utility of his life as a pattern for emulation. But at the same time the practical deification of Lafayette opened new paths of contact between the heroic model and his republican admirers. To the tremendous crowds that swarmed around the returned hero to see, to touch, to shake his hand if possible, the "sensible impression of the times of our fathers" that Ticknor expected Lafayette to convey might almost have depended on a magical physical contact. If already by 1784, as one of his biographers has concluded, Lafayette "had become a kind of national patron saint," [105] forty years later he stood, in the words of a Transylvania sophomore,

> . . . a PRECIOUS RELICK in our sight
> Of *ancient worthies,* still in MEMORY bright.[106]

Here again, Americans were determined to prevent themselves from being misunderstood. Describing the press to

[104] *New-York American,* September 15, 1824.

[105] Gottschalk, *Lafayette between the American and the French Revolution,* p. 144.

[106] *The Order of Exercises in the Chapel of Transylvania University, A Collection of original pieces in honour of the arrival of General La Fayette* . . . (Lexington, Ky., 1825), p. 8.

approach Lafayette on the Yorktown battleground, an editor explained:

Dearer—far dearer to them was the simple act of taking by the
hand the virtuous La Fayette, the champion of their liberties,
and of the rights of man, than could be to the pious anchorite
the relics of his patron saint. Such are the feelings which ani-
mate the independent yeomanry of our country, and constitute the best safeguard to the purity of our republican institutions.[107]

Clearly enough, while Lafayette's "disinterestedness" was
solitary, individual, and effectually "god-like" in its disregard of self, a republican religion of virtue of which he was
the center provided an easily shared mass value by which
the "independent yeomanry" could justify themselves
through reference to their own "feelings." At a time when
the possibility of Lafayette's brand of virtue, the virtue attributed to the life-giving Fathers, seemed problematical,
the communal entertainment of Lafayette, by allowing
an imaginative re-entry into a virtuous past, provided the
ritual substitute for a desired republican grace.

As Lafayette pressed on into one after another of the
twenty-four states of the Union it became evident, despite
the disclaimers of men like Holley, that the subtler ramifications of the American "JUBILEE OF LIBERTY" did
indeed hinge upon the famous visitor's personal qualities
to a surprising extent. While it was true enough that the
adulation heaped upon *"the Man"* aimed at something beyond him, it was also plain that the life of this man alone,
and not of just any distinguished Revolutionary survivor,
could supply the materials for the kind of drama that was
being played out on a nationwide scale. If ritual may be
described as the symbolic solution of problems that can
neither be faced nor mastered, the noticeable absence of
ritual in American life might have perhaps been ascribed
to the fact that the Puritans never flinched from facing the

[107] *Norfolk and Portsmouth Herald,* October 22, 1824.

unfaceable in the spiritual life, while the problems of the life of nature seemed to yield uniformly to handy techniques. By its patently sacramental function the American reception of Lafayette testified to a general awareness that the production of the type of virtue upon which "the purity of . . . republican institutions" depended could no longer be safely left to time alone. Time, which had always seemed to work providentially in the service of American purposes, as the unbroken record of material and social progress demonstrated, no longer wore an unambiguous face. The vaunted evidence of change was itself proof that a gulf had opened in American republican life. The more Americans insisted on the "spontaneous," and hence pure, character of the national gratitude to the returned representative of the Fathers, the more shaky appeared their own self-confidence in the moral continuity of American history. A disturbing feeling was abroad that the American world of the 1820's, with its dedication to a cheerful commercialism, might have parted company somewhere with the shades of the *"ancient worthies."* Heard over and over again, toasts such as one by Commodore David Porter were capable of taking on an odd ring: "That happy land where man mingles with his fellow men, unawed by power, and undazzled by wealth—. . . where he exalts himself by paying honor to worth." [108] Through constant repetition even so positive an assertion could start sounding like a question.

The American people recognized that in the person of the returning Lafayette a unique set of meanings had coalesced, making him the peculiarly suitable central figure in what turned out to be something close to a ritual of mass reconciliation.[109] For, in a sense, the instinct of those

[108] *Ibid.*

[109] Throughout this chapter my discussion has drawn upon W. Lloyd Warner, *The Living and the Dead;* Joseph Campbell, *The Hero with a Thousand Faces* (New York, 1949); Mircea Eliade, *Patterns in Comparative Religion* (New York, 1958); Sidney Hook,

who expected Lafayette's return to perform a healing function was sure. It was not, after all, to be a political schism which his hosts used Lafayette to reseal, but a fissure between generations, between the *then* and the *now*, between the fast-disappearing era of the Founders and the already arrived age of steam.

But there was one striking respect in which the virtues of Commodore Porter's "happy land" were less than totally congruent to the "times when there were giants in the land." This had to do with the dark fact of American Negro slavery. The celebration of a national "JUBILEE OF LIBERTY" was bound to draw attention to the most prominent of American ideological contradictions. Furthermore, the Founders with whom Lafayette had associated were known to have considered slavery an evil that they hoped was headed toward extinction, while the practical opposition of Lafayette himself to the institution was of long standing. For years he had been busy with international schemes to stop the slave trade, to emancipate slaves, and to colonize free Negroes.[110] But the America to which he returned in 1824, and which claimed so vociferously to have fulfilled the Revolutionary ideals, was a land where slavery had not only failed to disappear, but where its burgeoning power and geographical expansion now found the most respectable of defenders and advocates. When the public excitement over the libertarian values for which Lafayette stood could draw a plea for justice in behalf of the imprisoned debtor—"the slave of a brutal and miser-made law"—the plight of the Negro could hardly avoid attention.[111] Yet almost complete silence was the American

---

The Hero in History (New York, 1943); and Emile Durkheim, *The Elementary Forms of the Religious Life,* trans. J. W. Swain (London and New York, [1915]).

[110] Melvin D. Kennedy, *Lafayette and Slavery, from his Letters to Thomas Clarkson and Granville Sharp* (Easton, Pa., 1950).

[111] New York *National Advocate,* September 3, 1824. After his departure from America, Lafayette was reported to have sent money to ransom a Revolutionary officer from debtor's prison (*Niles' Weekly*

response to the challenge of an issue which provided a ready-made opportunity for Americans to confront the past with the present. Even though nearly all of the speeches addressed to Lafayette at receptions and banquets included descriptions and analyses of American economic development, the presence in the United States of an enormous mass of unfree labor was studiously ignored.

This was all the more difficult since Lafayette himself did not ignore it. With a persistence which gave evidence of that consistency to principle for which Americans so much praised him, he did not shrink from recognizing the Negro as an American whenever he could appropriately do so without the risk of offending his hosts. When he inspected New York City's schools he did not neglect the African Free School operated by the New York Manumission Society, of which he had been an honorary member for many years. Calling attention to the role of the race in the Revolution he publicly greeted at Richmond a Negro who had performed spying missions for him, and later drank champagne with his old manservant, Pompey, in Columbia, South Carolina. "I have often during the War of Independence," Lafayette remarked at New Orleans, "seen African blood shed with honor in our ranks for the cause of the United States." When he arrived in the half-French village of Gallipolis, Ohio, after his journey through the South, Lafayette "expatiated largely on the disadvantages of Slavery and congratulated the French people of Gallipolis on their location in a land where Slavery cannot breathe." So well known were Lafayette's

---

Register, XXIX [December 24, 1825], 262). On slavery see a curious poem, "Address to Gen. Lafayette, from 'The Slaves' in the Land of Freedom" (Boston *Columbian Centinel,* October 20, 1824). In a preface, the editor explained why he was printing the poem: "The great evil complained of . . . may be irremediable; . . . Still it is deemed to be the duty of the Christian Philanthropist to embrace the occasion which the great visit presents, to point out more forcibly a glaring inconsistency."

feelings that even the Indians greeted him as "one who in his affection for the inhabitants of America, had never made a distinction in blood or colour; and . . . was the honoured father of all races of men dwelling on that continent." [112] These discreet attempts to call attention to the question of slavery evoked little interest in the North, while the attitude of the South was fairly reflected in the published notices at several places that police authorities would "take into custody all such negroes and persons of color, as may be found at all trespassing upon, or attending the procession, parades, etc., during the stay of General LAFAYETTE in this city." [113]

In view of such strenuous efforts on the part of Lafayette's hosts to identify themselves with whatever could earn the otherworldly benediction of the Fathers, and to avoid areas where approval was doubtful, Lafayette's descent into Washington's tomb appears a highly representative act. In him it was the nation itself that stood before the coffin seeking the judgment of "the father of his country." [114] What could have been more natural, then, but that an eagle should have followed Lafayette from the Potomac and

continued *flying over the tomb of Washington*. . . . It seemed to have an inspiration in its actions. It would not quit the scene. It displayed those feelings which would seem to indicate that it was a special messenger, sent to welcome our illustrious

[112] New York *Evening Post,* September 11, 1824; *Pilgrimage,* pp. 60–61, 181–82, 351; *Guest,* III, 121; Levasseur, *Lafayette in America,* II, 75. Levasseur may have composed or doctored this Indian speech, but it could well have been authentic. Indians did travel long distances to meet the warrior Lafayette whom they or their fathers remembered from the Revolutionary War. And the racial emphasis fits the bitterness and despondency of the Indians in the old Southwest—where the speech was supposed to have been delivered—at the impending loss of their lands through an unfair Georgia treaty.

[113] *Savannah Georgian,* March 14, 17, 19, 1825.

[114] "The hero blessed by the father returns to represent the father among men. . . . To see him is to perceive the meaning of existence" (Campbell, *The Hero with a Thousand Faces,* p. 347) .

guest on his visit to the sacred repose of the first of men—his friend and the friend of mankind—After the general had fulfilled his pious devotions, this bird, representing the gratitude of the nation and emblematically the spirit of Washington, took its final departure.

To its report of the event the Alexandria *Herald* did not really have to add: "There is no doubt whatever of the fact which we communicate above. We could give the testimony of hundreds of the most respectable names of its correctness." [115]

One effect of Lafayette's visit, Horace Holley had said, would be the opportunity it gave Americans to know themselves more completely. And reflecting on the event a few years later, George Ticknor saw a national bearing of "testimony . . . to the great cause of liberty." It was true that sympathy for the revolutions in Greece and South America also provided an occasion for such a testimony, Ticknor thought, but only Lafayette, by presenting an object "so free from the alloy of doubt and human imperfection," allowed Americans, "in recognizing his merit, to reassert the principle to which his life had been consecrated." [116]

Implicit in Ticknor's terms was an understanding of the urgent need that a consecrated nation had to be purged "from the alloy of doubt and human imperfection" in order to feel again the reality of that moral dedication which was its title to being. Only the purity of a Lafayette, which had come down stainless from the days of the Fathers, could bring about such a time-defying reunion of the generations as was spoken of by President John Quincy Adams in his farewell to the old hero:

You have been received with rapture by the survivors of your earliest companions in arms: you have been hailed as a long absent parent by their children, the men and women of the

[115] Alexandria *Herald,* October 20, 1824.
[116] "Lafayette in America," *North American Review,* XXX (January, 1830), 220.

present age: And a rising generation, the hope of future time, in numbers surpassing the whole population of that day when you fought at the head and by the side of their forefathers, have vied with the scanty remnants of that hour of trial, in acclamations of joy at beholding the face of him whom they feel to be the common benefactor of all. You have heard the mingled voices of the past, the present, and the future age.[117]

Sometime during the decade after the War of 1812 America turned the corner into the nineteenth century. Looking back with a stabbing sense of loss, the nation pressed Lafayette to its heart in a last communion with its youthful self. When he was gone the world of the Founders had vanished forever.

[117] *Niles' Weekly Register,* XXIX (September 17, 1825), 42.

CHAPTER FIVE

The Priesthood of
Democratic Believers

Less than a dozen years after the *Brandywine* carried Lafayette out of Chesapeake Bay he and the last Revolutionary Fathers were dead. With them passed the line of
charismatic witnesses who were capable in their own persons of justifying the prosperous present before the memory of a simpler past. To conscript that past into the service of the present and future an American historian of
power and eloquence was needed, one who could transmute the well-known materials of the colonial experience
into a structure that would encompass all of American history and arch forward over the coming time.

The ten editions through which the first volume of his
History of the United States went from 1834 to 1844
demonstrated in spectacular fashion how well George Bancroft succeeded in estimating and satisfying the requirements of his public. "Whence did this immediate and unbounded popularity and acceptance arise?" asked an
American historiographer in the year of Bancroft's death,
more than half a century later.

Mainly, I believe, from the fact that the historian caught, and with sincere enthusiastic conviction repeated to the American people, the things which they were saying and thinking concerning themselves. . . . Bancroft's first volume succeeded mainly because it was redolent of the ideas of the new Jacksonian democracy,—its exuberant confidence, its uncritical self-laudation, its optimistic hopes. The Demos heard, as an undercurrent to his narrative, the same music which charmed its ears in the Fourth of July oration.[1]

Jameson's assertion that Bancroft's ideas were "the ideas of America in the year 1834," only partly applicable to the first volume, is an oversimplification also in regard to the two subsequent volumes that came out before Martin Van Buren left the White House. Certainly, the historical form of Bancroft's classic and the effectiveness of its message were related to each other and to the age that gave them birth. But to say this alone is to overlook the creative originality that gave it power as a moral force. For it is as a moralist in the role of epic-maker that George Bancroft served his generation.

In the more philosophical second volume of his *Democracy,* which appeared in 1840, Tocqueville expressed the opinion that as a result

of the continual movement that agitates a democratic community, the tie that unites one generation to another is relaxed or broken; every man there readily loses all trace of the ideas of his forefathers or takes no care about them.[2]

Admittedly, as he explained to John Stuart Mill, Tocqueville was describing no existing society but "the general features of democratic societies; no complete specimen of which can yet be said to exist." [3] The extreme social and physical mobility that so impressed him in the United

[1] J. Franklin Jameson, *The History of Historical Writing in America* (Boston and New York, 1890), pp. 103–04.

[2] *Democracy in America,* II, 4.   [3] *Ibid.,* I, xxxiv.

States was the basis for his observation about "the continual movement that agitates a democratic society," but the conclusion savored more of Gallic logic than American experience. The phenomenal success of Bancroft's initial volumes in the years since Tocqueville had left America would probably not have been known to him, since he had deliberately sealed himself off from current literature in order to guard the integrity of his original impressions.[4] Still, during his days in the United States it would have been practically impossible for him to have missed noticing that the most characteristic feature of that strikingly American phenomenon, the Fourth of July ritual oration, was its historical nature.

To glance at the productions of only two of the most popular practitioners in the genre, Daniel Webster and Edward Everett, is to recognize immediately that the traditional hours-long sermon on the election and perseverance of the saints had given way to a detailed historical narrative, although still informed by the spirit of the earlier theme. The familial kinship between Bancroft's *History,* of very recent origin, the Fourth of July oration, which was somewhat more venerable, and the Puritan sermon, whose spiritual prestige derived from two centuries of American usage, might have suggested to Tocqueville's generalizing mind that the American "cared" a great deal about "the ideas of his forefathers," but that his concern took the form of moral exhortation. The successful performance of this latter function, for reasons copiously documented in Tocqueville's analysis of "the continual movement that agitates a democratic community," was a requirement which Americans were ready to demand of a national history appearing in the 1830's.

While rusticating unhappily at Groton, Massachusetts, in the middle of the decade, Margaret Fuller, always a voracious reader, turned to a new subject: "American His-

[4] George Wilson Pierson, *Tocqueville and Beaumont in America* (New York, 1938), p. 742.

tory! Seriously, my mind is regenerating as to my country, for I am beginning to appreciate the United States and its great men." She lamented that her education had not included much acquaintance with the history of the nation. With characteristic fervor she exclaimed, "Had I but been educated in the knowledge of such men as Jefferson, Franklin, Rush!" [5] Even with her idiosyncratic upbringing she probably knew as much American history as the average product of an academic curriculum. In 1826, Jared Sparks, whose own activities were directed toward the amelioration of the condition he described, could state that "no work approaching to the character of a complete history of America, or of the United States or of the American Revolution, has yet appeared." [6] The following year several articles on historical subjects in the *North American Review* underscored the fact that the study of American history had only a short time before "formed no part of our system of education either at school or at college." As a result, "There are few things of which the American youth are more ignorant, than the history of this country. Nine times in ten they can tell you more about the fabulous ages of antiquity." Especially did this seem to be true of the pre-Revolutionary ages, which were commonly regarded "as a state of preexistence." Whereas Margaret Fuller, in the manner of a loyal Democrat, would rejoice in heroes of the republican tradition, the *North American Review* noted with pleasure that Americans were at last learning

to trace our present free and happy condition to its remote as well as proximate causes, to acknowledge our obligations not only to the statesmen and soldiers, who conducted the war of independence, but to those sages from whom we derived the principles, institutions, and habits, which render independence desirable.[7]

[5] *Memoirs of Margaret Fuller Ossoli,* ed. Ralph Waldo Emerson et al. (Boston, 1852), I, 149.

[6] *North American Review,* XXIII (October 1826), 276.

[7] *Ibid.,* XXIV (January, 1827), 23–24, 225.

To the influence of the past, Americans were also ready to ascribe certain less benevolent inheritances. When Tocqueville at Boston sought clues toward an understanding of American society, he was assured by Alexander Hill Everett that "the starting point of a people has an immense bearing, the consequences for good or ill have an influence by which one is unceasingly surprised." A member at that time of the state legislature, and an advocate for the abolition of imprisonment for debt, Everett pointed out the English roots of this inherited encumbrance, adding, "So difficult to conquer are the habits that its origin gives a nation." [8] This observation, together with Sparks's remark about Massachusetts that "our origin is the fact which best explains our government and our ways," found quick lodgment in the early pages of *Democracy in America*. With confidence Tocqueville recorded:

If we carefully examine the social and political state of America, after having studied its history, we shall remain perfectly convinced that not an opinion, not a custom, not a law, I may even say not an event is upon record which the origin of that people will not explain.[9]

Yet when he came to describe "that people" he was so impressed by the strong forces of antitraditionalism he saw all around him, the powerful sense of newness and self-determination, that he painted the portrait of a society bereft of history, detached and isolated from any contact with an effective past. After all, it seemed it was not really America he was searching for but "the image of democracy itself, with its inclinations, its character, its prejudices, and its passions." [10]

This ghostly image of democracy bore a more than coincidental resemblance to Tocqueville's image of democratic man, the being whose spiritual home was America, and whose destinies would someday be sung by as yet nonexist-

[8] Pierson, *Tocqueville and Beaumont*, p. 398.
[9] *Democracy in America*, I, 28.   [10] *Ibid.*, I, 14.

ent American poets. This was the "man [who] springs out of nothing, crosses time, and disappears forever in the bosom of God; he is seen but for a moment, wandering on the verge of the two abysses, and there he is lost." In the absence of a past it was man without a past, man spotlighted on the ridge of now, who would provide subject matter for the poets of democracy. It would be "man himself . . . with his passions, his doubts, his rare prosperities and inconceivable wretchedness . . . [who would] become the chief, if not the sole, theme of poetry among these [democratic] nations." [11]

For what he saw in the United States Tocqueville preferred the "novel expression" *Individualism*. Whereas ordinary selfishness consisted of an exaggerated self-love and self-preference, "Individualism," Tocqueville explained,

is a mature and calm feeling, which disposes each member of the community to sever himself from the mass of his fellows and to draw apart with his family and his friends, so that after he has thus formed a little circle of his own, he willingly leaves society at large to itself.

Selfishness, at any rate, was old and not particularly determined by a set of social arrangements, but "individualism is of democratic origin, and it threatens to spread in the same ratio as the equality of condition." The reason lay, Tocqueville continued, in the especially dissolvent effect of democracy upon the social bonds of community. Where it was possible "among aristocratic nations" for families to exist in a relatively stable form over a period of centuries, an identification of the present with the past and the future, and a consequent willingness to revere the one and sacrifice oneself for the other, were promoted. With the temporal extension of personality in two directions went obligation to both the dead and the unborn. Meanwhile, realization of the structured and interconnected

[11] *Ibid.*, II, 76.

nature of such a society gave rise to a sense of duty toward particular persons at least, if not toward the amorphous "mankind" worshiped by democrats.

Because the extreme fluidity of the American social situation worked against the maintenance of a close-knit family establishment over several generations, it seemed to Tocqueville that

the woof of time is every instant broken and the track of generations effaced. Those who went before are soon forgotten; of those who will come after, no one has any idea: the interest of man is confined to those in close propinquity to himself.

At the same time, while the chain of community binding together the class-ridden society was being destroyed, a new type of democratic man was making his appearance, a type whose prime characteristic was his sense of sovereign independence:

They owe nothing to any man, they expect nothing from any man; they acquire the habit of always considering themselves as standing alone, and they are apt to imagine that their whole destiny is in their own hands.

Cut off equally from social community with the past, present, and future, this time-bereft man against the sky, as Tocqueville envisioned him, was thrown "back forever upon himself alone," to be imprisoned finally, perhaps, "entirely within the solitude of his own heart." [12]

From the dangerous consequences of such alienation, an alienation that was bound to lead eventually to the selfishness which "blights the germ of all virtue," Americans were saved by the centripetal influences of their free institutions. Forced to work closely with one another on public projects and to rely on the public approbation for election to office, Americans realized "that they cannot do without the people who surround them." It is "local freedom,"

[12] *Ibid.*, p. 98.

therefore, which counteracts the centrifugal forces of equality and overcomes them.[13]

Although Tocqueville had succeeded here to his own satisfaction in restoring to the Americans that sense of human solidarity of which his previous discussion would seem to have deprived them, he did not return upon his path to consider the effect of his collectivist and coopera- tive conclusions upon the "Sources of Poetry Among Dem- ocratic Nations." There he had declared that "all that be- longs to the existence of the human race taken as a whole, to its vicissitudes and its future, becomes an abundant mine of poetry." In their pursuit after the essential charac- ter of this "whole," after "the ideal," poets would spurn the unpoetical subject matter provided by the "language, the dress, and the daily actions of men in democracies" in favor of "the scrutiny of the hidden depths in the immate- rial nature of man." For Americans, a people whom he had already labeled natural Cartesians, the next step in the poetic process would seem to be simplicity itself. For, Toc- queville went on,

I need not traverse earth and sky to discover a wondrous object woven of contrasts, of infinite greatness and littleness, of in- tense gloom and amazing brightness, capable at once of excit- ing pity, admiration, terror, contempt. *I have only to look at myself* [italics added].[14]

But, what would the American see when he looked at himself? The subtleties of Tocqueville's own examination into the implications of democratic society had resulted in the description of a democratic man who was pulled toward the opposite poles of isolation and community.[15]

[13] *Ibid.,* pp. 103–04.   [14] *Ibid.,* pp. 75–76.

[15] This vision of the democratic man was obviously one of the major preconceptions which Tocqueville brought with him to Amer- ica. It was already a staple of European romanticism, and Tocque- ville was clearly bent upon "discovering" in America its objective correlative.

The facial lineaments of that self which would be celebrated in a coming "Song of Myself" were left shadowed in ambiguity. One thing was clear, however: Tocqueville had left no role or any effective influence for the past upon men in a democratic society. If they were to be saved alive from the bond-destroying social maelstrom in which they were immersed, it would not be through any sense of genetic relationship—although Americans had their share of "those disinterested and spontaneous impulses that are natural to man"—but simply because they had found out that things worked better the other way. In fact, Tocqueville told his French readers, Americans prided themselves on their mastery of an enlightened selfishness, and preferred to explain "almost all the actions of their lives by the principle of self-interest rightly understood." [16]

The "principle of self-interest rightly understood" was, of course, the great regulator of public order in the philosophy of John Locke. The familiar ease with which Americans could speak of themselves in such terms proved the charm that an artificial and mechanical rationale of society had for them as an everyday rule of thumb. Inclined to be legalistic, Americans preferred to be strictly committed only by the exact terms of the bond. Understandably, the "principle of self-interest rightly understood" was popular because of its double usefulness: the first part of the formula left full freedom of action in the hands of each individual, while the efficacy of the "rightly understood" saved the day for all those spheres of benevolent cooperation in which, as Tocqueville was so impressed to note, Americans delighted to participate.[17]

As a practical matter, then, Americans were preserved from the logical implications of their own philosophy. Nevertheless, the acceptance of such a formula involved, as many thoughtful Americans fully recognized, just such an element of social peril as Tocqueville's acute reasoning

[16] *Democracy in America,* II, 122.   [17] *Ibid.,* Ch. 5.

had uncovered. The years of Andrew Jackson's administrations provided the peculiarly appropriate setting for a sharper delineation of all the ramifications of this problem, and witnessed a major attempt by George Bancroft to coerce the American past toward its solution.

Exactly what were the points at issue? Ranged in order and adorned with the most approved rhetoric of the time they can be heard reverberating through an address which the already distinguished lawyer Rufus Choate delivered at Salem in the year before Bancroft published the first volume of his *History*. Choate and Bancroft had several things in common: they were descendants of old Massachusetts Puritan families; they were high-powered intellectuals with more than the usual freight of classical and literary erudition; and their careers were to be marked by a sporadic participation in politics carried on from an outside base. As Bancroft was to be considered the acknowledged master of American historians, Choate gained the reputation of being perhaps the most skillful trial attorney of his time. Most important, since they were almost the same age—Choate was born in 1799, Bancroft in 1800—they belonged to the generation of born Americans for whom colonial society and the Revolutionary era were a memory imparted by tradition and not a matter of living experience.[18] Both came of age in an American world far different from that which their fathers had known, a world in which it was quite apparent that the

alliance between the magistracy, the clergy, property, and culture, was collapsing. The eclipse of the Federalists, who were the living image of government by leaders, robbed it of one of its strongest supports. The influence of the clergy, which had been one of the main props of the Federalists, was being thrust out of lay society.[19]

[18] Choate's biography is in Samuel Gilman Brown, *The Works of Rufus Choate with a Memoir of His Life,* 2 vols. (Boston, 1862).

[19] M. Ostrogorski, *Democracy and the Organization of Political Parties,* trans. Frederick Clarke (New York, 1902), II, 26–27.

The dissolution of institutional ties that Ostrogorski thus described presented the members of the Bancroft-Choate generation with the necessity of formulating and defending a program for social cohesion capable of holding together the whirling elements into which the relatively static world of their fathers had been transformed. As Massachusetts, and by extension the entire country, had been founded upon the reality of a Godly Commonwealth, such a task was bound to be moral and patriotic at the same time. Rufus Choate was a leading conservative; George Bancroft made himself the spokesman for a libertarian doctrine of progress and those social forces that Choate most feared. At bottom, however, they shared some common assumptions which gave them a not dissimilar outlook toward the function of history in their time.

Choate's 1833 oration at Salem was entitled "The Importance of Illustrating New England History by a Series of Romances Like the Waverly Novels." [20] "The history of the United States," Choate began by declaring,

from the planting of the several Colonies out of which they have sprung, to the end of the war of the Revolution, is now as amply written, as accessible, and as authentic, as any other portion of the history of the world, and incomparably more so than an equal portion of the history of the origin and first ages of any other nation that ever existed.

There was no need, therefore, for more conventional history of the type which served well "lawyers, politicians, and for most purposes of mere utility, business, and intellect." What was now needed was a recasting of the existing record into "a form in which it should speak directly to the heart and affections and imagination of the whole people." America needed a thousand Walter Scotts to project

a series of romantic compositions . . . the scenes of which should be laid in North America, somewhere in the time be-

[20] *Works,* I, 319–46. The following discussion is based on this oration.

fore the Revolution, and the incidents and characters of which should be selected from the records and traditions of that, our heroic age.

The happy result would be the "mingling [of] the tones of a ravishing national minstrelsy with the grave narrative, instructive reflections, and chastened feelings of Marshall, Pitkin, Holmes, and Ramsay."

From one point of view Choate's voice was another in the chorus that had for a number of years been calling for the creation of an original American literature.[21] For it would be the work of the American Scott to

begin with the landing of the Pilgrims, and pass down to the War of Independence, from one epoch and one generation to another, like Old Mortality among the graves of the unforgotten faithful, wiping the dust from the urns of our fathers,— gathering up whatever of illustrious achievement, of heroic suffering, of unwavering faith, their history commemorates, and weaving it all into an immortal and noble national literature.

But the form which that literature ought to take, according to Choate, was the conscious creation, in an age of national sophistication, of a filio-pietistic epical series that would bypass the Revolutionary era and concentrate upon the "incidents and events . . . of our heroic age." Such a literature, Choate insisted, would be no departure from the truth, but an elaboration of valuable historical materials presented in a manner more impressive than could be attempted by conventional scholars. "The Iliad and Odyssey of Homer," Choate asked, "—what are they but great Waverly Novels!" And yet they were important historical sources. In the same way, he went on, by revivifying the social milieu of early American history, "*our* Iliad and Odyssey . . . when they come to be written, will help to

[21] The references are collected in G. Harrison Orians, "The Rise of Romanticism, 1805–1855," *Transitions in American Literary History*, ed. Harry Hayden Clark (Durham, N.C., 1953), p. 202, n. 58.

illustrate and to complete and to give attraction to that history."

It is important to note that the "history" to which the productions of the coming American Homers were to give "attraction" was to be in substance that presented in "the grave narrative, instructive reflections, and chastened feelings of Marshall, Pitkin, Holmes, and Ramsay." All four had written to a certain extent about the years of colonial dependency, but their principal interest lay in the Revolutionary era of which they were all contemporaries. Ungraceful writers, they presented a narrative which was unquestionably "sober"; about its "instructiveness," however, there may have been less unanimity. Except for Ramsay they had extended their histories into the early national period, and while Pitkin and Holmes were perhaps only mildly pro-Federalist and pro-Hamiltonian, Marshall's *Life of Washington* had become notorious among the followers of Jefferson for its obvious bias. A scandal to the Republicans for a quarter of a century, the book had been reissued by the aged Chief Justice in the year before Choate spoke at Salem.[22]

It was, then, American history as written by these men that Rufus Choate felt was already adequate for "lawyers, politicians, and for most purposes of mere utility, business, and intellect"—in short, for all those who wished only to know the truth and had the intellectual capacity and education to make use of it. Choate's audience could not mistake him: the thinking man's history already existed. Now something was needed to bring home the facts to "the heart and affections and imagination of the whole people." Nor could his audience miss this reference to a Democratic

[22] Michael Kraus, *The Writing of American History* (Norman, Okla., 1953), pp. 72–73, 84–86, 100–03; John Marshall, *The Life of George Washington . . .* , 2 vols. (2d ed.; Philadelphia, 1832); Timothy Pitkin, *A Political and Civil History of the United States of America . . .* , 2 vols. (New Haven, 1828); Abiel Holmes, *The Annals of America . . .* , 2 vols. (2d ed.; Cambridge, 1829).

electorate whose emotional, and therefore presumably mindless, attachment to Andrew Jackson was a staple of Whig polemics. The muse Rufus Choate was bidding arise had her work cut out for her; not for her would it be to sing the causes of that fatal enmity between Jefferson and Hamilton. In the interest of re-establishing national rapport, Choate proposed to abandon the dark and bloody foreground of recent American history in order to hymn the glories of a pre-Revolutionary "heroic age." This was for him now the area of *the usable past,* the innocent, disengaged past, whose elements alone were suitable for molding and coloring into therapeutic romances.

There was yet another, equally cogent reason that made the choice of the pre-Revolutionary era for this purpose deeply satisfying to both Choate and his hearers. They were agonizingly aware that the avalanche of social change, of which the presidency of Andrew Jackson was but the most painful sign, threatened to sweep from New England's grasp the historic scepter of social leadership that was hers by ancient right. Already, the home of the divinely directed Puritans and the original seat, as New Englanders were firmly convinced, of free institutions in the New World had felt what it was to have its counsels rejected and its ideals scorned. To the men of Salem, as to most New Englanders, colonial history was pre-eminently Puritan history; any refocusing of attention upon those great days long before the growth of a Jacksonian West would recover for New England some measure of the prestige that now seemed to be slipping away from her.

What could be more natural, therefore, when Choate cast about to pluck from the "thousand" subjects "connected with the history of New England in that era, which deserve, and would reward, the fullest illustration which learning and genius and philosophy could bestow," that he would know immediately of "two or three." And that the one of these which he should first choose to enlarge upon should be "the *old Puritan character,*" which was from all viewpoints "an extraordinary mental and moral phenomenon." Its accomplishments in New England were "inscribed upon all the sides of our religious, political, and literary edifices, legibly and imperishably." "But while," Choate continued,

we appreciate what the Puritans have done, and recognize the divine wisdom and purposes in raising them up to do it, something is wanting yet to give to their character and fortunes a warm, quick interest, a charm for the feelings and imagination, an abiding-place in the heart and memory and affections of *all* the generations of the people to whom they bequeathed these representative governments and this undefiled religion. It is time that literature and the arts should at least cooperate with history [italics added].

In the plea of the eloquent counselor Choate for "an abiding-place in the heart and memory and affections of all the generations" for his Puritan plaintiffs, lay an appeal to the heart of the nation by Jacksonian New England that she be loved. New England knew well that she was *right,* as she had always been; but the anguishing fact was that the American world was no longer one in which that was enough. In reaching out for that community of the generations which Tocqueville saw wanting in democratic society, New England sought to quiet her anxieties amid the familiar security of long-known and cherished values. In light of her historically sober temperament, the degree of her need could be measured by Choate's announced willingness to "put in requisition alternately music, poetry, eloquence, and history, and speak by turns to the senses, the fancy, and the reason of the world."

It would be the function of Choate's magnificent literary pageant not only to prevent the effacement of what Tocqueville was to call "the track of generations," but also to guard against Tocqueville's disease of individualism: the community-destroying canker of selfishness. Before an

audience who felt themselves besieged by a horde of new
men, empty of the past, who disregarded all the proprieties
in a clamorous scramble for every form of social power,
Choate invoked the regulating authority of an American
history "full of instruction, and written for instruction."
And what was most valuable in its instruction, Choate
declared, was "its moral lessons," which elevate for "our
emulation and love great models of patriotism and virtue."
It was by holding up such commonly accepted models that
American history combated the forces making for the isolation of men from one another and from their shared
past. "It corrects," Choate contended,

the cold selfishness which would regard ourselves, our day, and
our generation, as a separate and insulated portion of man
and time; and, awakening our sympathies for those who have
gone before, it makes us mindful, also, of those who are to follow, and thus binds us to our fathers and to our posterity by a
lengthening and golden cord.

As implicitly present-minded as Choate's oration had
thus far been, he turned at its close to make explicit the
application of his argument to the current political scene.
He was speaking to a New England that had received a
severe jolt by the "brinkmanship" of South Carolina over
a point of principle which went to the very heart of the national existence. Choate's own concern was deep and genuine, and he put forward the suggestion that such a literature as he had recommended "might do *something* to per-
petuate the Union itself." In preparation for this conclusion he now enlarged the temporal and geographical
boundaries within which he had been working to envisage
a grand literature "embodying the romance of the whole
revolutionary and ante-revolutionary history of the United
States." At the same time he reworked and expanded the
principal Puritan virtue—character—into a unifying concept with national scope. "Poems and romances," said
Choate,

which shall be read in every parlor, by every fireside, in every
school-house, behind every counter in every printing-office, in
every lawyer's office, at every weekly evening club, in all the
States of this Confederacy, must do something, along with
more palpable if not more powerful agents, toward moulding
and fixing that final, grand, complex result,—the national
character.

Let such a literature once exist, Choate went on, and

it would perhaps not be so alarming if demagogues should
preach, or governors practise, or executives tolerate nullification. Such a literature would be a common property of all the
States,—a treasure of common ancestral recollections,—more
noble and richer than our thousand million acres of public
land; and unlike that land, it would be indivisible. It would
be as the opening of a great fountain for the healing of the
nations. . . . Reminded of our fathers, we should remember
that we are brethren. The exclusiveness of State pride, the
narrow selfishness of a mere local policy, and the small jealou-
sies of vulgar minds, would be merged in an expanded, comprehensive, constitutional sentiment of old, family, fraternal
regard. It would reassemble, as it were, the people of America
in one vast congregation. It would rehearse in their hearing
all things which God had done for them in the old time; it
would proclaim the law once more; and then it would bid
them join in that grandest and most affecting solemnity,—a
national anthem of thanksgiving for the deliverance, of honor
for the dead, of proud prediction for the future!

Since the element of the Puritans' character that Choate
had stressed was their lack of worldly ambition and self-
seeking, it is not difficult to see how he would utilize their
virtue for wider ends. In Jacksonian America "self-interest
rightly understood" had signally failed to produce fellow-
feeling. The remedy Choate prescribed was a return in
spirit to the period of disinterested harmony.

The harmony of that earlier time was one which refused to entertain the idea of Tocqueville's democratic
man, the man who owed nothing to anybody, expected

nothing from anybody, and insisted upon "standing alone." Choate's references to fraternalism and family feeling were deliberately made. They were indicative of the kind of social chaos he felt around him in his own time. The rise of industry, the development of canals, railroads, and steamboats—the westward trails choked with American humanity on the move—had eroded what patriarchal authority remained from colonial days. For if the distinguishing mark of a true American had come to be his insistence that he owed nothing to inheritance but everything to his own pluck and energy, what was he doing but proclaiming himself an orphan. Indeed, the prime example of the American as Orphan sat in the White House. As an element in the prestige of President Jackson himself, orphanhood had now become a distinction.[23]

To Choate a nation of self-seeking orphans offered no security for social peace. Here he was at one with that spearhead of the Congregational-Presbyterian coalition to conquer the West, Lyman Beecher, who in his *Lectures on Scepticism,* published in the year of Choate's address, thundered,

Let the belief and feeling of accountability fail from the public mind, and poverty, and envy, and ambition, and lust, be summoned to a crusade against religion, and purity, and property, and law, and how long would the police of our cities protect us? How soon would the laws of the land be cobwebs, and crime roll over us its wave of desolation, as once the waters of the flood swept over the earth!

Only a mass reconversion to Calvinist religion, Beecher insisted, could keep chained those self-regarding inclinations whose triumph would mean the downfall of civilization. The disestablishment of Congregationalism in Massachusetts that same year was only another in a long series of unfortunate events which made it easy for Beecher to associ-

[23] John William Ward, *Andrew Jackson: Symbol for an Age,* Chap. IX. See also William R. Taylor, *Cavalier and Yankee,* p. 132.

ate the general abandonment of moral responsibility with the veneration for a "numerical majority at the polls." [24] Both Beecher and Choate expressed concern for the fate of "the law" at the hands of such majorities, and one of the principal functions of Choate's set of romantic epics was to proclaim "the law once more." For Choate, the current movement to abandon the old common law in favor of constructed codes, an innovation which he vigorously opposed, was the counterpart of Beecher's disestablishment, and its implications were as terrifying.

Finally, at the close of his address, Choate pointed shrewdly to the considerable ritual value that the possession of such a literature as he proposed would confer upon the nation. So far, he declared, America had not been able to match the richness of the ancient world in this respect. While the tribes of Israel had foregathered thrice yearly at great national festivals in the capital to celebrate "the triumphs of their fathers by the Red Sea, at the fords of Jordan, and on the high places of the field of Barak's victory," the United States, said Choate, had no such set feasts. Similarly, the Greeks contributed to common temples, consulted a common oracle, and attended a common festival "to hear their glorious history read aloud, in the prose of Herodotus, the poetry of Homer and of Pindar." In comparison, the Americans had "built no national temples but the Capitol; . . . [consulted] no commmon oracle but the Constitution." Neither was it possible for them all to come together at one time for a national communion. Nevertheless, Choate reminded his hearers, America did indeed have one remarkable agency whose prepotent influence was capable of repairing all these lacks. That agency was the press. It was the press whose

thousand tongues . . . clearer far than the silver trumpet of the jubilee,—louder than the voice of the herald at the games —may speak and do speak to the whole people, without call-

[24] *Lectures on Scepticism,* pp. 87–88.

ing them from their homes or interrupting them in their employments.

In thus recognizing the powerful role of myth and rite in the creation of a national spirit Choate was attempting to counter not only the divisiveness of an interest-directed society but the alarmingly successful irrationalism of Jacksonian Democracy. When he pointed out the absence in America of institutions with a central focus he had before him the vision of such an institution, the Second Bank of the United States, assailed by enemies making full use of a powerful mythology. Since his partisanship saw the Jacksonians as the enemy to be combated, he was unprepared to acknowledge, even should it have occurred to him, that perhaps the rise of equalitarian democracy had already given birth to the kind of communal "congregation" he was calling for.

As he watched the Democratic victory march through the streets of New York City in November, 1834, Michel Chevalier had a feeling that this was not just another big parade. By torchlight, in a line almost a mile long, Democrats with banners and mottoes came on under portraits of Jackson, Jefferson, and Washington, accompanied by "a real live eagle—tied by the legs, surrounded by a wreath of leaves and hoisted upon a pole, after the manner of the Roman standards." The whole thing reminded Chevalier of the religious processions of Mexican Indians, following the Eucharist with holy candles. It was a panorama asking for the genius of a master painter to transmit its glory to the future:

For this is something more than the grotesque fashion of scenes immortalized by Rembrandt; it belongs to history, this belongs to the sublime; these are episodes of a wondrous epic which will bequeath a lasting memory to posterity, *the memory of the coming of democracy* [italics added].[25]

[25] Chevalier, *Society, Manners, and Politics,* pp. 307–08.

Six years later, after Rufus Choate and the Whig party had reached the same conclusion, thousands of erstwhile Democrats poured libations in hard cider round the log-cabin manger of a champion who had risen from lowly beginnings to shed his blood for them on the field of Tippecanoe.

Choate's high-toned depiction, in 1833, of a quasi-historical romance which would reintroduce the sense of social solidarity could almost serve as an anticipation of Bancroft's *History*. Opposite as were their stands on the political controversies of the time, both were anxious to reestablish connection with a living past and to use that past for the assuagement of present social griefs. In Choate's words, to open "a great fountain for the healing of the nations." But while Choate sought to rally allegiance to an ancient fortress of prestigious values—garrisoned, he had no doubt, by men of his own temper and background—- George Bancroft, a defector from the social-intellectual hierarchy of old New England, was already switching the insignia on the walls and turrets to the pennants and banners of democracy.

This difference in historical strategy reflected a difference in the hosts who were led and in the leaders themselves. Choate did not feel that he had to prove the worth of those principles by which his party lived. If he feared moral anarchy his solution was to bring round the dissident hordes, the new rulers in Egypt, to the remembrance of the Joseph of New England. Himself a representative of the law, Choate spoke from a secure and self-assured institutional framework. Bancroft, of course, was the son of the revered Aaron, but as one of the handful of Americans to have taken a doctorate in Germany, he had returned from hearing Schleiermacher and Hegel ill suited to join his father in the pulpit. Indeed, he had so far forgotten himself upon landing in New York as to greet the Reverend Andrews Norton with kisses on both cheeks. Afterward, a venture at schoolmastering on advanced principles was followed by conversion to the party of Andrew Jackson and the position of resident intellectual to "The Democracy." [26]

As much perhaps for Bancroft as for the democratic legions whose cause he espoused, the conquest of the past was a ploy for the capture of a present where their joint claims still battled for acceptance. Part of the strong animus toward John Locke which Bancroft displayed in his *History* may have come from the consciousness that he was dealing with a professional competitor. The preface to the *Second Treatise,* however unhistorically, proclaimed the author's intention

to establish the Throne of our Great Restorer, Our present King William; to make good his Title, in the Consent of the People, . . . And to justify to the World, the People of England, whose love of their Just and Natural Rights, with their Resolution to preserve them, saved the Nation when it was on the very brink of Slavery and Ruine.[27]

As the national historian, Bancroft tried to do for the American people as a whole what Locke had done for Wililam III: *to establish* the popular dominion; *to make good its title* to the repository of social wisdom; and *to justify to the American world* the historic role of the popular virtues.

For the accomplishment of the first two of these aims it was necessary to mount a spirited assault against Locke's theory of knowledge, to convert a libertarian *doctor angelicus* into the *bête noire* of democratic history. In a famous oration that he delivered in 1835, Bancroft proclaimed:

[26] M. A. DeWolfe Howe, *The Life and Letters of George Bancroft,* 2 vols. (New York, 1908); Russel B. Nye, *George Bancroft, Brahmin Rebel* (New York, 1944).

[27] *Two Treatises of Government, A Critical Edition* . . . , ed. Peter Laslett (Cambridge, England, 1960), p. 155. On its unhistoricity see *ibid.,* pp. 45 ff.

Reason exists within every breast. I mean not that faculty which deduces inferences from the experiences of the senses, but that higher faculty, which from the infinite treasures of its own consciousness, originates truth, and assents to it by the force of intuitive evidence; that faculty which raises us beyond the control of time and space, and gives us faith in things eternal and invisible.[28]

To Locke, reason had been exactly "that faculty which deduces inferences from the experiences of the senses." It neither originated truth nor had access to intuitive evidence, but proceeded to conclusions through the exercise of discrimination, reflection, and judgment. As these were all qualities amenable to training and discipline it followed inexorably that, although all men might reason, some men might reason more truly than others. While men of the Enlightenment, such as Thomas Jefferson, looked with satisfaction toward the creation of an aristocracy of talent by means of education, an intellectual leveler like Bancroft found such a result highly uncongenial. By removing the "treasures" of reason "beyond the control of time and space," Bancroft successfully nullified the advantages of special culture and depreciated the value of the trained intelligence. If reason needed only to dip for truth into "the infinite treasures of its own consciousness," then it was indeed plausible, as Bancroft went on to claim, that "there is not the difference between one mind and another, which the pride of philosophers might conceive." [29]

Thus Bancroft attempted to overcome any invidious distinction between minds by localizing, in the "breast," a source of truth which was apparently available on easier terms than those which the head demanded. Primarily a literary man, Bancroft was unsystematic in his use of terms. The cognitive properties of the "breast" he at other

[28] "The Office of the People in Art, Government, and Religion" (1835), *Literary and Historical Miscellanies,* p. 409.
[29] *Ibid.*

times attributed to "the soul" and even "the mind," but what he meant was plain enough.[30] He was concerned to endow every individual with the ability to intuit general propositions, universals which were "beyond the control of time and space." Locke had insisted that knowledge had to stick close to experiential facts which were time- and space-ridden, and that "general and universal belong not to the real existence of things, but are inventions and creatures of the understanding, made by it for its own use." The pragmatic tentativity of human judgments Locke saw as sufficient to "our condition," since it enabled men to acquire as much truth as they needed "to live and talk and act like other people." [31] Such epistemological moderation cramped the scope of the democratic electorate as Bancroft envisioned their function. To their judgments, Bancroft would have it, belonged the absolute truth and certainty which the Lockean analysis of experience denied men.

Thus exalting and guaranteeing the validity of the popular wisdom, Bancroft went on to give an extended demonstration of the long-term, providential efficacy of the nonself-serving virtues of the heart throughout American history. "The diagnosis of any human existence, whether of an individual, a people or an age," Ortega y Gasset has written, "must begin by establishing the repertory of its convictions. . . . and to this end it must establish before all else which belief is fundamental, decisive, sustaining and breathing life into all the others." [32] Bancroft aspired to write the authentic history of his people, that is, the one in which they should be willing to recognize themselves.

[30] For example, *ibid.*, ff.

[31] *Essay Concerning Human Understanding* (28th ed.; London, 1838), Bk. III, Ch. 3, Par. 11; Bk. I, Ch. 1, Par. 5; R. G. Collingwood, *The Idea of History* (New York, 1956), p. 73. For the attack on Locke generally in this period see Merle Curti, "The Great Mr. Locke: America's Philosopher, 1783–1861," in *Probing Our Past* (Gloucester, Mass., 1962), pp. 69–118.

[32] *History as a System* . . . (New York, 1961), pp. 166–68.

Given the nature of American society, the problem of convictions presented itself as one of moral mission, the discovery of the moral repertory with which Americans imagined themselves moving through history. To legitimize the present and the future such an image was bound to include an element of dream and desire, the idea not alone of what the American had been, but what he sought to become. In this quality of something-yet-to-be America demanded of its aspiring historian that he project from out of the past its own living wish for the future, that genuine American self which was to be realized.

Regarded in Ortega's terms as a sort of moral diagnosis of his people's beginnings, Bancroft's first volume illustrated copiously the lineaments of that self to which Americans were inclined to give credence. Not surprisingly, it was a dynamic and progressing self; but its prosperity and progress came about practically unsought for by direct attention to material interests. Obvious self-interest was the blackest sin in Bancroft's catalogue of vices; wherever he spotted its presence he hurled his fiercest denunciations. Already early in the settlement of Virginia, Bancroft showed, "it became necessary to depose Wingfield, the avaricious president, who was charged with engrossing the choicest stores." He described how the burdens of the colonists were increased by "the angry covetousness of a greedy . . . corporation," which basely "grasped at sudden emoluments," and consistently demonstrated "an avarice which would listen to no possibility of defeat." Thus were greed and avarice on the one side from the first, and opposed on the other by their natural correlative, then embodied in the Captain John Smith who was "not covetous to find gold." Fortunately the thirst for gain sometimes tended to its own destruction, and the later "indiscriminate rapacity" of deputy-governor Argall, like that of Wingfield, brought on his displacement. Although Bancroft admitted that the colonists could be guilty themselves of "covetousness," as when they brutally seized Indian lands, corporations were the worst offenders by their very nature, a nature insensible to any merely human appeal. For since "gain" was the "object" of their organization, success meant only that the settlers were "made subservient to commercial avarice." Whereas the individual could be appealed to through such virtues as "magnanimity" or "benevolence," it was plain to Bancroft that "corporate ambition is deaf to mercy, and insensible to shame."

The Pilgrims of Plymouth also suffered from a business arrangement favoring "only the cupidity of the proprietors," a grant which "yielded everything to the avarice of the corporation." Though saved from the rigor of this bargain by the very excessiveness of its demands, their own kindliness did not preserve them from the threat of Indian attacks to which they were exposed by the "graspings of avarice" in another colony. That colony, organized solely to exploit the fur trade, failed "after having boasted of their strength, as far superior to Plymouth, which was enfeebled they said, by the presence of children and women." Its misfortune was for Bancroft a sign of the superiority of altruistic benevolence over self-interest.[33]

The virtues which Bancroft praised in the first volume of his *History* he went on to single out thereafter. As he poured out his scorn upon "cupidity," "avarice," "selfishness," "self-love," "covetousness," "greediness," and the "passion for gain" generally, so he picked out and held up for emulation examples of "benevolence," "disinterested conduct," and "redeeming love." His saints were Thomas Hooker and Roger Williams and, above all, William Penn and the Quakers. His treatment of Quaker virtue was one extended panegyric on the excellence of their "self-denial" and "disinterested virtue." Pre-eminently was the Quaker "no slave to avarice . . . [but] to him the love of money for money's sake was the basest of passions." Indeed, the

[33] *History of the United States* (Boston, 1834–1874), I (1834 and 1837), Chaps. IV, V, VIII.

image of Bancroftian virtue wore a face of almost ascetic devotion to an unworldly set of aims.

What was to the Quaker "the basest of passions," the single-minded pursuit of wealth, seemed to many the ruling passion of that worldly American society which enthusiastically received Bancroft's successive editions. Moralizers, foreign and domestic, were practically unanimous on this point. But there was no secret to Bancroft's popular appeal; his narrative was, after all, a grand success story from the material as well as the spiritual standpoint, whose happy ending was well known to all. Puritan-Quaker virtue had eventuated in an affluent society, while, as Bancroft assured his readers when he concluded Volume II, "we shall still see that the selfishness of evil defeats itself, and God rules in the affairs of men." [34]

Yet Bancroft's reception showed that a society straining to snap the last barriers against unrestricted economic competition felt a strong need to re-emphasize its genetic and spiritual congruity with a past believed to be based on the highest of altruistic motives. Bancroft's one-to-one identification of democracy with the practitioners of selfless virtue, coupled with his pervasive doctrine of progress, made it easy for his public to still any disquieting pricks of conscience over the apparent moral disproportion between past and present. In the spread of equalitarian democracy, in the dismantling of the last props to social and political domination by property interests, Americans were carrying out the mission of their remote past, bringing to fruition the dreams of godly ancestors.

To consider Bancroft's *History* merely as a sustained paean to Jacksonian democracy is to overlook its most striking characteristic: its quality as a multivolume sermon against "selfishness." The danger of anarchic selfishness was the other side of excessive individualism, Tocqueville realized. And selfishness was one of the principal vices to be curbed by Choate's romantic virtue-literature. Both

[34] *Ibid.*, II (1837), Chaps. XII, XVI, XVII, XVIII.

these men valued the role of institutional sanctions as reg-
ulators of the social machinery; both feared majority
rule as only another name for the reign of an unchecked
mass egoism. The fulminations of Lyman Beecher were
only a cruder exposition of essentially the same argument.
As a brief for the defense of popular sovereignty against a
moral attack too important to be ignored, Bancroft's *History* reflected the insecure position of the man of progress
who accepts the assumptions of the past without being
quite sure just how he fits into their pattern.

Bancroft's quarrel with John Locke was one good way of
returning the charge of selfishness upon the enemy. By
basing society upon contract, Bancroft asserted contemp-
tuously, Locke was simply appealing to selfish interest.
Did not Locke have men enter into political life in order
to secure benefits for themselves, to satisfy their personal
desires? With a close eye on his own times Bancroft identified the entire corpus of Lockean virtue with the idea of
contract, which became in his pages a thoroughly amoral
piece of *meum-tuum, quid-pro-quo* bargaining. Furthermore, a reverential attitude toward prescriptive property
rights had thrown repeated roadblocks in the path of the
colonies to independence. But genuine virtue could of
course not be expected from a philosophy based upon
sense experience. Fortunately, Bancroft wrote, "the school
that bows to the senses as the sole interpreter of truth, had
little share in colonizing our America." The colonial fathers were men who knew the reality of God, the soul, and
a moral imperative not derivable from sense impressions.
It was hardly contract, then, to which they owed the noble
framework of their society. In the case of the Pilgrims, the
acknowledged rectitude of their social order nowhere even
rested on the standard prop of a charter, Bancroft boasted.
"It was therefore in the virtues of the colonists themselves,
that their institutions found a guaranty for stability." [35]

To those like Choate who viewed the current attack

[35] *Ibid.*, Chaps. XIII, XVI, XVIII; I, Chap. VIII.

upon contract rights, epitomized in the famous Charles River Bridge case of 1837, as a breach in the dike of morality, Bancroft offered the protection afforded by the virtues of the people themselves as a "guaranty for stability." The antinomianism of the Quakers proved triply useful for this purpose. To Lyman Beecher and his authoritarian Evangelical cohorts, Bancroft was able to proffer the example of a people of appealing virtue, whose extreme devotion to social peace even to the point of pacifism was based upon an equally extreme moral rigorism. While to the defenders of contract and prescriptive property rights the Quaker concern for others constituted a sharp rebuke. For all who feared the heart-chilling atmosphere surrounding the new democratic "man against the sky" the Quakers proved that a noninstitutional community of spirit could have all the best social consequences.

The nature of Bancroft's task obliged him to take the field against John Locke, and the suitability of the Quaker example for his argument made it understandable that he would pay them more than ordinary attention. Yet Bancroft's treatment of another factor in the American story demonstrated a considerable amount of ingenuity and novelty. That was the use to which he put the great Calvinist theologian Jonathan Edwards. As Locke was the philosophical champion of the secular enemies to equalitarian democracy, so Edwards was the Aquinas of the ecclesiastical forces which insisted on emphasizing the total moral incapacity of unaided men for a life of virtue. In contrast to Bancroft's warm belief in the doctrine of secular progress and the capacity of men to shape their own destinies, the Edwardsian tradition concentrated on man's natural depravity, his utter will-lessness, his hapless subordination to a divine fate not of his making. Nothing would appear to have been less useful for Bancroft's purposes than such a doctrine. Yet he managed skillfully to press even Edwards into historical service.

As an American historian Bancroft had ready at hand a

traditional master key to history, the doctrine of Providence. The providential nature of their history had long been a root assumption with Americans of all political persuasions. It was to be expected that Bancroft would seek to enlist its prestige on the side of his version of that history, as he announced at the very beginning of his work his intention "to follow the steps by which a favoring Providence, calling our institutions into being, has conducted the country to its present happiness and glory." It was just as natural for the cold and logical John Quincy Adams, on the Fourth of July, 1837, to ask at Newburyport:

Is it not that, in the chain of human events, the birth-day of the nation is indissolubly linked with the birth-day of the Saviour? That it forms a leading event in the progress of the gospel dispensation? Is it not that the Declaration of Independence first organized the social compact on the foundation of the Redeemer's mission upon earth? That it laid the cornerstone of human government upon the first precepts of Christianity, and gave to the world the first irrevocable pledge of the fulfilment of the prophecies, announced directly from Heaven at the birth of the Saviour and predicted by the greatest of the Hebrew prophets six hundred years before? [36]

For Bancroft and his countrymen American history was deadly serious, and it was its providential nature that gave it its heavy freight of meaning. The same Providence that guided and preserved the Pilgrims was, for Bancroft, the Providence that established and guaranteed the sovereignty of the people in his own time. The doctrine of Providence, the doctrine of the power of God in human history, Bancroft shared with Jonathan Edwards.

"The wheels of providence," Edwards had said, "are not turned round by blind chance, but are full of eyes round about, (as Ezekiel represents them,) and are guided by the Spirit of God." Ezekiel's wheels rolled onward to unfold, as the title of his last, unfinished manuscript announced, *A*

[36] *An Oration delivered before the inhabitants of the Town of Newburyport . . . July 4, 1837*, pp. 5–6.

History of the Work of Redemption. "The *glorious issue* of this whole affair," according to Edwards, "[lies] in the perfect and eternal destruction of the wicked, and in the consummate glory of the righteous." To that end was it carried on through a succession of miracles and divinely appointed events, ever increasing in excellence as the final purpose grew nearer to accomplishment. For that reason, he explained, "the work of the new creation is more excellent than the old. So it ever is, that when one thing is removed by God to make way for another, the new excels the old." [37] This brief remark Bancroft wrenched happily from the corpus of Edwards' writings, and flourished aloft as a proof that the mighty theologian believed in his own brand of secular progress. "The meek New England divine," Bancroft exulted, "in his quiet association with the innocence and simplicity of rural life, knew that, in every succession of revolutions, the cause of civilization and moral reform is advanced." Quietly, Bancroft proceeded next to extract cause for optimism out of a watered-down version of the doctrine of an unfree will. For "nothing appears more self-determined than the volitions of each individual; and nothing is more certain than that the providence of God will overrule them for good." Herein lay the guarantee for the triumphant upward trend of history, and herein lay

the reason why evil is self-destructive; why truth, when it is once generated, is sure to live forever; why freedom and justice, though resisted and restrained, renew the contest from age to age, confident that messengers from heaven fight on their side, and that the stars in their courses war against their foes.[38]

Thus did Bancroft turn Edwards' providentialism into a secular doctrine of progressivism. But the most important

[37] Jonathan Edwards, *Works* (New York, 1829–1830), III, 429, 426.

[38] Bancroft, III (1840), Chap. XXIV.

idea which he drew from the New England thinker was the concept of "disinterested virtue." [39] For Edwards the most difficult of attainments, and dependent upon supernatural grace, in the hands of Bancroft it became the great possession of the common people, and freely accessible to all. Undertaking to write the history of his people, and finding Edwards athwart the way, Bancroft had wasted no time in argument but had calmly taken him into camp. Once disinterested virtue became the ordinary property of the masses, the secularization and democratization of Calvinism could be said to have become complete.

Like that of Edwards, Bancroft's *History* was a history of redemption. But the promise of salvation which had before been doubtful, contingent, and only for a few, was now made certain, absolute, and for the many. From it all cosmic risk had been eliminated. Similarly, Locke had asked men to question their ordinary perceptions and values, and put them to the hazardous test of experience. But Bancroft soothingly insisted things were pretty much what they seem. Both Edwards and Locke had summoned men to begin a perilous journey; Bancroft assured the American "man against the sky" that he had never, after all, left home.

[39] The idea of disinterested virtue had a vigorous life of its own in the eighteenth century, and influenced humanitarianism. I am concerned here with what might be called its politicization in Bancroft's hands. As in many other places, I am greatly indebted to Perry Miller's article, "From the Covenant to the Revival," in *Religion in American Life,* eds. James Ward Smith and A. Leland Jamison (Princeton, N. J., 1961), I, 322–68, and his last book, *The Life of the Mind in America from the Revolution to the Civil War* (New York, 1965).

ENDWORD

Elder Brewster's Benison

GLENDOWER: I can call spirits from the
  vasty deep.
HOTSPUR: Why, so can I, or so can any man;
  But will they come when you do call for them?

When the New England Society of New York met to
celebrate the two hundred and thirtieth anniversary of the
Pilgrim landing, they invited Secretary of State Daniel
Webster to the dinner. Webster, as the whole country
knew, had been born in New Hampshire before the close
of the Revolutionary War, and his family had lived in
New England since 1636. During his lifetime this area had
been irrevocably transformed into a prosperous commercial
and industrial community. No man in public life had done
more to further the transformation. But the Union upon
which national prosperity depended, and for whose preservation Webster had expended his strength, had now entered upon a crisis from which many believed it would not
emerge intact. And Webster himself, in his effort to allay
that crisis, had been made a target for contempt and abuse

by hundreds of New Englanders who had been brought up to revere his name. Unwell, and with less than two years to live, Webster accepted the Society's invitation in December, 1850, and took the train up to New York.[1]

There was no featured speaker at that year's dinner, but Webster certainly knew he would be expected to say a few words, and he was ready when the time came to reply to a toast. Inviting the banqueters to imagine themselves landing on Plymouth Rock that day long ago, Webster then prayed, "Thanks to Almighty God, who, from that distressed early condition of our fathers, has raised us to a height of prosperity and of happiness which they neither enjoyed, nor could have anticipated!" Warming to his task, a few minutes later the old man launched into what had always been one of his most appreciated oratorical tricks, the dramatic resurrection of a historical figure in whose name Webster could speak to the crowd. This time, from out of the Mayflower band the "tall and erect" Elder William Brewster entered through the door of the great hall to look upon the assembled diners. "Are ye," asked Brewster,

are ye our children? Does this scene of refinement, of elegance, of riches, of luxury, does all this come from our labors? Is this magnificent city, the like of which we never saw nor heard of on either continent, is this but an offshoot from Plymouth Rock? . . . Is this one part of the great reward for which my brethren and myself endured lives of toil and of hardship? We had faith and hope. God granted us the spirit to look forward, and we did look forward. But this scene we never anticipated. Our hopes were on another life. . . . And yet, let me say to you who are our descendants, who possess this glorious country and all it contains, who enjoy this hour of prosperity and the thousand blessings showered upon it by the God of your fathers, we envy you not, we reproach you not. Be rich, be prosperous, be enlightened. Live in pleasure, if such be your allot-

[1] Claude M. Fuess, *Daniel Webster* (Boston, 1930), II, 267–69.

ment on earth; but live, also, always to God and to duty. Spread yourselves and your children over the continent, accomplish the whole of your great destiny, and if it be that through the whole you carry Puritan hearts with you, if you still cherish an undying love of civil and religious liberty, and mean to enjoy them yourselves, and are willing to shed your heart's blood to transmit them to your posterity, then will you be worthy descendants of Carver and Allerton and Bradford, and the rest of those who landed from stormy seas on the rock of Plymouth.[2]

Elder Brewster could do no more. It would remain for one of Daniel Webster's greatest admirers to say upon a later occasion:

Yet, if God wills that . . . all the wealth piled by the bondsman's two hundred and fifty years of unrequited toil shall be sunk, and . . . every drop of blood drawn with the lash shall be paid by another drawn with the sword, as was said three thousand years ago, so still it must be said, "The judgments of the Lord are true and righteous altogether." [3]

[2] *Works,* IV, 217–18; 221–22.
[3] "Second Inaugural Address" (March 4, 1865), Richardson, *Messages and Papers,* VI, 276–77.

Selected Bibliography
(of works cited in the notes)

PRIMARY SOURCES

Newspapers

Albany Daily Advertiser, 1824.
Cahawba Press and Alabama State Intelligencer, 1824.
Charleston Courier, 1825.
City Gazette (Charleston), 1825.
Columbian Centinel (Boston), 1824.
Commercial Advertiser (New York), 1824.
Evening Gazette (Boston), 1824.
Evening Post (New York), 1824.
Evening Post (Philadelphia), 1824.
Georgia Journal (Milledgeville), 1825.
Herald (Alexandria, D.C.), 1824.
Illinois Gazette (Shawneetown), 1825.
Kentucky Reporter (Lexington), 1825.
Liberty Hall and Cincinnati Gazette, 1825.

Massachusetts Spy [and] *Worcester Advertiser,* 1824.
Nashville Whig, 1825.
National Advocate (New York), 1824.
National Gazette and Literary Register (Philadelphia), 1824.
New-Hampshire Gazette (Portsmouth), 1824.
New-Jersey Eagle (Newark), 1824.
New-York American, 1824–1825.
Niles' Weekly Register (Baltimore), XXVI–XXIX, 1824–1827.
Norfolk and Portsmouth Herald, 1824.
Providence Gazette, 1824.
Raleigh Register and North Carolina State Gazette, 1825.
Richmond Enquirer, 1824.
Salem Gazette, 1824.
Savannah Georgian, 1824–1825.
Troy Sentinel, 1824.
True American (Trenton), 1824.
Virginia Herald (Fredericksburg), 1824.
Washington Gazette, 1824.

Articles

Beecher, Lyman. "The Gospel the Only Security for Eminent
   and Abiding National Prosperity," *American National
   Preacher* . . . , III (March, 1829), 145–51.
——. "Propriety and Importance of Efforts to Evangelize the
   Nation," *American National Preacher,* III (March, 1829),
   151–55.
Bushnell, Horace. "Barbarism the First Danger," *American
   National Preacher,* XXI (September, 1847), 197–219.
Cable, Joseph. Speech in Congress, March 10, 1852, *Congres-
   sional Globe,* XXV (1852), 1st Sess., 32d Cong.
[Anon.] "Existing Commercial Embarrassments," *Christian
   Examiner,* 22 (July, 1837), 329–406.
Flint, Timothy. "America," *Western Monthly Review,* I
   (July–August, 1827), 164–75, 217–26.
Holdich, Joseph. "Elements of Political Economy," *Method-
   ist Magazine and Quarterly Review,* XIX (1837), 405–32.

[Anon.] "Outline of the United States," *North American Review*, XXI (April, 1825), 446–48.

[Sparks, Jared]. "Materials for American History," *North American Review*, XXIII (1826), 275–94.

[Ticknor, George]. "Lafayette," *North American Review*, XX (January, 1825), 147–80.

——. "Lafayette in America," *North American Review*, XXX (January, 1830), 216–37.

Tucker, George. "Dangers to be guarded against in the Progress of the United States," *The American Review: A Whig Journal . . .*, V (June, 1847), 614–29.

[Anon.] "Winthrop's History of New England," *North American Review*, XXIV (January, 1827), 23–37.

Books

Adams, John, and John Quincy Adams. *Selected Writings*. Eds. Adrienne Koch and William Peden. New York: Knopf, 1956.

——, and Thomas Jefferson. *The Adams-Jefferson Letters*. Ed. Lester J. Cappon. 2 vols. Chapel Hill, N.C.: University of North Carolina Press, 1959.

Adams, John Quincy. *An Oration delivered before the inhabitants of the Town of Newburyport . . . July 4th, 1837*. Newburyport: Morss and Brewster, [1837?].

Alcott, A. Bronson. *Journals*. Ed. Odell Shepard. Boston: Little, Brown, 1938.

Allen, William. *Memoir of John Codman, D.D. . . .* Boston: Marvin and Whipple, 1853.

Ames, Fisher. *Works*. Boston: T. B. Wait, 1809.

Anderson, Charles. *An Address on Anglo Saxon Destiny . . . December 20, 1849*. Cincinnati: John D. Thorpe, 1850.

Arthur, W. E. *An Oration delivered on the Fourth of July, 1850, before the Citizens of Covington, Ky*. Covington: Davis and Bedinger, 1850.

Atkinson, Thomas. *A Sermon in St. Peter's Church, Baltimore . . . the 12th day of December*. Baltimore: D. Brunner, 1845.

Audubon and His Journals. Eds. Maria R. Audubon and Elliott Coues. 2 vols. New York: Scribner's, 1898.

Baird, Robert. *Religion in America.* . . . New York: Harper, 1845.

Baldwin, Elihu W. *Considerations for the American Patriot: A Sermon delivered on . . . December 12, 1827.* New York: John P. Haven, 1828.

Ballou, Maturin. *Biography of Rev. Hosea Ballou.* Boston: Abel Tompkins, 1852.

Bancroft, George. *History of the United States from the Discovery of the American Continent.* 10 vols. Boston: Little, Brown, 1834–1874.

——. *Literary and Historical Miscellanies.* New York: Harper, 1855.

Barlow, Joel. *The Columbiad: A Poem.* London: Phillips, 1809.

Beecher, Lyman. *Lectures on Scepticism.* 3d ed. Cincinnati: Corey and Webster, 1835.

Bigelow, Andrew. *God's Charge Unto Israel: A Sermon . . . at the Annual Election, on Wednesday, January 6, 1836.* Boston: Dutton and Wentworth, 1836.

Bingham, Caleb, ed. *The Columbian Orator.* . . . Boston: Caleb Bingham, 1817.

[Bishop, Isabella (Bird)]. *The Englishwoman in America.* London: John Murray, 1856.

Botkin, B. A., ed. *A Treasury of American Folklore.* New York: Crown, 1944.

Brainerd, Cephas, and Eveline Warner Brainerd, eds. *New England Society Orations.* 2 vols. New York: Century, 1901.

Brandon, Edgar Ewing. *A Pilgrimage of Liberty, a contemporary account of the triumphal tour of General Lafayette through the southern and western states in 1825, as reported by the local newspapers.* Athens, Ohio: Lawhead Press, 1944.

——, comp. and ed. *Lafayette, Guest of the Nation, a contemporary account of the triumphal tour of General Lafayette through the United States in 1824–1825, as reported by the local newspapers.* 3 vols. Oxford, Ohio: Oxford Historical Press, 1950–1957.

Browne, Sir Thomas. *Works.* Ed. Simon Wilkin, F.L.S. 3 vols. London: Bohn, 1852.

Brownson, Orestes A. *Works.* Collected by Henry F. Brownson. 20 vols. Detroit: Thorndike, Nourse, 1884.

Bryan, Daniel. *The Lay of Gratitude; consisting of poems occasioned by the recent visit of Lafayette to the United States.* Philadelphia: Carey and Lea, 1826.

Bryant, William Cullen. *Poems.* Philadelphia: Carey and Hart, 1849.

Burnap, George W. *Lectures on the Sphere and Duties of Woman.* . . . Baltimore: John Murphy, 1841.

———. *The Philosophical Tendencies of the American Mind.* . . . Baltimore: John D. Toy, 1852.

———. *The Voice of the Times; a sermon . . . on Sunday, May 14, 1837.* Baltimore: John D. Toy, 1837.

Cairns, William B., ed. *Selections from Early American Writers, 1607–1800.* New York: Macmillan, 1910.

Calhoun, John C. *Works.* Ed. Richard K. Crallé. 6 vols. New York: Appleton, 1854–1860.

Carey, H[enry] C. *The Past, the Present, and the Future.* Philadelphia: Carey and Hart, 1848.

Carey, M[athew]. *Miscellaneous Essays.* . . . Philadelphia: Carey and Hart, 1830.

Channing, William Ellery. *Memoir of William Ellery Channing, with Extracts from his Correspondence and Manuscripts.* Ed. W. H. Channing. 2 vols. London and New York: George Routledge, n.d.

Chastellux, Marquis de. *Travels in North America in the Years 1780, 1781 and 1782.* Rev. trans. by Howard C. Rice, Jr. 2 vols. Chapel Hill: University of North Carolina Press, 1963.

Chesterton, Gilbert K. *Orthodoxy.* New York and London: John Lane, 1909.

Chevalier, Michael [Michel]. *Society, Manners, and Politics in the United States: Letters on North America.* Ed. John William Ward. Anchor Books ed. Garden City, N.Y.: Doubleday, 1961.

Choate, Rufus. *Works.* Ed. Samuel Gilman Brown. 2 vols. Boston: Little, Brown, 1862.

Clay, Henry. *Speeches*. Ed. Calvin Colton. 2 vols. New York: Barnes, 1857.

Cobbett, William. *Rural Rides*. Ed. James Paul Cobbett. London: A. Cobbett, 1853.

[Coffin, Robert S.] *Oriental Harp: Poems of the Boston Bard*. Providence, R.I.: Smith and Parmenter, 1826.

The Columbian Orator. See Bingham.

Cooper, James Fenimore. *The Crater, or Vulcan's Peak*. Mohawk ed. New York and London: n.d.

——. *Home as Found*. Mohawk ed. New York and London: n.d.

——. *Letters and Journals*. Ed. James Franklin Beard. Vols. I–IV. Boston: Harvard University Press, 1960–1964.

——. *Notions of the Americans: picked up by a Travelling Bachelor*. 2 vols. Philadelphia: Carey, Lea and Carey, 1828.

Crèvecoeur, J. Hector St. John de. *Letters from an American Farmer*. Everyman's Library; New York: Dutton, 1926.

Cushing, Caleb. *A Eulogy on John Adams and Thomas Jefferson, pronounced in Newburyport, July 15, 1826. . . .* Cambridge, Mass.: Hilliard and Metcalf, 1826.

——. *An Oration, on the National Growth and Territorial Progress of the United States . . . on the Fourth of July, 1839*. Springfield, Mass.: Merriam, Wood, 1839.

Cutler, Benjamin. *A Sermon delivered in . . . Brooklyn, on Sunday following the celebration of our national independence, MDCCCXXXVI*. New York: Protestant Episcopal Press, 1836.

Daveis, Charles S. *An Address delivered on the Commemoration at Fryeburg, May 19, 1825*. Portland, Me.: James Adams, Jr., 1825.

Dewey, Orville. *A Sermon . . . on the Moral Importance of Cities, and the moral means for their reformation. . . .* New York: David Felt, 1836.

Dickens, Charles. *American Notes for General Circulation*. London: Chapman and Hall, 1850.

Dwight, Timothy. *Travels in New England and New York*. 4 vols. New Haven: Converse, 1821–1822.

Edwards, Jonathan. *The Works of President Edwards: with*

a memoir of his life. Ed. Sereno E. Dwight. 10 vols. New York: S. Converse, 1829–1830.

Emerson, Ralph Waldo. *The Complete Works of Ralph Waldo Emerson.* Ed. Edward Waldo Emerson. 12 vols. Boston: Houghton, Mifflin, 1903–1904.

——. *Journals.* Ed. Edward Waldo Emerson and Waldo Emerson Forbes. 10 vols. Boston: Houghton, Mifflin, 1909–1914.

Everett, Alexander H. *New Ideas on Population: with Remarks on the Theories of Malthus and Godwin.* Boston: Oliver Everett, 1822.

Everett, Edward. *Orations and Speeches on Various Occasions.* 4 vols. 9th ed.; Boston: Little, Brown, 1878–1879.

——. *Recollections of the Last Ten Years.* Boston: Cummings, Hilliard, 1826.

Freneau, Philip. *The Last Poems of Philip Freneau.* Ed. Lewis Leary. New Brunswick, N.J.: Rutgers University Press, 1945.

Fuller Ossoli, Margaret. *At Home and Abroad, or Things and Thoughts in America and Europe.* Ed. Arthur B. Fuller. 2d ed. Boston: Crosby Nichols, 1856.

——. *Life Without and Life Within.* Ed. Arthur B. Fuller. New York: Tribune Association, 1869.

——. *Memoirs.* Ed. Ralph Waldo Emerson *et al.* 2 vols. Boston: Phillips, Sampson, 1852.

[Anon.] *A General Outline of the United States of North America, her Resources and Prospects with a Statistical Comparison.* . . . Philadelphia: Tanner, 1824.

Gray, John Chipman. *An Oration, . . . on the Fourth of July, 1822, at . . . Boston.* . . . Boston: Charles Callender, 1822.

Greenough, Horatio. *A Memorial of Horatio Greenough, consisting of a Memoir, Selections from his Writings and Tributes to his Genius.* Ed. Henry T. Tuckerman. New York: G. P. Putnam, 1853.

Gregg, Jarvis. *Eulogy on Lafayette, delivered in the chapel of Dartmouth College, July 4, 1834.* Hanover, N.H.: Thomas Mann, 1834.

Grund, Francis J. *The Americans in their Moral, Social, and*

Political Relations. 2 vols. London: Longman *et al.*, 1837.
——, ed. [*sic*]. *Aristocracy in America.* 2 vols. in 1. London: Richard Bentley, 1839.

Haven, Samuel F. *An Historical Address delivered before the citizens of the Town of Dedham, on the Twenty-first of September, 1836. . . .* Dedham: Mann, 1837.

Hawthorne, Nathaniel. *The Marble Faun . . .* (1860). Riverside ed. Boston: Houghton, Mifflin, 1888.

Hegel, G. W. F. *Lectures on the Philosophy of History.* Trans. J. Sibree. London and New York: George Bell and Sons, 1894.

Hickok, Laurens P. *A Nation Saved from Its Prosperity Only by the Gospel. . . .* New York: American Home Missionary Society, 1853.

Hillhouse, James A. *An Oration, Pronounced at New Haven . . . August 19, 1834,* in commemoration of . . . General Lafayette. New Haven: H. Howe, 1834.

[Anon.] *Historical Sketches of the Life of M. DE LAFAYETTE; and the Leading Events of the American Revolution. By An American.* New York: Printed for the Author, 1824.

Holmes, Abiel. *The Annals of America. . . .* 2d ed. 2 vols. Cambridge: Hilliard and Brown, 1829.

Hone, Philip. *Diary . . . 1828–1851.* Ed. Allan Nevins. 2 vols. New York: Dodd, Mead, 1927.

Hunt, Gilbert J. *The Tour of General La Fayette through the U. States, from his departure from France until his departure from America, in 1825. . . .* New York: The Compiler, 1825.

Ingersoll, Charles Jared. *An Oration delivered before The Philadelphia Association for Celebrating the Fourth of July . . . 1832.* Philadelphia: Jesper Harding, 1832.

Ives, L. Silliman. *The Introductory Address of the Historical Society of North Carolina . . . June 5th, 1844.* Raleigh: T. Loring, 1844.

Jay, John. *Correspondence and Public Papers.* Ed. Henry P. Johnston. 4 vols. New York: Putnam's, 1890–1893.

Jefferson, Thomas. *Writings.* Eds. Albert A. Lipscomb and

Albert Ellery Bergh. 20 vols. Washington, D.C.: Thomas Jefferson Memorial Association, 1905.

[Johnson, Captain Edward]. *Wonder-Working Providence of Sions Saviour in New England.* Ed. William Frederick Poole. Andover: Warren F. Draper, 1867.

Johnston, James F. W. *Notes on North America.* . . . 2 vols. Edinburgh and London: Blackwood, 1851.

Kennedy, Melvin D., ed. *Lafayette and Slavery, from his letters to Thomas Clarkson and Granville Sharp.* Easton, Pa.: American Friends of Lafayette, 1950.

Ibn Khaldun. *The Muqaddimah.* Trans. Franz Rosenthal. 3 vols. New York: Pantheon, 1958.

Kingsbury, Harmon. *The Sabbath: A brief history of* . . . *the Christian Sabbath.* 2d ed. New York: J. Leavitt, 1841.

Klinkowström, Baron Axel L. *Baron Klinkowström's America, 1818–20.* Trans. and ed. Franklin D. Scott. Evanston, Ill.: Northwestern University Press, 1952.

Knapp, Samuel L. *Lectures on American Literature* . . . (1829). Reprinted as *American Cultural History, 1607–1829.* Intro. and Index by Richard Beale Davis and Ben Harris McClary. Gainesville, Fla.: Scholars' Facsimiles and Reprints, 1961.

[Knapp, Samuel L.] *Memoirs of General Lafayette, with an Account of his Visit to America.* . . . Boston: E. G. House, 1824.

Konkle, Burton Alva. *The Life and Speeches of Thomas Williams.* 2 vols. Philadelphia: Campion, 1905.

[Anon.] *Lafayette, or Disinterested Virtue.* Boston: Office of the Christian Register, 1825.

Lafayette: The Nation's Guest. Winterthur, Del.: The Henry Francis Dupont Winterthur Museum, 1957.

Lawrence, Amos. *Extracts from the Diary and Correspondence of the late Amos Lawrence.* . . . Ed. William R. Lawrence. Boston: Gould and Lincoln, 1855.

Lawrence, D. H. *Studies in Classic American Literature.* Anchor Book. Garden City, N.Y.: Doubleday, n.d.

[Anon.] "Letters on India—By a Lady," *The Mother's Magazine,* V (November, 1837).

Levasseur, A. *Lafayette en Amérique, en 1824 et 1825.* . . . 2 vols. Paris: Baudouin, 1829.

——. *Lafayette in America in 1824 and 1825.* . . . Trans. John D. Godman, M.D., 2 vols. Philadelphia: Carey and Lea, 1829.

Lieber, Francis. *The Stranger in America, or, Letters to a Gentleman in Germany.* . . . Philadelphia: Carey, Lea and Blanchard, 1834.

Lincoln, Abraham. *The Collected Works of Abraham Lincoln.* Ed. Roy P. Basler. 9 vols. New Brunswick, N.J.: Rutgers University Press, 1953–1955.

Locke, John. *An Essay Concerning Human Understanding.* 28th ed. London: T. Tegg and Son, 1838.

——. *Two Treatises of Government: A Critical Edition.* . . . Ed. Peter Laslett. Cambridge: Cambridge University Press, 1960.

Lyell, Sir Charles. *A Second Visit to North America.* 2 vols. London: John Murray, 1855.

Mann, Horace. *Common School Journal.* Excerpted in *American Issues,* ed. Merle Curti. Chicago: Lippincott, 1941.

——. *An Oration, delivered before the authorities of the City of Boston, July 4, 1842.* 5th ed. [Boston: W. B. Fowle and N. Capen, 1842?].

Marryat, Captain Frederick. *Diary in America (1837–38).* Ed. Jules Zanger. Bloomington, Ind.: Indiana University Press, 1960.

Marshall, John. *The Life of George Washington.* . . . 2d ed. 2 vols. Philadelphia: James Crissy, 1832.

Martineau, Harriet. *Autobiography.* Ed. Maria Weston Chapman. 2 vols. Boston: James R. Osgood, 1877.

——. *Retrospect of Western Travel.* 2 vols. London: Saunders and Otley; New York: Harper, 1838.

——. *Society in America.* 2d ed. 3 vols. London: Saunders and Otley, 1839.

Mellen, Grenville. "The True Glory of America," *The Poets and Poetry of America to the Middle of the Nineteenth Century.* Ed. Rufus Griswold. 10th ed., rev. Philadelphia: Carey and Hart, 1850.

Melville, Herman. *Letters.* Eds. Merrill R. Davis and William

H. Gilman. New Haven: Yale University Press, 1960.

———. *Mardi, and a Voyage Thither.* Standard ed. reissue. 2 vols. New York: Russell & Russell, 1963.

———. *Moby Dick.* Standard ed. reissue. 2 vols. New York: Russell & Russell, 1963.

Miller, Perry, and Thomas H. Johnson, eds. *The Puritans.* New York: American Book Co., 1938.

Minutes of the Common Council of the City of New York 1784–1831. 19 vols. New York: Pub. by the City, 1917.

Moreau de St. Méry's American Journey (1793–1798). Trans. and ed. Kenneth Roberts and Anna M. Roberts. Garden City, N.Y.: Doubleday, 1947.

Nevins, Allan, comp. and ed. *American Social History as Recorded by British Travelers.* New York: Holt, 1923.

New England Society Orations. See Brainerd.

New-York Literary Gazette, I (1825).

Nichols, Thomas Low. *Forty Years of American Life.* 2 vols. London: J. Maxwell, 1864.

Noah, M[ordecai] M[anuel]. *Oration delivered . . . before Tammany Society . . . to Celebrate the 41st Anniversary of American Independence.* New York: J. H. Sherman, 1817.

Official Report of the Debates and Proceedings in the State Convention, assembled May 4th, 1853, to revise and amend the Constitution of the Commonwealth of Massachusetts. 3 vols. Boston: White and Potter, 1853.

The Order of Exercises in the Chapel of Transylvania University. A collection of original pieces in honour of the arrival of General La Fayette, the hero, patriot, and philanthropist, A defender of American independence, a companion of Washington, and a devoted friend of Liberty and Equal laws in Europe and America. Lexington, Fayette County, Kentucky, n.p., May, 1825.

Paine, Thomas. *The Rights of Man.* Everyman's Library; London: J. M. Dent; New York: E. P. Dutton, 1935.

Parkman, Francis. *Journals. Ed.* Mason Wade. 2 vols. London: Eyre and Spottiswood, [1946?].

Peabody, Ephraim. *A Sermon delivered . . . April 2, 1846.* Boston: Leonard C. Bowles, 1846.

Peirce, Charles Sanders. *Collected Papers*. Ed. Charles Hart-shorne and Paul Weiss. 6 vols. Cambridge: Harvard University Press, 1934.

Pitkin, Timothy. *A Political and Civil History of the United States of America.* . . . 2 vols. New Haven: Hezekiah Howe, *et al.*, 1828.

Poe, Edgar Allen. *The Complete Tales and Poems*. Modern Library ed.; New York: Random House, 1938.

Prescott, Edward G. *An Oration* . . . *on the Fifty-eighth* [*sic*] *anniversary of American Independence*. Boston: J. H. Eastburn, 1833.

Quincy, Josiah. *Figures of the Past, From the Leaves of Old Journals*. 9th ed. Boston: Little, Brown, 1901.

Rafinesque, C[onstantine] S. *A Life of Travels and Researches in North America.* . . . Philadelphia: F. Turner, 1836. Reprinted with original pagination by *Chronica Botanica*, VIII, no. 2 (Spring 1944), Waltham, Mass.

——, Constantine S. *Western Minerva, or, American Annals of Knowledge and Literature*. Vol. 1, no. 1 (January, 1820). Lexington, Ky.: T. Smith, 1821. Repub. in facsimile ed. New York: P. Smith, 1949.

Ramsay, David, M.D. *History of the American Revolution*. 2 vols. Philadelphia: R. Aitken and Son, 1789.

Report of the Committee of the New-York Historical Society, on a National Name, March 31, 1845. [New York, 1845?].

Richardson, James D., ed. *A Compilation of the Messages and Papers of the Presidents, 1789–1897*. 10 vols. Washington: Government Printing Office, 1896–1899.

Riddle, David D. *Our Country for the Sake of the World, a sermon* . . . *preached in* . . . *New York and Brooklyn, May, 1851*. New York: Baker, Godwin, 1851.

Saxe-Weimar Eisenach, Duke of. *Travels Through North America, during the Years 1825 and 1826*. 2 vols in 1. Philadelphia: Carey, Lea and Carey, 1828.

Schaff, Philip. *America, A Sketch of its Political, Social, and Religious Character* (1855). Ed. Perry Miller. Cambridge: Harvard University Press, 1961.

Schurz, Carl. *Speeches, Correspondence, and Political Papers.*

Ed. Frederic Bancroft. 6 vols. New York and London: Putnam's, 1913.

Scrapbook, containing newspaper clippings of Lafayette's tour, 1824–1825. Library of Congress, Rare Book Room.

Sedgwick, Catharine Maria. *Life and Letters.* Ed. Mary E. Dewey. New York: Harper, 1871.

[Anon.]. *Sketch of the Life and Military Services of Gen. La Fayette, during the American Revolution. . . .* New York: printed and published for the editor, 1824.

Skidmore, Thos. *The Rights of Man to Property. . . .* New York: Alexander Ming, Jr., 1829.

[Smith, Joseph, Jr.]. *The Book of Mormon, translated by Joseph Smith, Jr.* Authorized ed. Independence, Mo.: Board of Pub. of the Reorg. Ch. of Jesus Christ of Latter Day Saints, 1948.

Stetson, Caleb. *A Discourse on the State of the Country . . . April 7th, 1842.* Boston: James Munroe, 1842.

Storrs, Richard. *Home Missions: As Connected with Christ's Dominion. . . .* New York: American Home Missionary Society, 1855.

Taft, Kendall B. *Minor Knickerbockers.* New York: American Book Co., 1947.

Tansill, Charles C. *Documents Illustrative of the Formation of the Union of the American States.* Washington, D.C.: Government Printing Office, 1927.

Taylor, William R. *Cavalier and Yankee.* New York: Braziller, 1961.

Thoreau, Henry David. *Writings.* Walden ed. 20 vols. Boston and New York: Houghton, Mifflin, 1906.

Tocqueville, Alexis de. *Democracy in America.* Ed. Phillips Bradley. 2 vols. New York: Knopf, 1945.

[Trollope, Frances]. *Domestic Manners of the Americans by "Mrs. Trollope."* 2 vols. 3d ed. London: Whittaker, Treacher, 1832.

Tryon, Warren, comp. and ed. *A Mirror for Americans: Life and Manners in the United States 1790–1870, as Recorded by American Travelers.* 3 vols. Chicago: University of Chicago Press, 1952.

Verplanck, Gulian C. *The Advantages and Dangers of the American Scholar. A discourse . . . at Union College, July 26, 1836.* New York: Wiley and Long, 1836.

Waln, Robert, Jr. *Life of the Marquis de La Fayette. . . .* Philadelphia: J. P. Ayres, 1825.

Webster, Daniel. *The Writings and Speeches of Daniel Webster.* National ed. 18 vols. Boston: Little, Brown, 1903.

Whitman, Walt. *Complete Poetry and Selected Prose.* Ed. James E. Miller, Jr. Riverside ed. Boston: Houghton, Mifflin, 1959.

——. *The Gathering of the Forces.* Ed. C. Rodgers and J. Black. 2 vols. New York: Putnam's, 1920.

——. *Lafayette in Brooklyn.* Intro. by John Burroughs. New York: George D. Smith, 1905.

Whittemore, Thomas. *An Oration, pronounced on the Fourth of July, 1821 . . . before the Republican Citizens of Milford, Mass. . . .* Boston: True, Field and Green, 1821.

SECONDARY SOURCES

Articles

Boas, Franz. "Liberty Among Primitive People," in *Freedom, Its Meaning,* ed. Ruth Nanda Anshen (New York: Harcourt, Brace, 1940), pp. 375–80.

Cady, George Johnson. *The Early American Reaction to the Theory of Malthus.* Chicago, 1931. Reprinted from *Journal of Political Economy,* XXXII (October, 1931), 601–32.

Curti, Merle. "The Great Mr. Locke: America's Philosopher, 1783–1861," in *Probing Our Past* (Gloucester, Mass.: Peter Smith, 1962), pp. 69–118.

Dahl, Curtis. "The American School of Catastrophe," *American Quarterly,* XI (Fall, 1959), 380–90.

Ekirch, Arthur A., Jr. "Parrington and the Decline of American Liberalism," *American Quarterly,* III (Winter, 1951), 295–308.

Geismar, Maxwell. "Was 'Papa' a Truly Great Writer?" *New York Times Book Review,* July 1, 1962, p. 1.

Mead, Sidney E. "The American People: Their Space, Time, and Religion," *Journal of Religion,* XXXIV (October, 1954), 244-55.

Miller, Perry. "From the Covenant to the Revival," in *Religion in American Life,* eds. James Ward Smith and A. Leland Jamison (4 vols.; Princeton, N.J.: Princeton University Press, 1961), I, 322-68.

Orians, G. Harrison. "The Rise of Romanticism, 1805-1855," in *Transitions in American Literary History,* ed. Harry Hayden Clark (Durham, N.C.: Duke University Press, 1955), pp. 163-244.

Persons, Stow. "The Cyclical Theory of History in Eighteenth Century America," *American Quarterly,* VI (Summer, 1954), 147-53.

Sanford, Charles L. Review of Leo Marx, *The Machine in the Garden, American Quarterly,* XVII, no. 2, Pt. 1 (Summer 1965), 272-76.

Spengler, Joseph. "Population Doctrines in the United States. I. Anti-Malthusianism; II. Malthusianism," *Journal of Political Economy,* XXXXI (1933), 433-67, 639-72.

Books

Boorstin, Daniel J. *The Lost World of Thomas Jefferson.* New York: Holt, 1948.

Campbell, Joseph. *The Hero with a Thousand Faces.* Bollingen Series, XVII, New York: Pantheon Books, 1949.

Collingwood, R. G. *The Idea of History.* Galaxy Book ed. New York: Oxford University Press, 1956.

Curti, Merle. *The Roots of American Loyalty.* New York: Columbia University Press, 1946.

Durkheim, Emile. *The Elementary Forms of the Religious Life.* Trans. J. W. Swain. London: George Allen and Unwin; New York: Macmillan, [1915].

Ekirch, Arthur A., Jr. *The Idea of Progress in America,* 1815-60. New York: Peter Smith, 1951.

Eliade, Mircea. *Myth of the Eternal Return*. Trans. Willard R. Trask. London: Routledge and Kegan Paul, 1955.

——. *Patterns in Comparative Religion*. Trans. Rosemary Sheed. New York: Sheed and Ward, [1958].

Elkins, Stanley M. *Slavery: A Problem in American Institutional and Cultural Life*. Chicago: University of Chicago Press, 1959.

Fuess, Claude M. *Daniel Webster*. 2 vols. Hamden, Conn.: Archon Books, 1963.

Fussell, Edward. *Frontier: American Literature and the American West*. Princeton, N.J.: Princeton University Press, 1965.

Gottschalk, Louis. *Lafayette and the Close of the American Revolution*. Chicago: University of Chicago Press, 1942.

——. *Lafayette between the American and the French Revolution (1783–1789)*. Chicago: University of Chicago Press, 1950.

——. *Lafayette Comes to America*. Chicago: University of Chicago Press, 1935.

——. *Lafayette Joins the American Army*. Chicago: University of Chicago Press, 1937.

Haroutunian, Joseph. *Piety Versus Moralism*. New York: H. Holt (1932).

Hook, Sidney. *The Hero in History*. New York: John Day, [1943].

Howe, M. A. DeWolfe. *The Life and Letters of George Bancroft*. 2 vols. New York: Scribner's, 1908.

Jameson, J. Franklin. *The History of Historical Writing in America*. Boston and New York: Houghton Mifflin, 1891.

Kraus, Michael. *The Writing of American History*. Norman, Okla.: University of Oklahoma Press, 1953.

Lewis, R. W. B. *The American Adam: Innocence, Tragedy, and Tradition in the Nineteenth Century*. Chicago: University of Chicago Press, 1955.

Mabee, Carleton. *The American Leonardo, A Life of Samuel F. B. Morse*. New York: Knopf, 1943.

Marx, Leo. *The Machine in the Garden: Technology and the Pastoral Ideal in America*. New York: Oxford University Press, 1964.

Meyers, Marvin. *The Jacksonian Persuasion: Politics and Belief.* Palo Alto: Stanford University Press, 1957.

Miller, Perry. *The Life of the Mind in America from the Revolution to the Civil War.* New York: Harcourt, Brace and World, 1965.

———. *The New England Mind, From Colony to Province.* Cambridge: Harvard University Press, 1953.

Moore, Arthur K. *The Frontier Mind, A Cultural Analysis of the Kentucky Frontiersman.* [Lexington, Ky.]: University of Kentucky Press, 1957.

Mumford, Lewis. *The Culture of Cities.* New York: Harcourt, Brace, 1938.

Nolan, J. Bennett. *Lafayette in America Day by Day.* Baltimore: Johns Hopkins Press, 1934.

Nye, Russel B. *George Bancroft, Brahmin Rebel.* New York: Knopf, 1944.

Ortega y Gasset, José. *History as a System and Other Essays toward a Philosophy of History.* Reprint of *Toward a Philosophy of History* (1941). New York: Norton, 1961.

Orwell, George. *Dickens, Dali and Others.* New York: Reynal and Hitchcock, 1946.

Ostrogorski, M. *Democracy and the Organization of Political Parties.* Trans. Frederick Clark. 2 vols. New York: Macmillan, 1902.

Parrington, Vernon Louis. *Main Currents in American Thought: An Interpretation of American Literature from the Beginnings to 1920.* 3 vols. in 1. New York: Harcourt, Brace, 1930.

Pierson, George W. *Tocqueville and Beaumont in America.* New York: Oxford University Press, 1938.

Rogers, Will. *The Will Rogers Book.* Ed. Paula McSpadden Love. Indianapolis: Bobbs Merrill, 1961.

Sanford, Charles L. *The Quest for Paradise: Europe and the American Moral Imagination.* Urbana, Ill.: University of Illinois Press, 1961.

Smith, Henry Nash. *Virgin Land: The American West as Symbol and Myth.* Cambridge: Harvard University Press, 1950.

Spengler, Oswald. *The Decline of the West.* Trans. Charles

Francis Atkinson. 2 vols. New York: Knopf, 1926–1928.

Tate, Allen. *Collected Essays*. Denver: Alan Swallow, 1959.

Van Zandt, Roland. *The Metaphysical Foundations of American History*. The Hague: Mouton, 1959.

Ward, John William. *Andrew Jackson: Symbol for an Age*. New York: Oxford University Press, 1955.

Warner, W. Lloyd. *The Living and the Dead, A Study of the Symbolic Life of Americans*. Yankee City Series, Vol. V. New Haven: Yale University Press, 1959.

Weinberg, Albert K. *Manifest Destiny, A Study of Nationalist Expansionism in American History*. Baltimore: Johns Hopkins Press, 1935.

Wright, Nathalia. *Horatio Greenough, The First American Sculptor*. Philadelphia: University of Pennsylvania Press, 1963.

Index

DATE DUE

GAYLORD			PRINTED IN U.S A.